CAT vs HUMAN

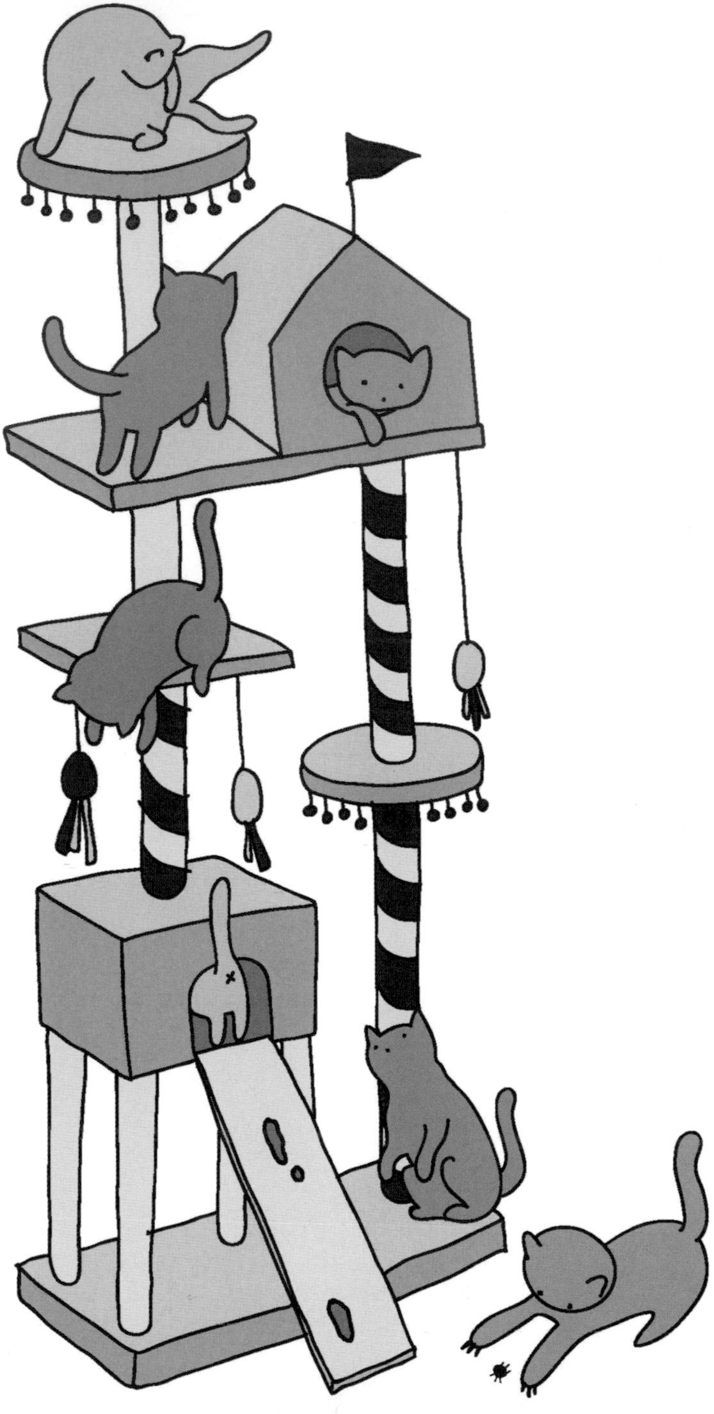

CAT vs HUMAN

YASMINE SUROVEC

Andrews McMeel
Publishing, LLC

Kansas City · Sydney · London

Andrews McMeel Publishing, LLC
an Andrews McMeel Universal company
1130 Walnut Street, Kansas City, Missouri 64106

www.andrewsmcmeel.com

11 12 13 14 15 TEN 10 9 8 7 6 5 4 3 2 1

ISBN: 978-1-4494-0865-7

Library of Congress Control Number: 2011925565

Attention: Schools and Businesses
Andrews McMeel books are available at quantity discounts
with bulk purchase for educational, business, or sales promotional use.
For information, please e-mail the
Andrews McMeel Publishing Special Sales Department:
specialsales@amuniversal.com

TO VICTOR, MY FAMILY,
PUPPY, OPRAH, SHELLEY,
MONEY, DUMPLING, AND
TO ALL CAT LADIES
AND GENTS

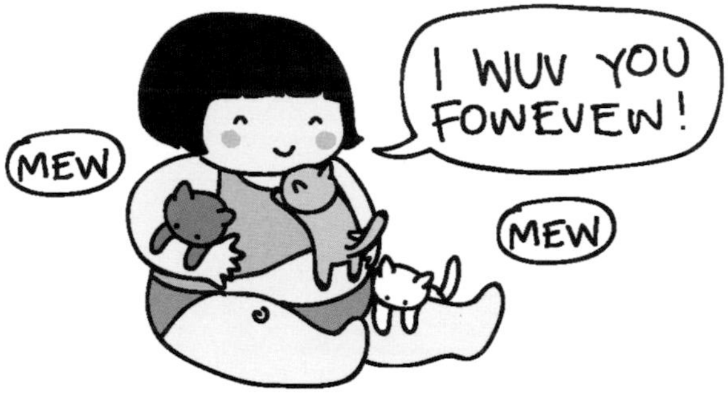
MEW
I WUV YOU FOWEVEW!
MEW

CAT vs HUMAN

ANATOMY OF A CAT LADY: APPEARANCE

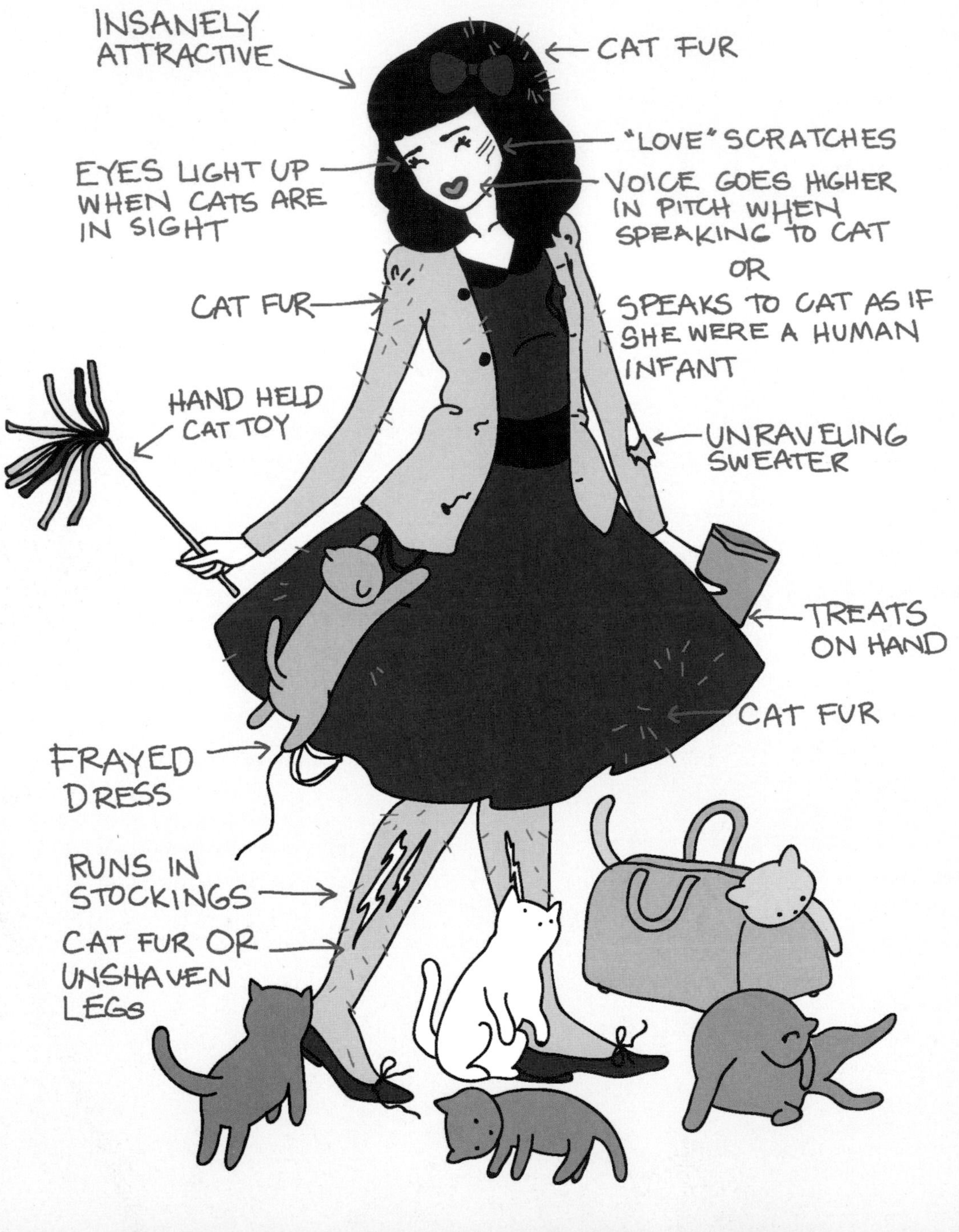
INSANELY ATTRACTIVE
CAT FUR
"LOVE" SCRATCHES
EYES LIGHT UP WHEN CATS ARE IN SIGHT
VOICE GOES HIGHER IN PITCH WHEN SPEAKING TO CAT
OR
SPEAKS TO CAT AS IF SHE WERE A HUMAN INFANT
CAT FUR
HAND HELD CAT TOY
UNRAVELING SWEATER
TREATS ON HAND
CAT FUR
FRAYED DRESS
RUNS IN STOCKINGS
CAT FUR OR UNSHAVEN LEGS

ANATOMY OF A CAT LADY: HOME

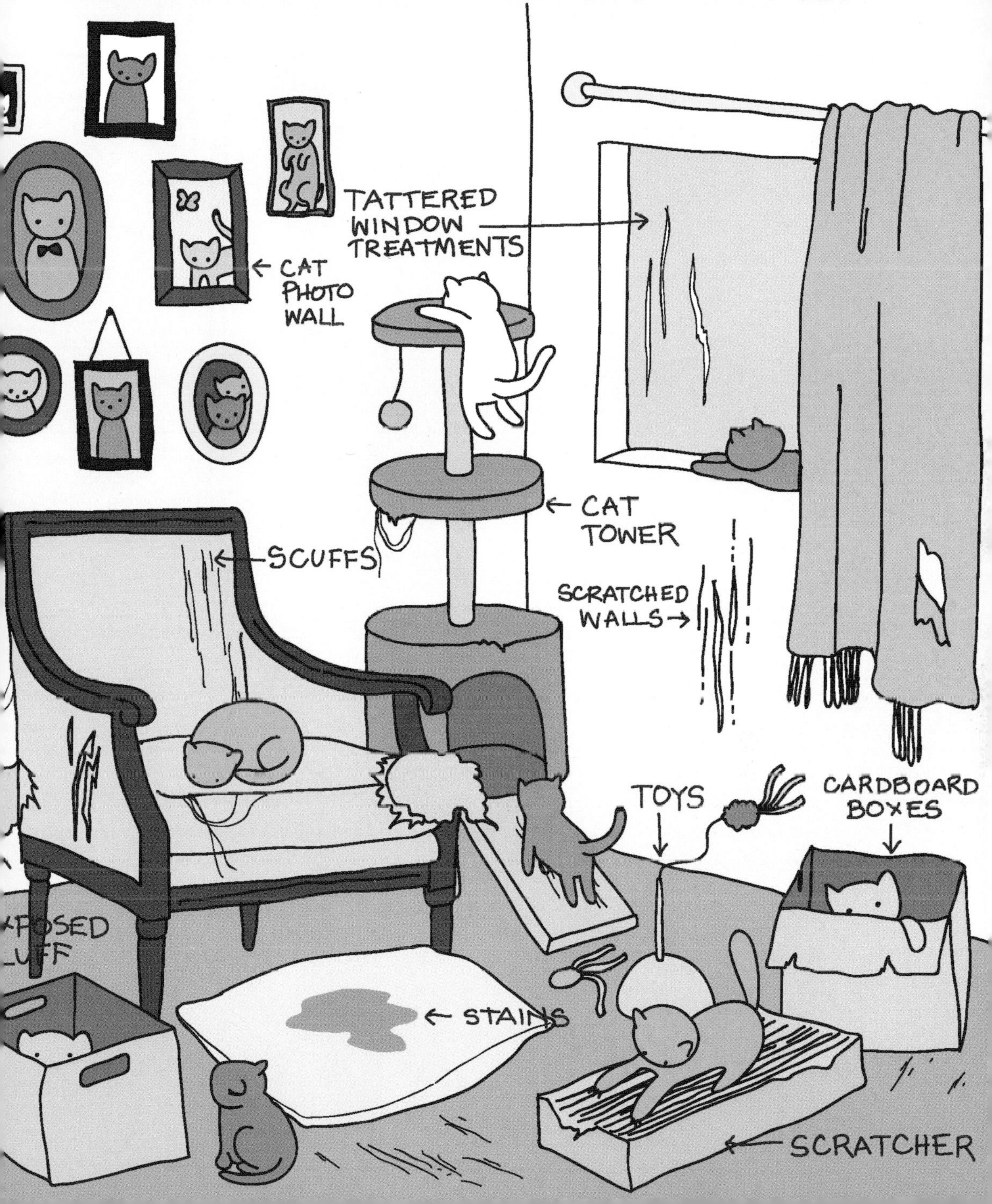

TATTERED WINDOW TREATMENTS
CAT PHOTO WALL
CAT TOWER
SCUFFS
SCRATCHED WALLS
TOYS
CARDBOARD BOXES
XPOSED LUFF
STAINS
SCRATCHER

ANATOMY OF A CAT LADY: DATING

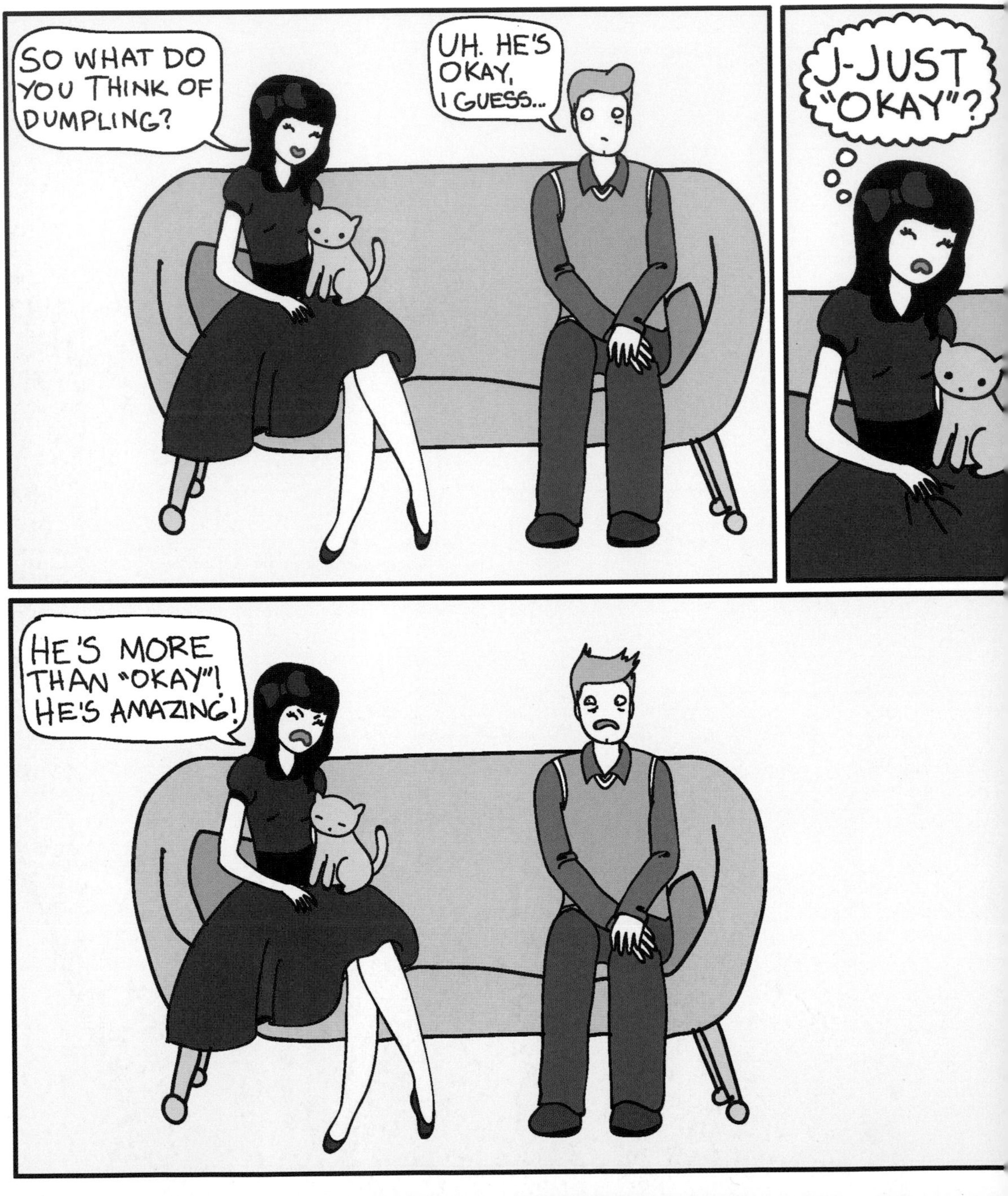
SO WHAT DO YOU THINK OF DUMPLING?
UH. HE'S OKAY, I GUESS...
J-JUST "OKAY"?
HE'S MORE THAN "OKAY"! HE'S AMAZING!

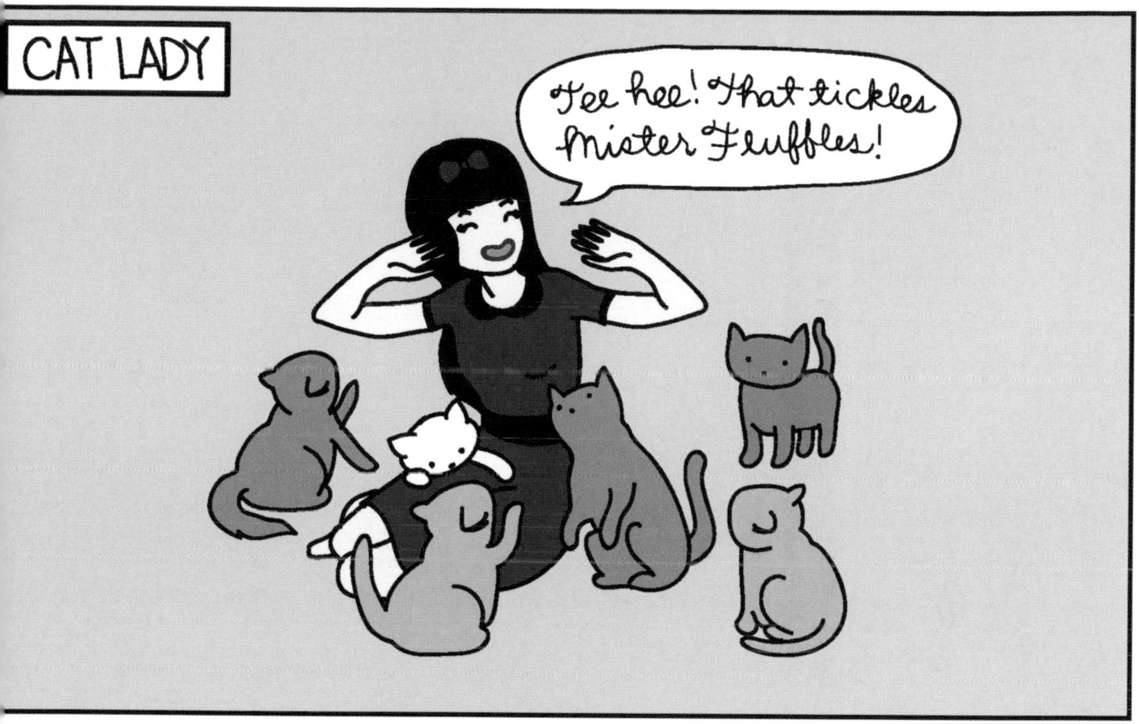
CAT LADY
Tee hee! That tickles Mister Fluffles!

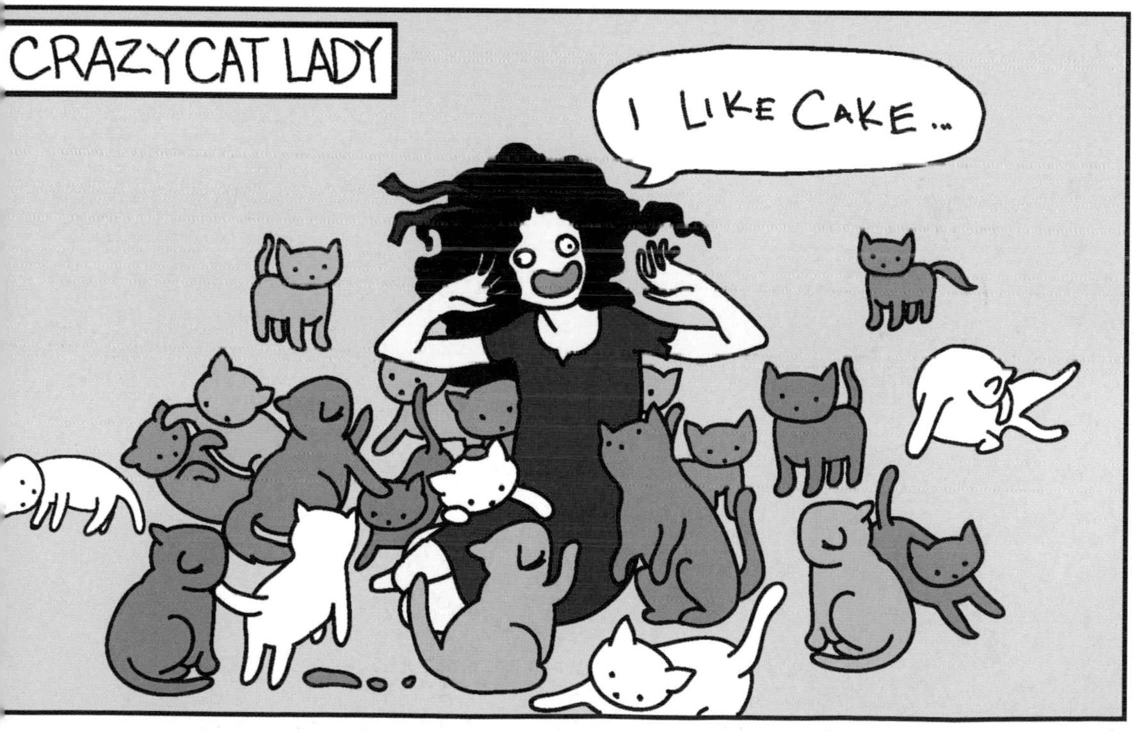
CRAZY CAT LADY
I LIKE CAKE...

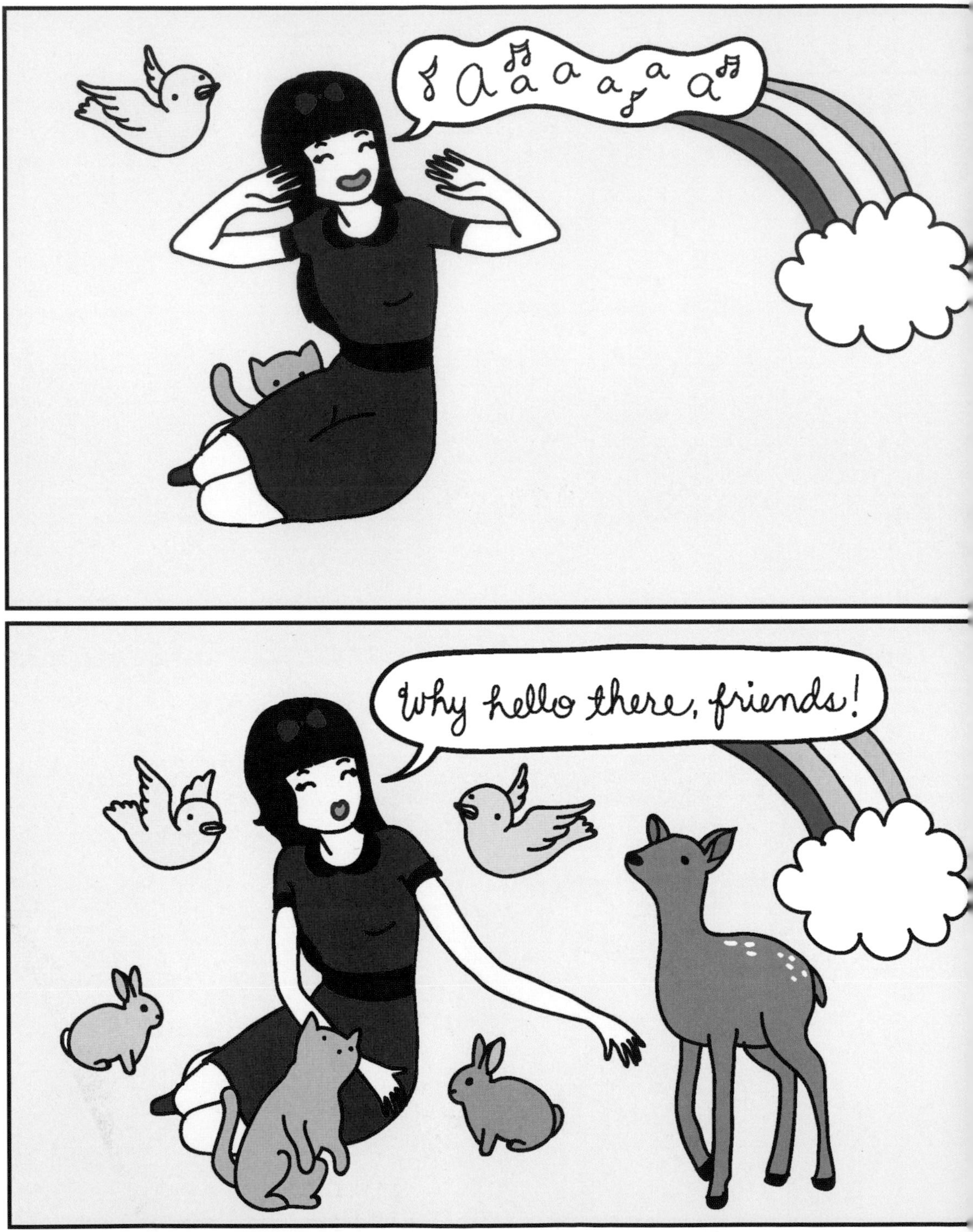
a a a a a a
Why hello there, friends!

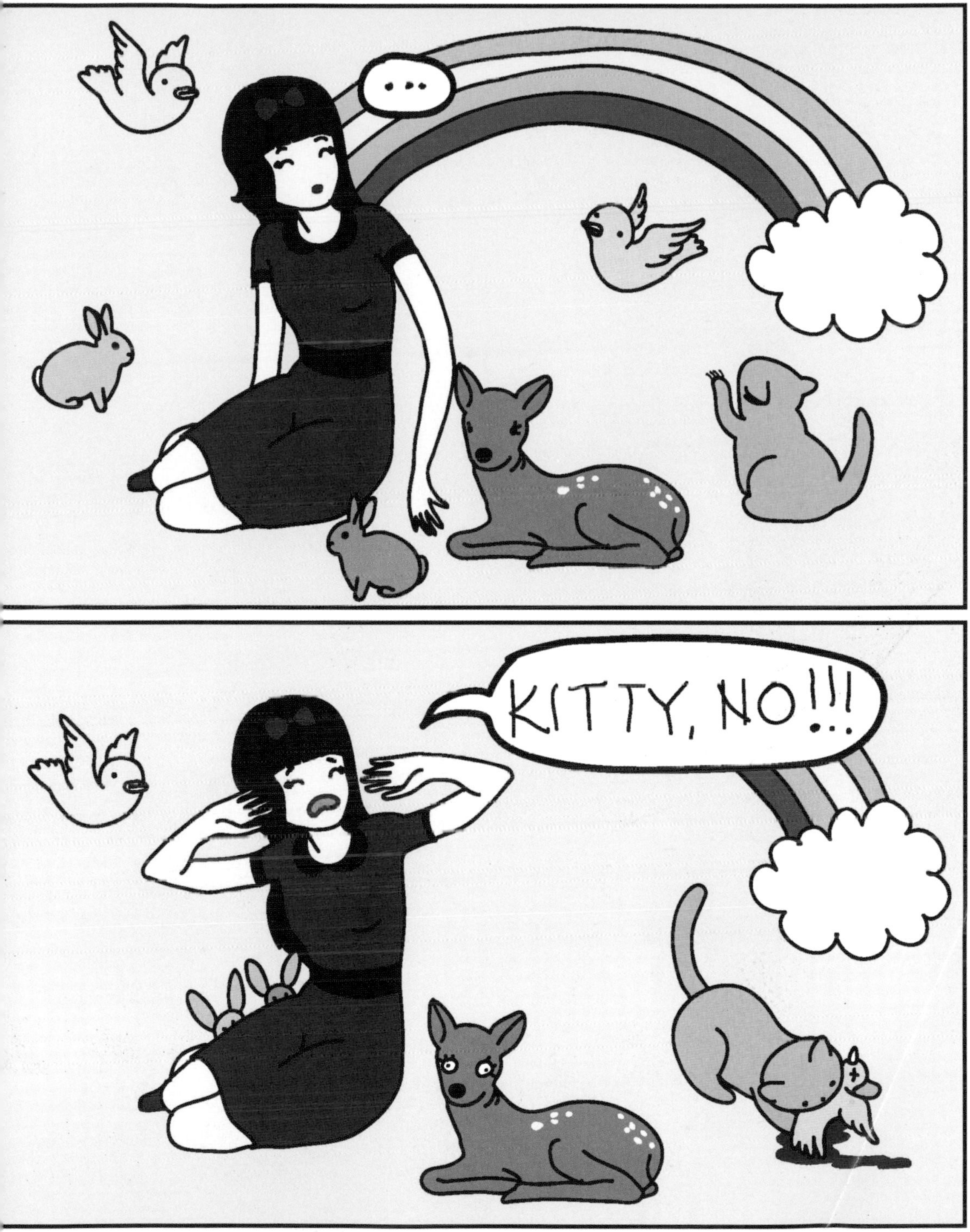
...
KITTY, NO!!!

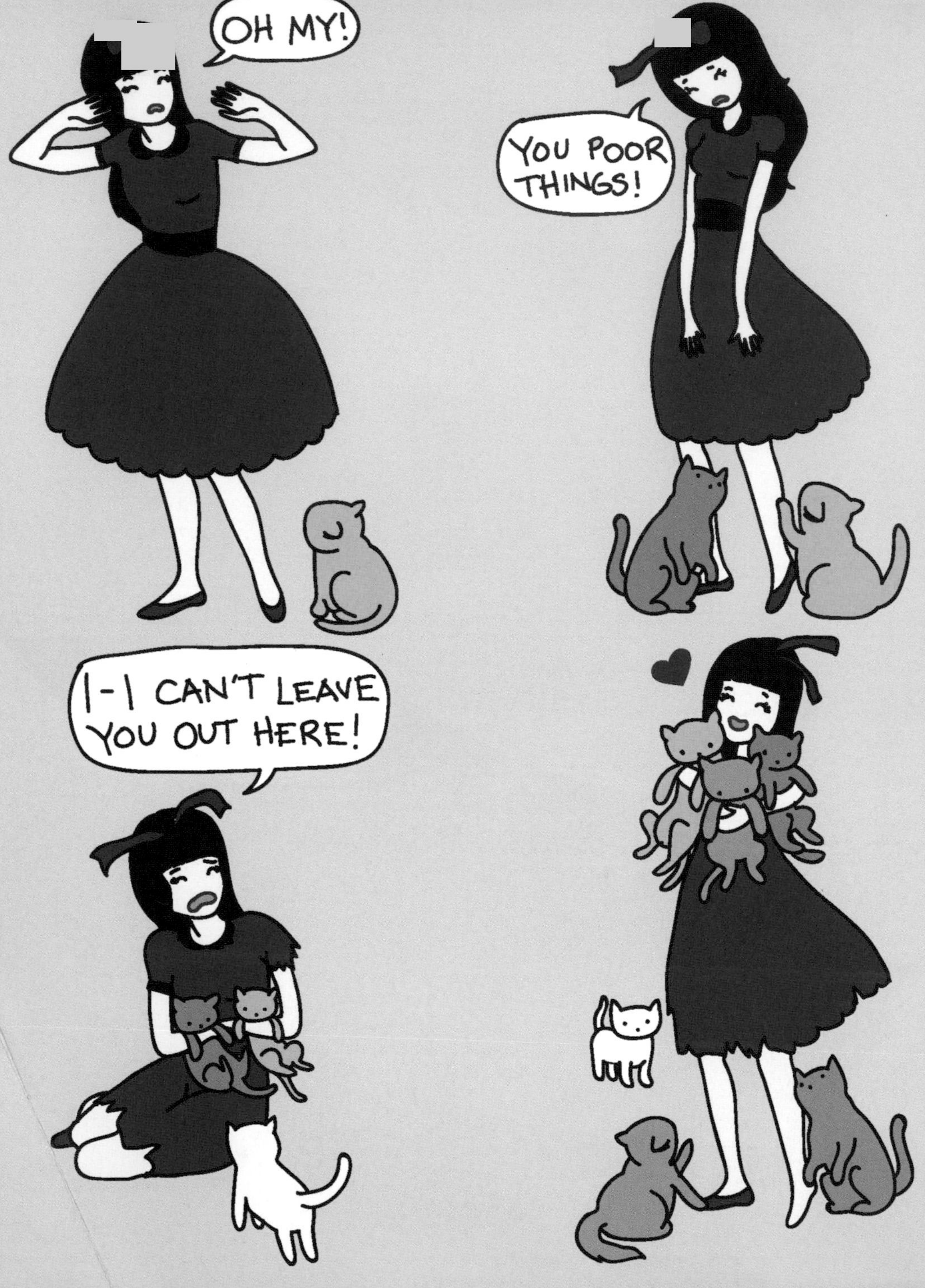
OH MY!
YOU POOR THINGS!
I-I CAN'T LEAVE YOU OUT HERE!

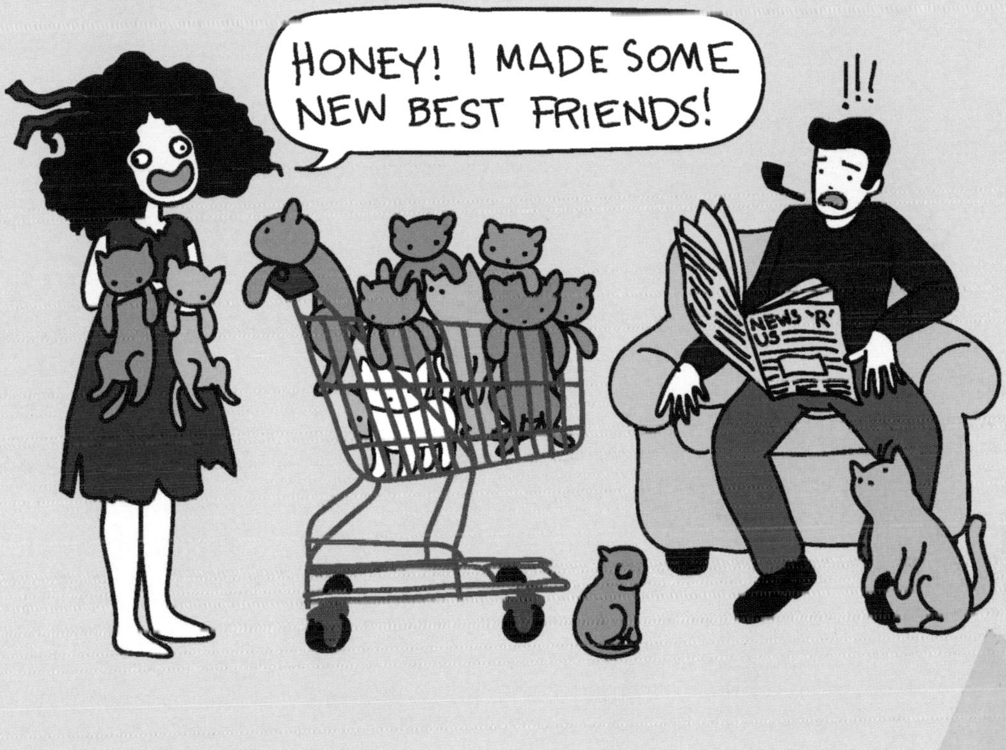
HONEY! I MADE SOME NEW BEST FRIENDS!
!!!
NEWS 'R' US

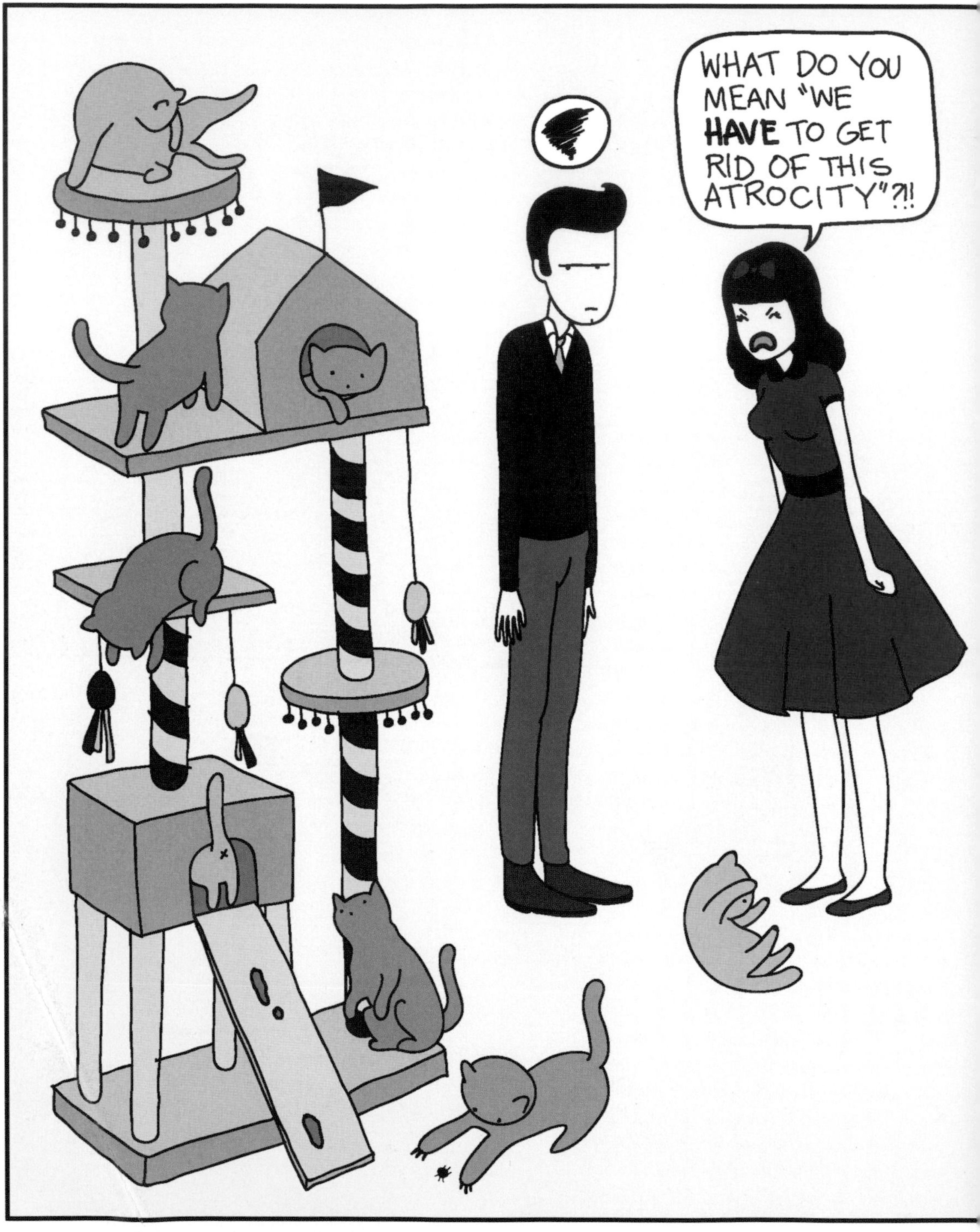
WHAT DO YOU MEAN "WE **HAVE** TO GET RID OF THIS ATROCITY"?!

A little tea party

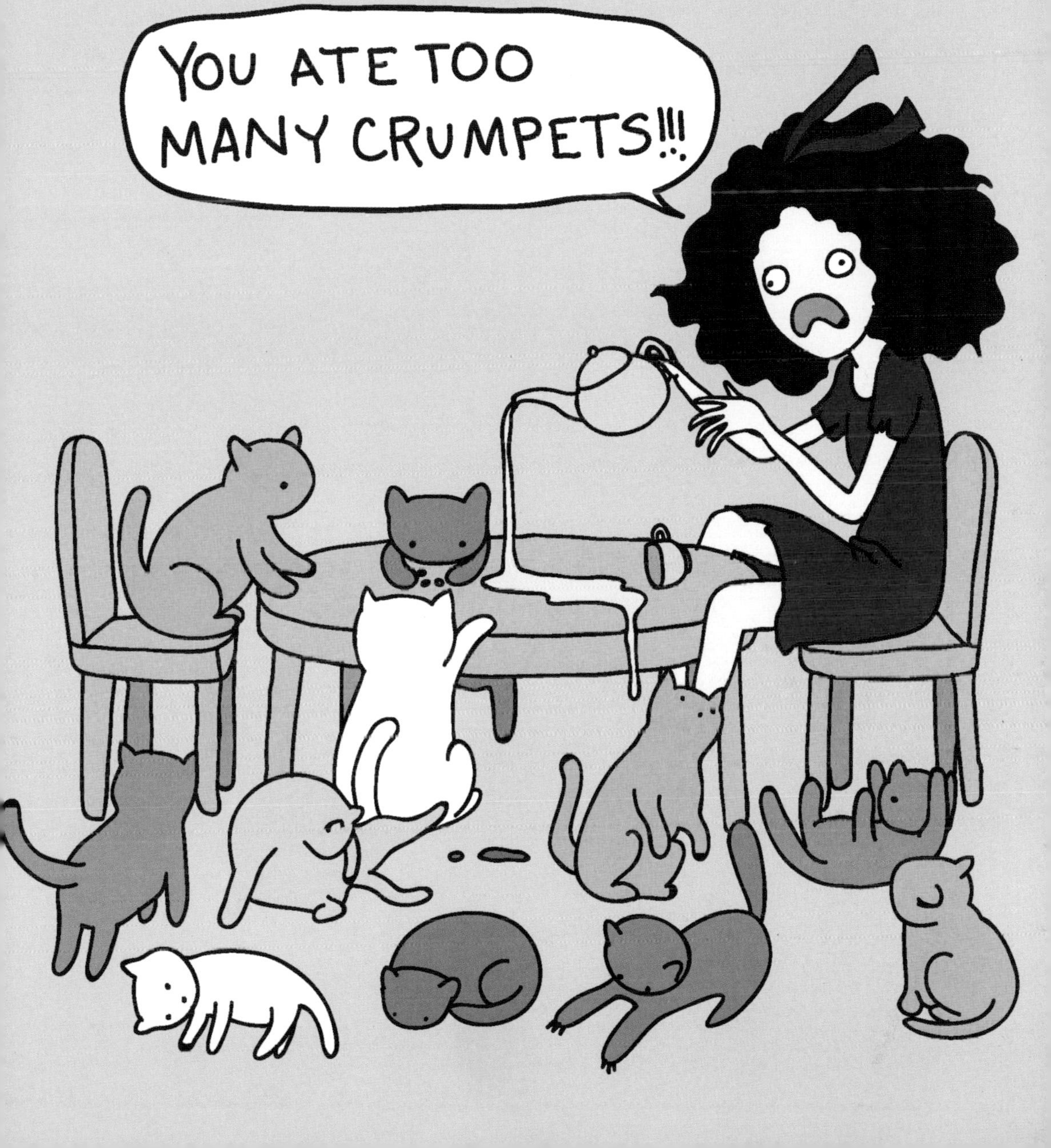
YOU ATE TOO MANY CRUMPETS!!!

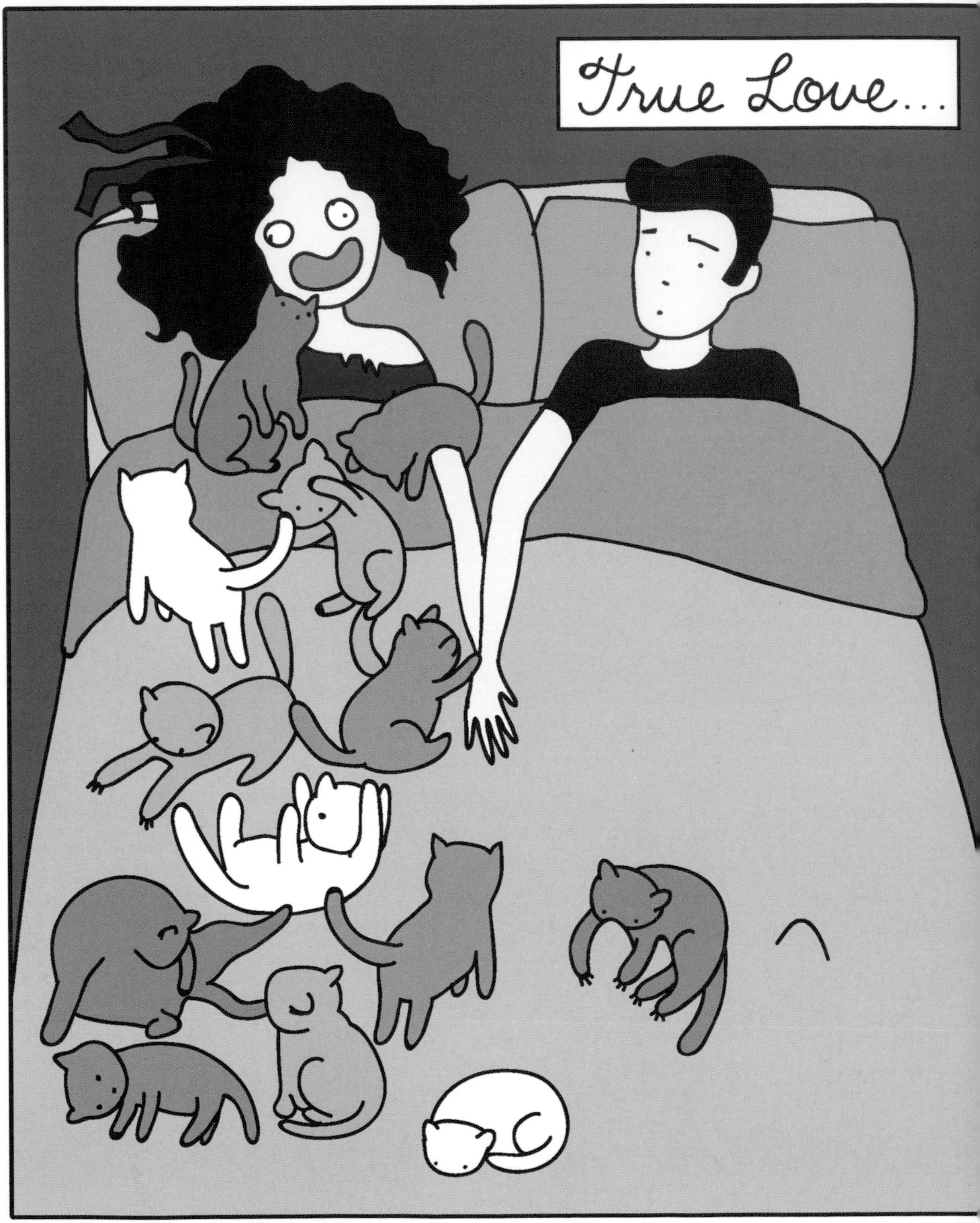
True Love...

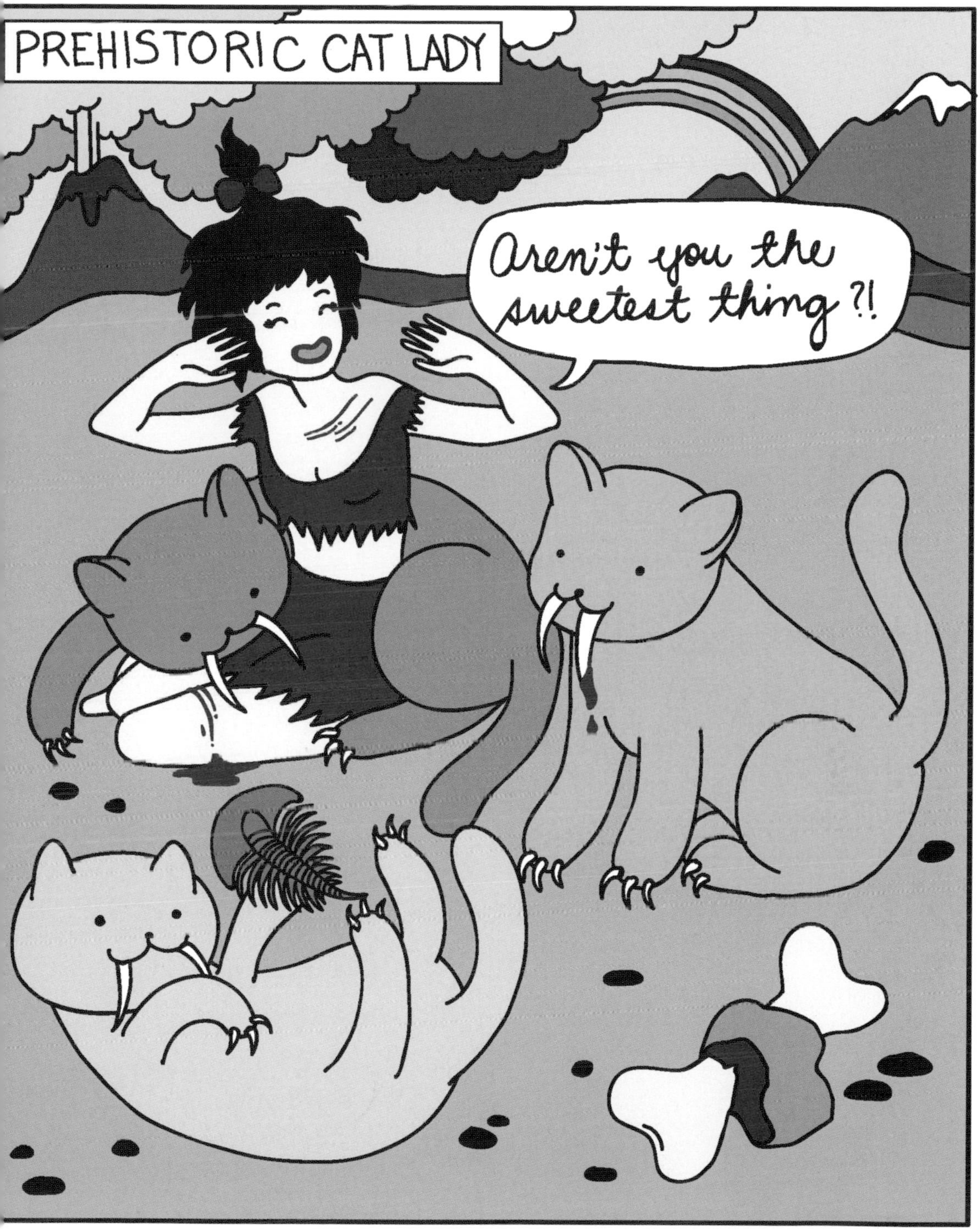
PREHISTORIC CAT LADY
Aren't you the sweetest thing?!

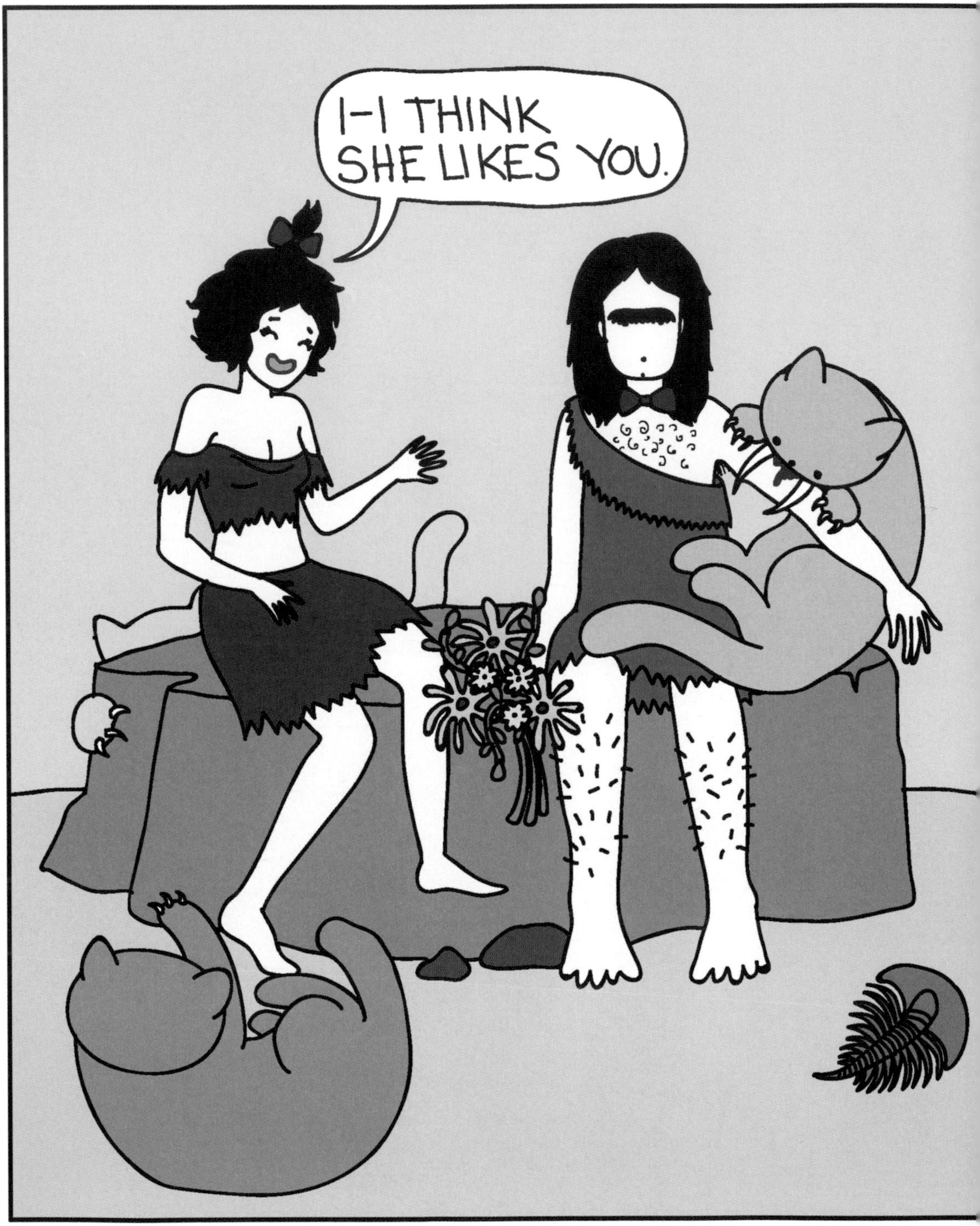
I-I THINK SHE LIKES YOU.

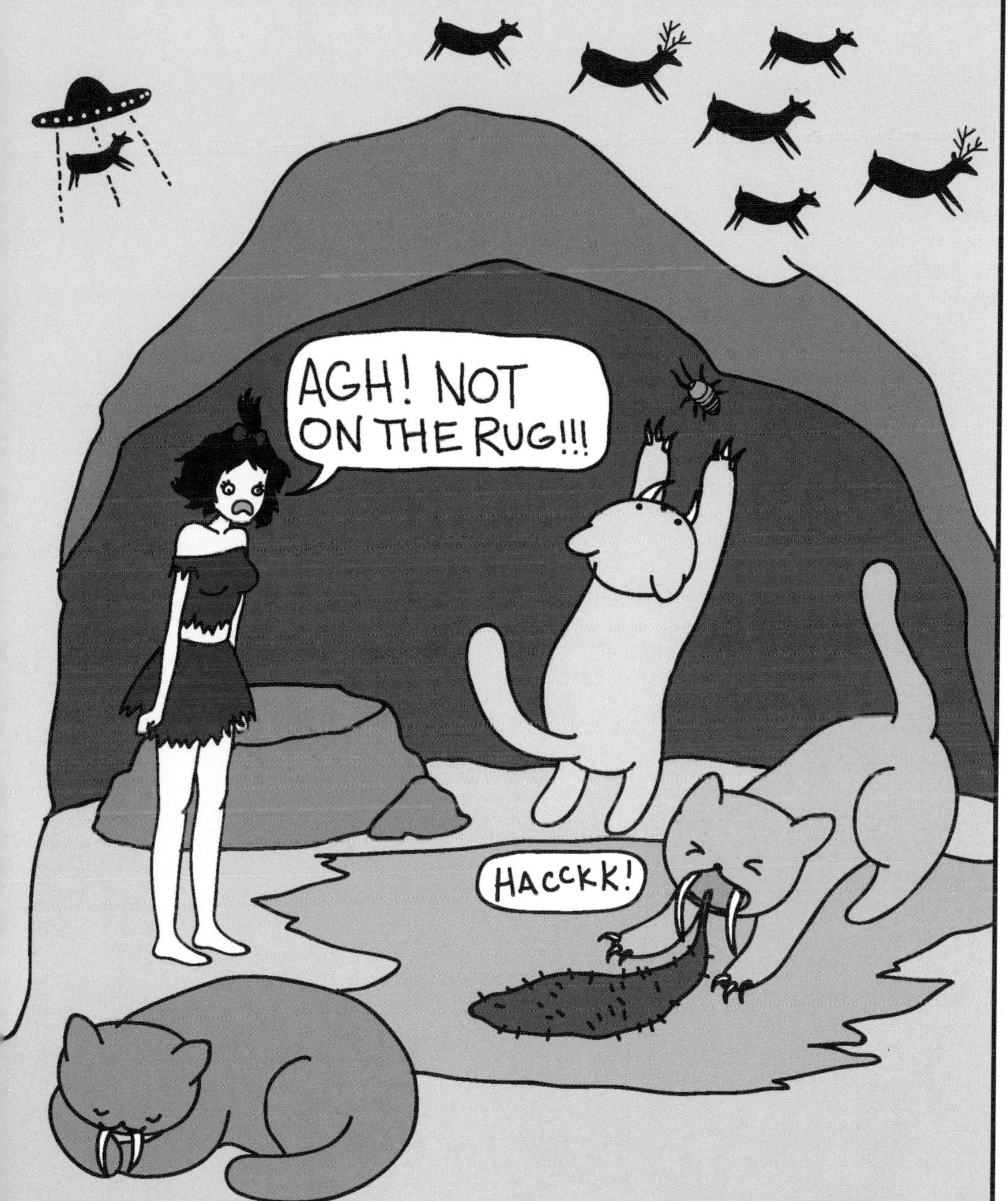
AGH! NOT ON THE RUG!!!
HACCKK!

IF HUMANS ACTED LIKE CATS

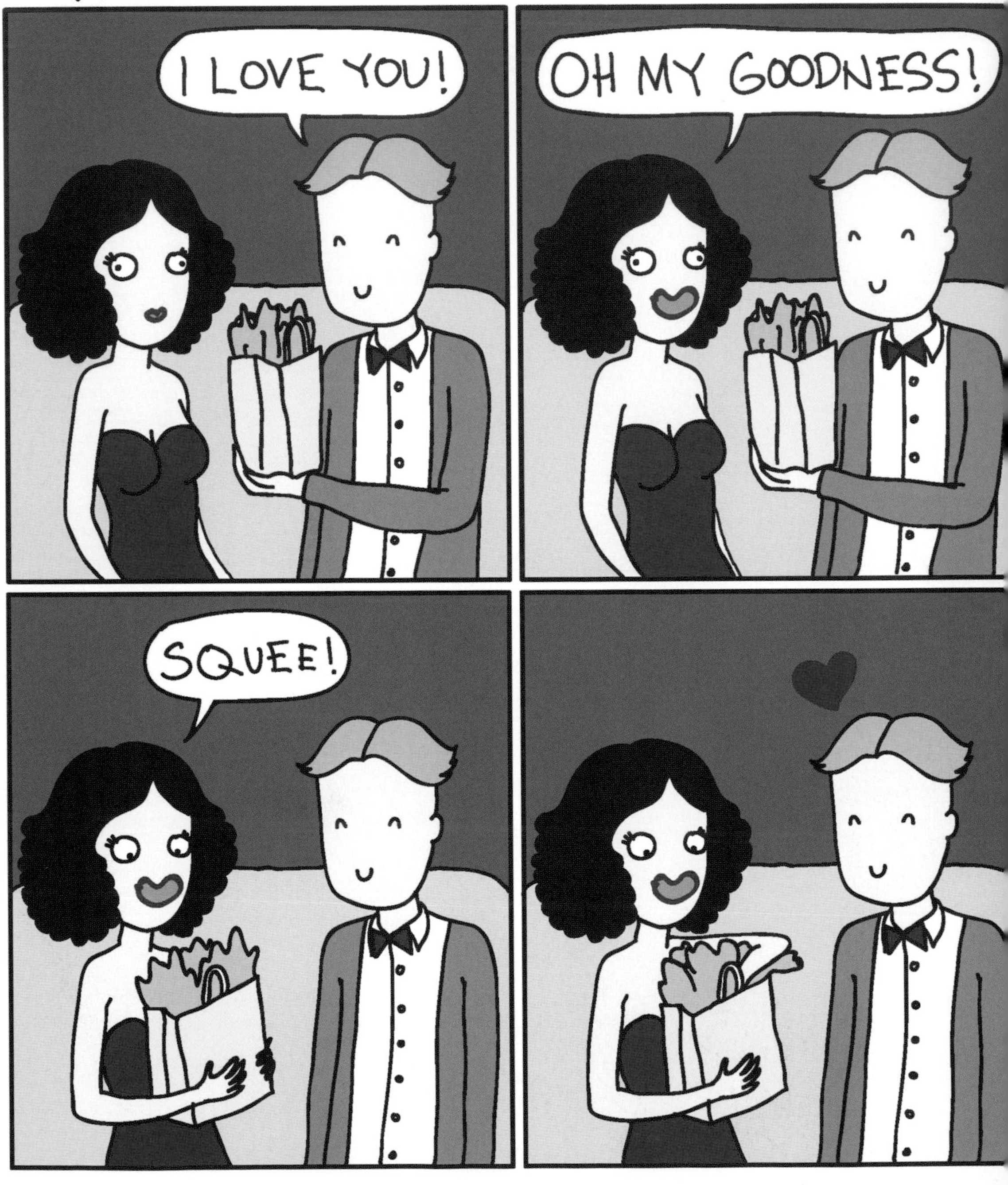
I LOVE YOU!
OH MY GOODNESS!
SQUEE!

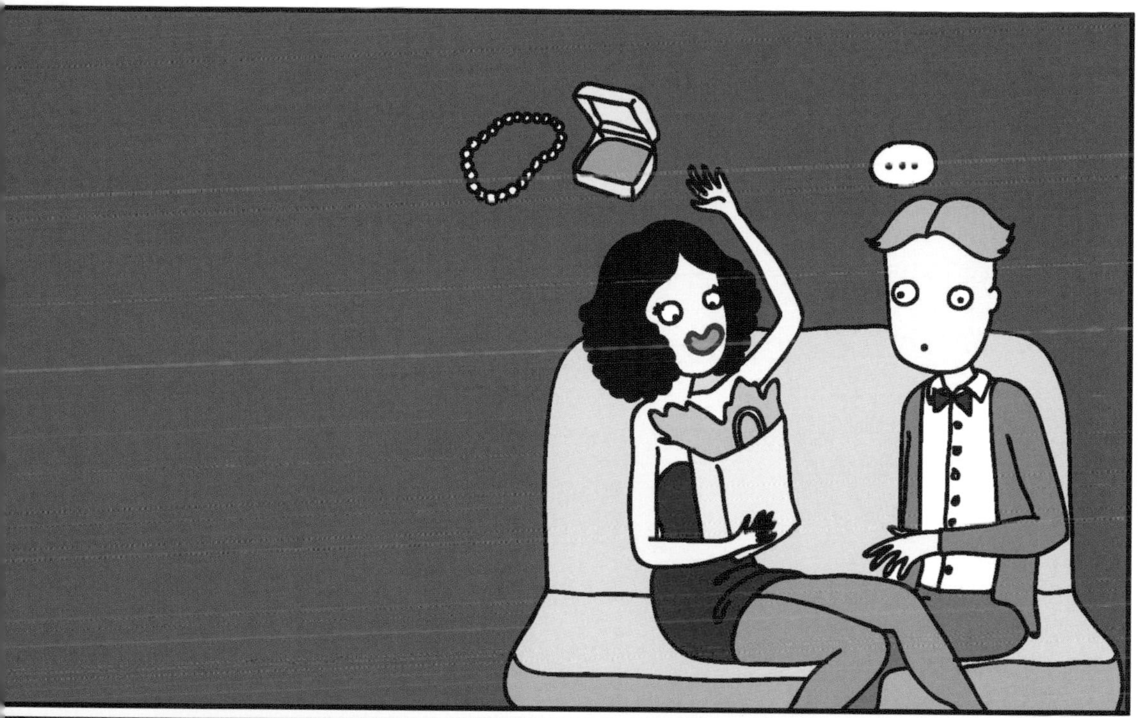
...

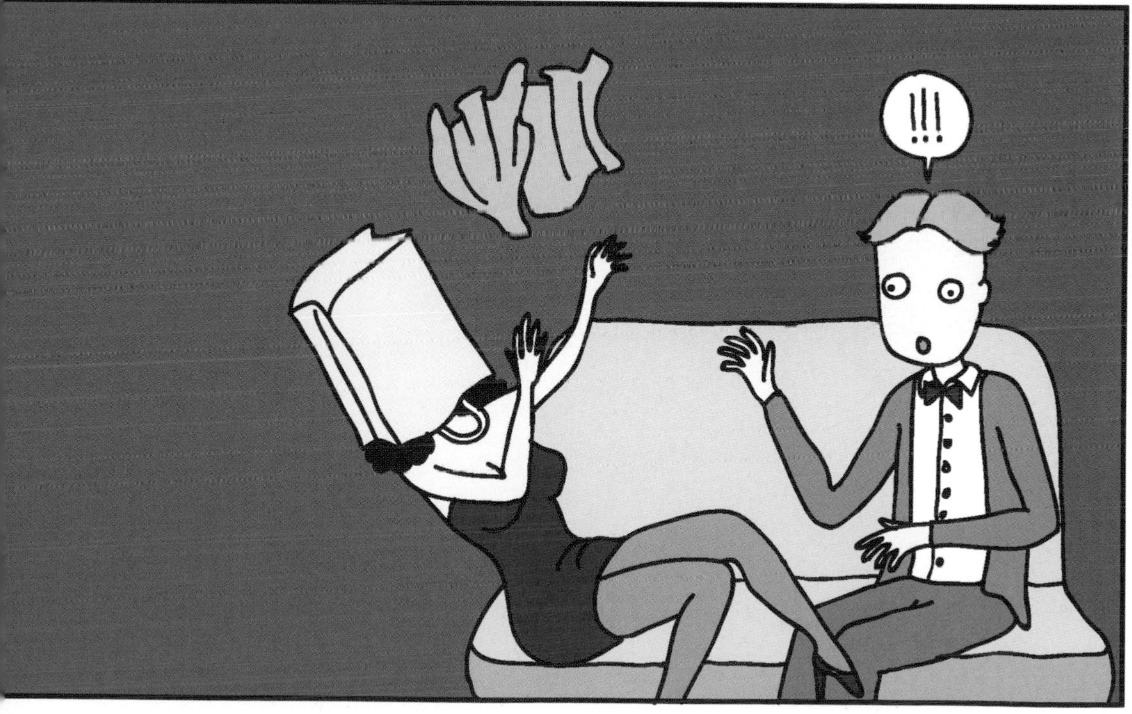
!!!

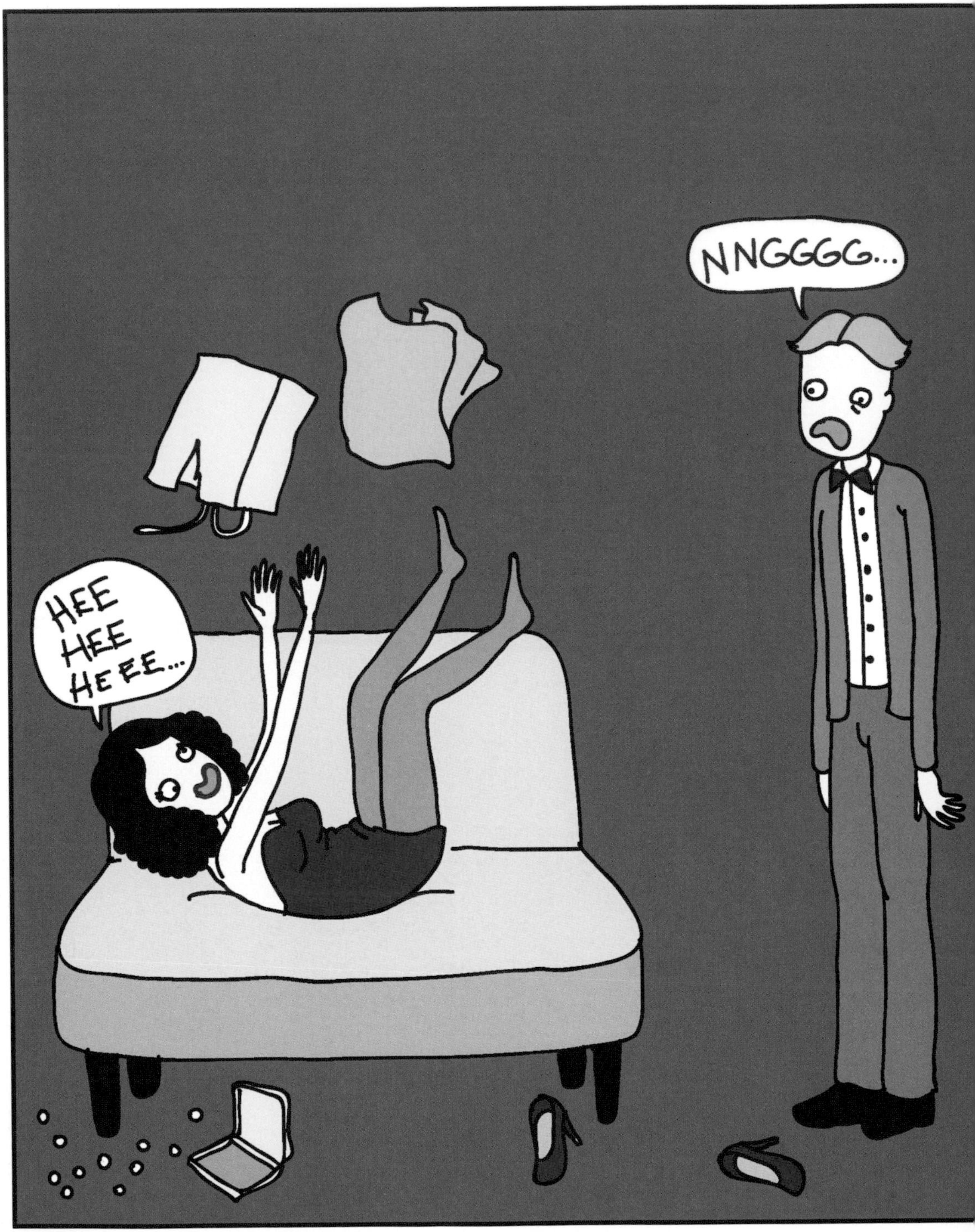
HEE HEE HEEE...
NNGGGG...

ADVENTURES IN PET SITTING

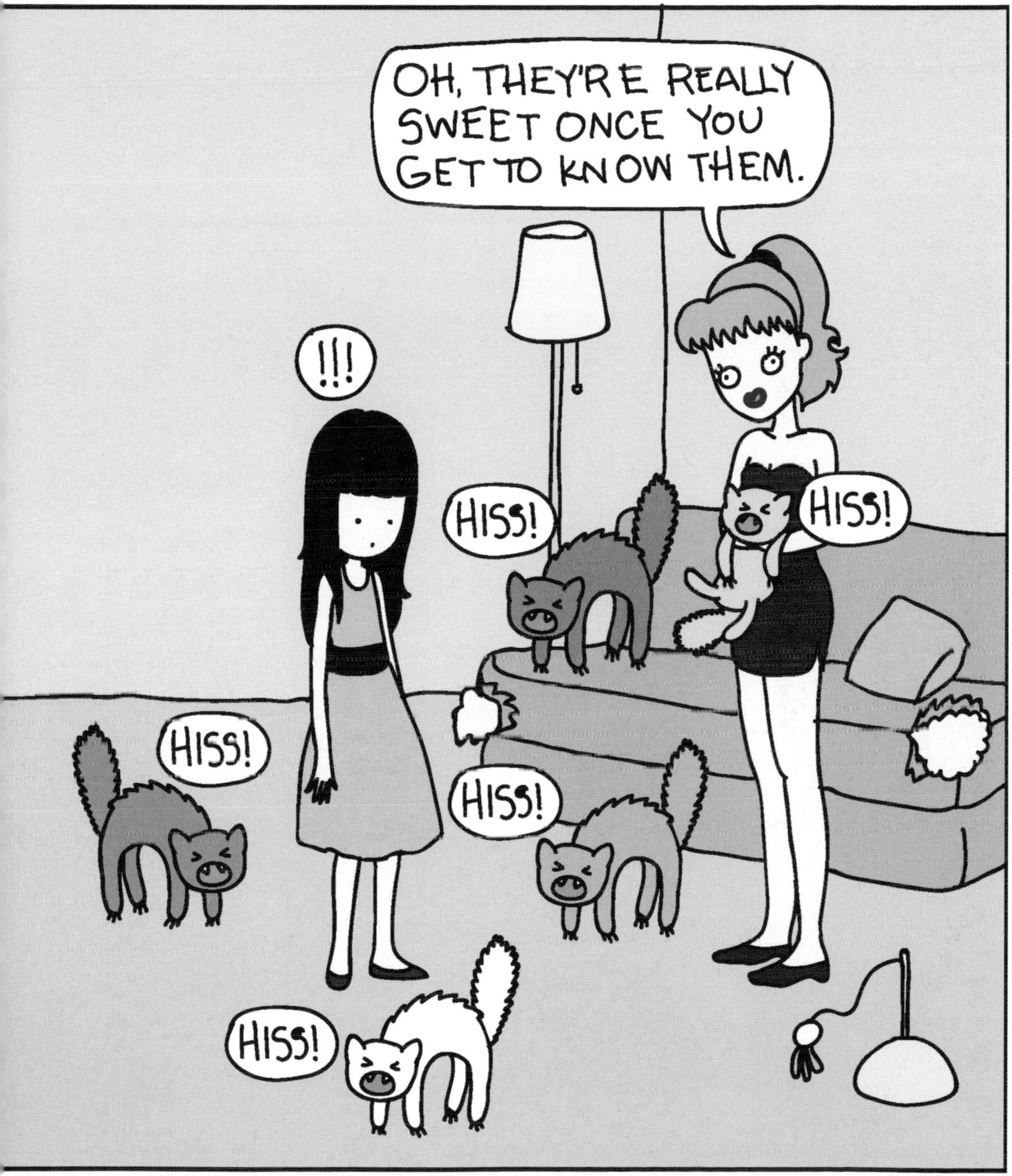
OH, THEY'RE REALLY SWEET ONCE YOU GET TO KNOW THEM.
!!!
HISS!
HISS!
HISS!
HISS!
HISS!

ADVENTURES IN PET SITTING

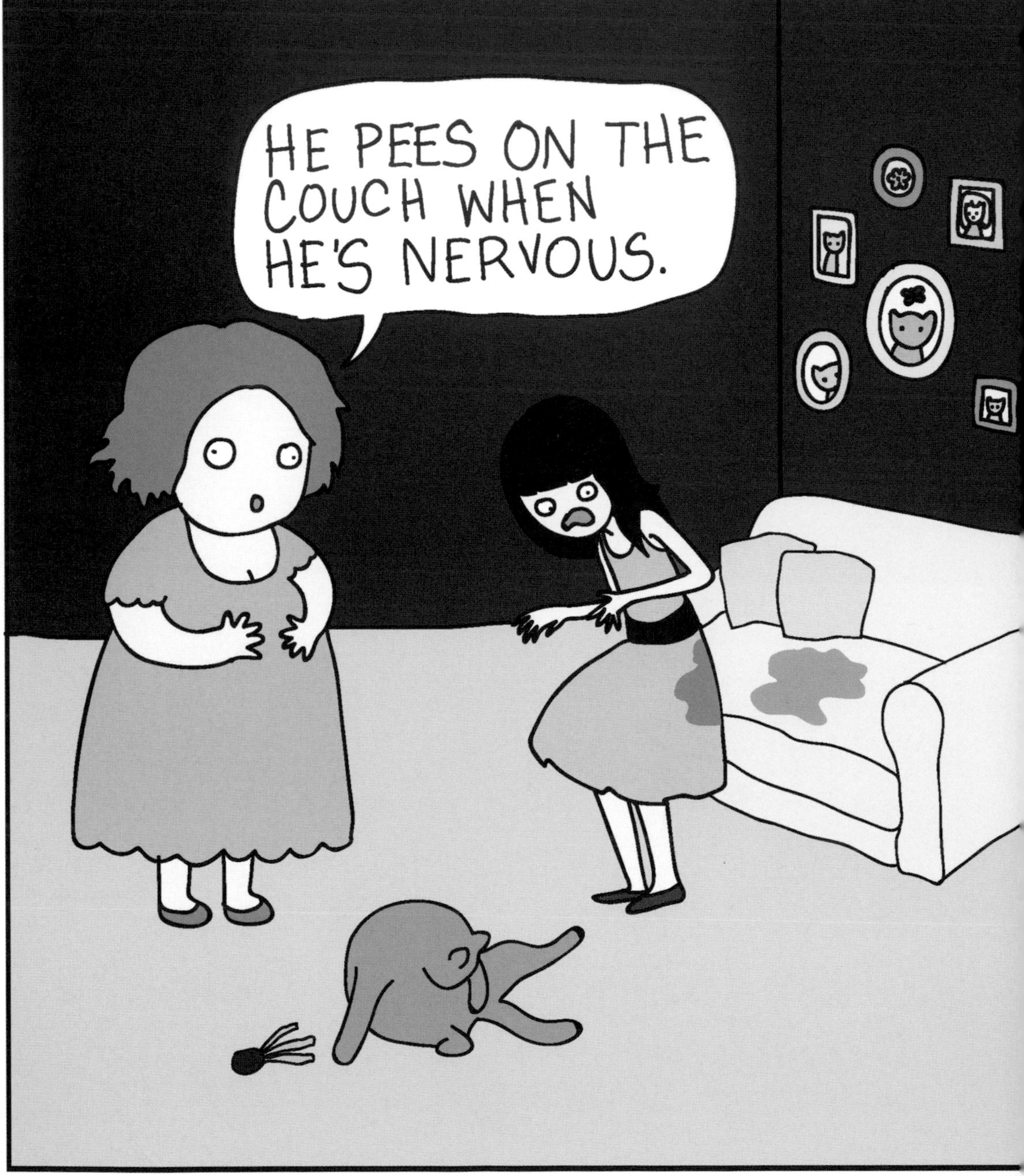
HE PEES ON THE COUCH WHEN HE'S NERVOUS.

ADVENTURES IN PET SITTING

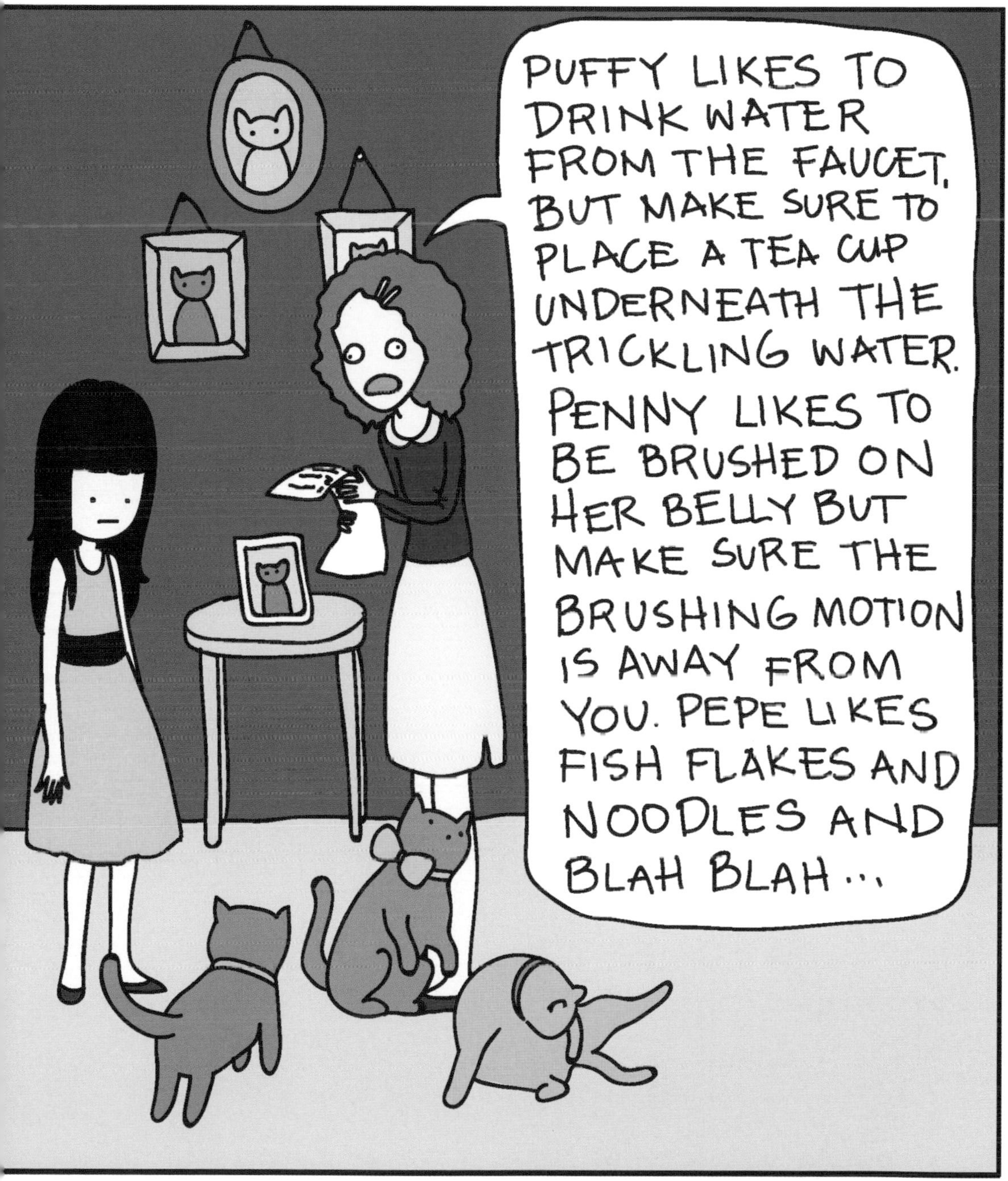
PUFFY LIKES TO DRINK WATER FROM THE FAUCET, BUT MAKE SURE TO PLACE A TEA CUP UNDERNEATH THE TRICKLING WATER. PENNY LIKES TO BE BRUSHED ON HER BELLY BUT MAKE SURE THE BRUSHING MOTION IS AWAY FROM YOU. PEPE LIKES FISH FLAKES AND NOODLES AND BLAH BLAH...

IF HUMANS ACTED LIKE CATS

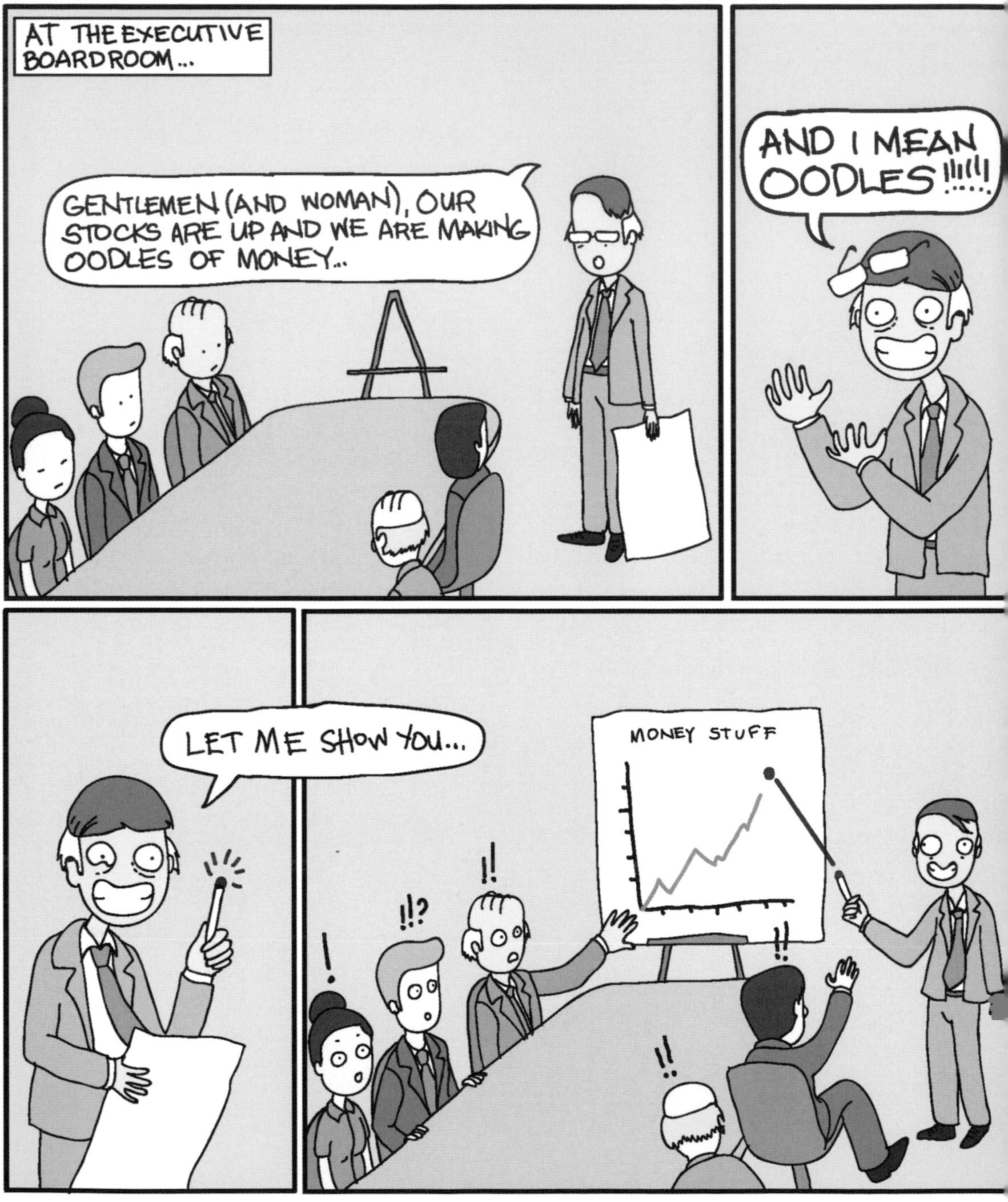
AT THE EXECUTIVE BOARDROOM...
GENTLEMEN (AND WOMAN), OUR STOCKS ARE UP AND WE ARE MAKING OODLES OF MONEY..
AND I MEAN OODLES!!!!!!
LET ME SHOW YOU...
MONEY STUFF
!
!!?
!!
!!
!!

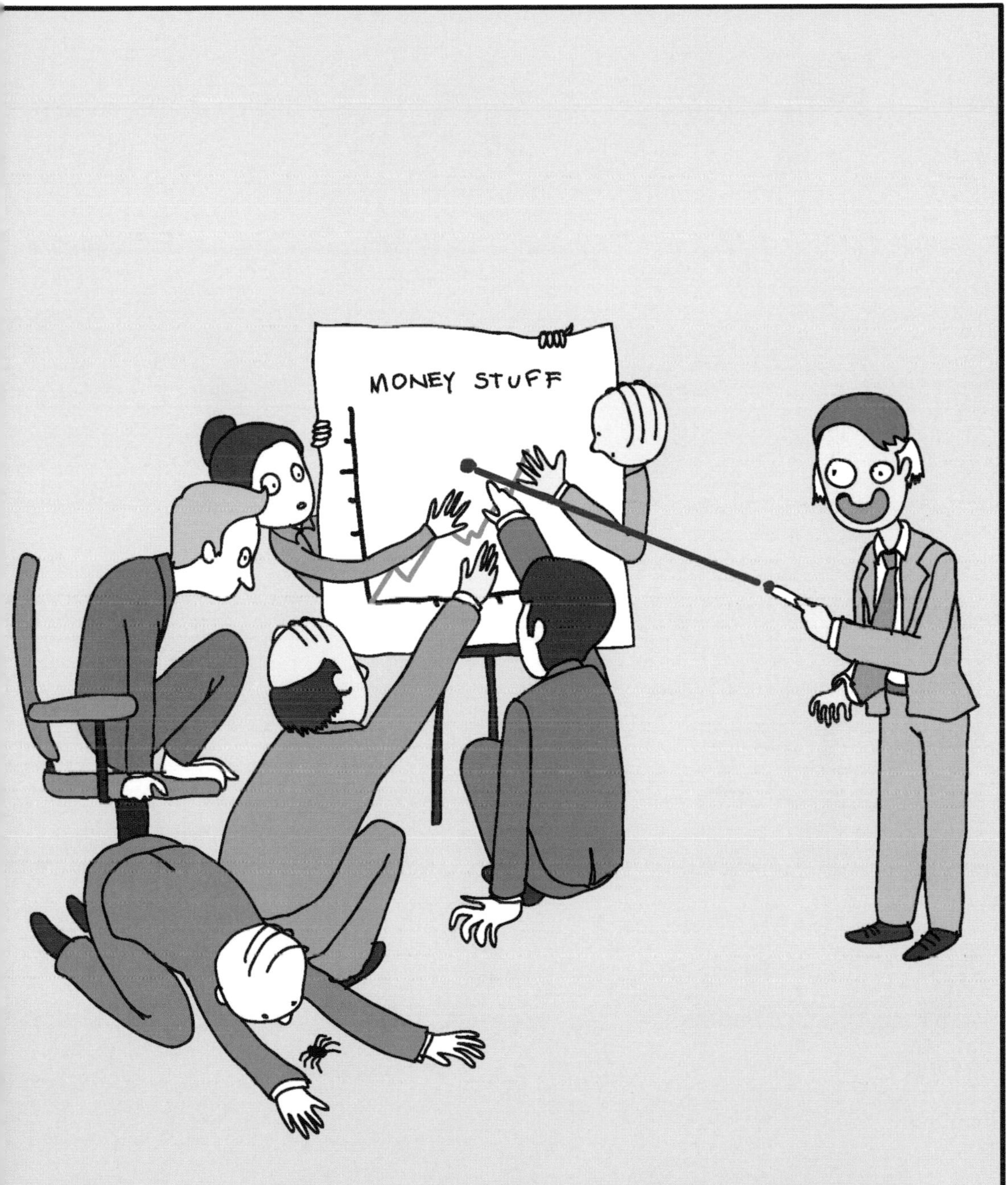
MONEY STUFF

An Adorable Stalker

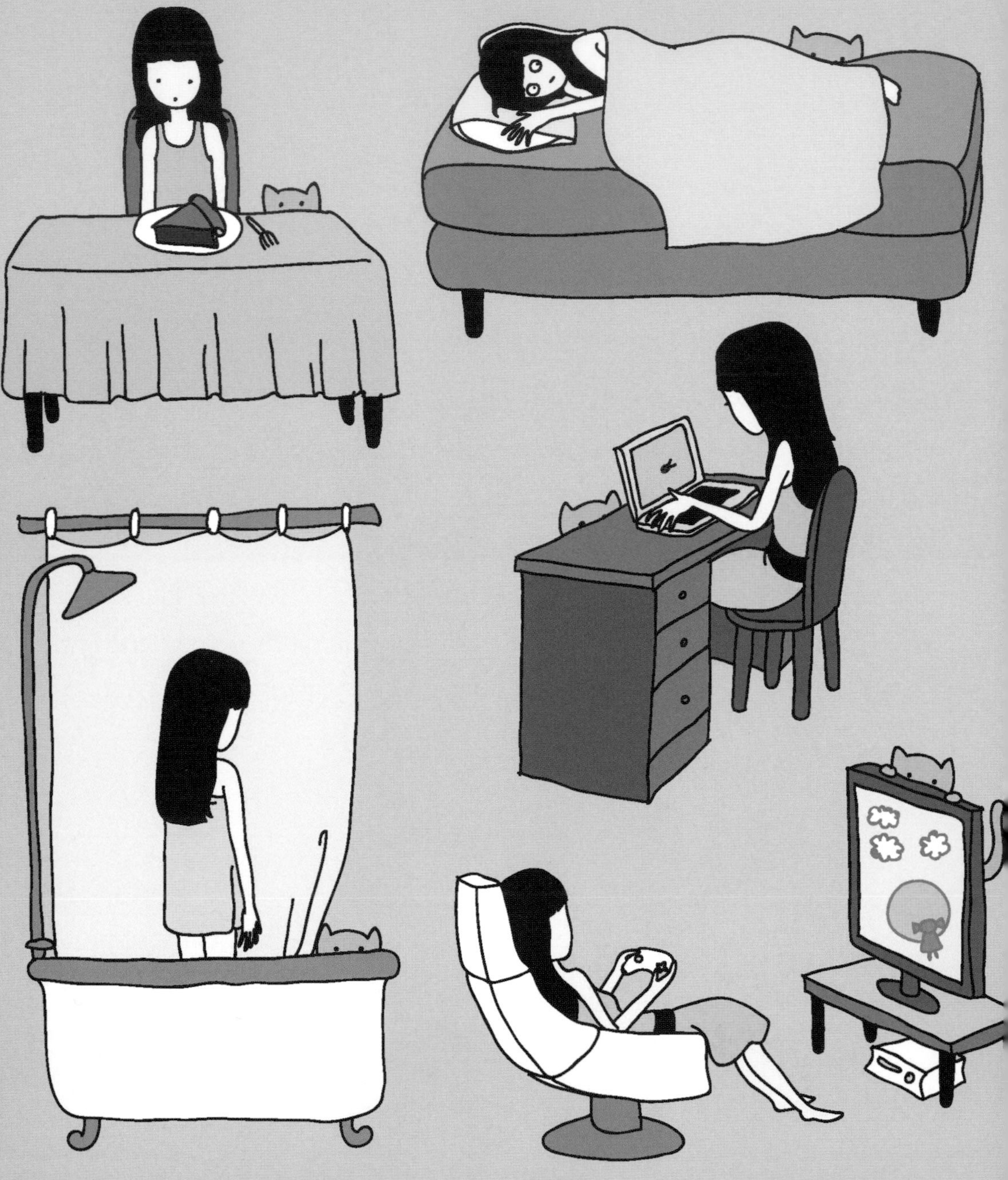

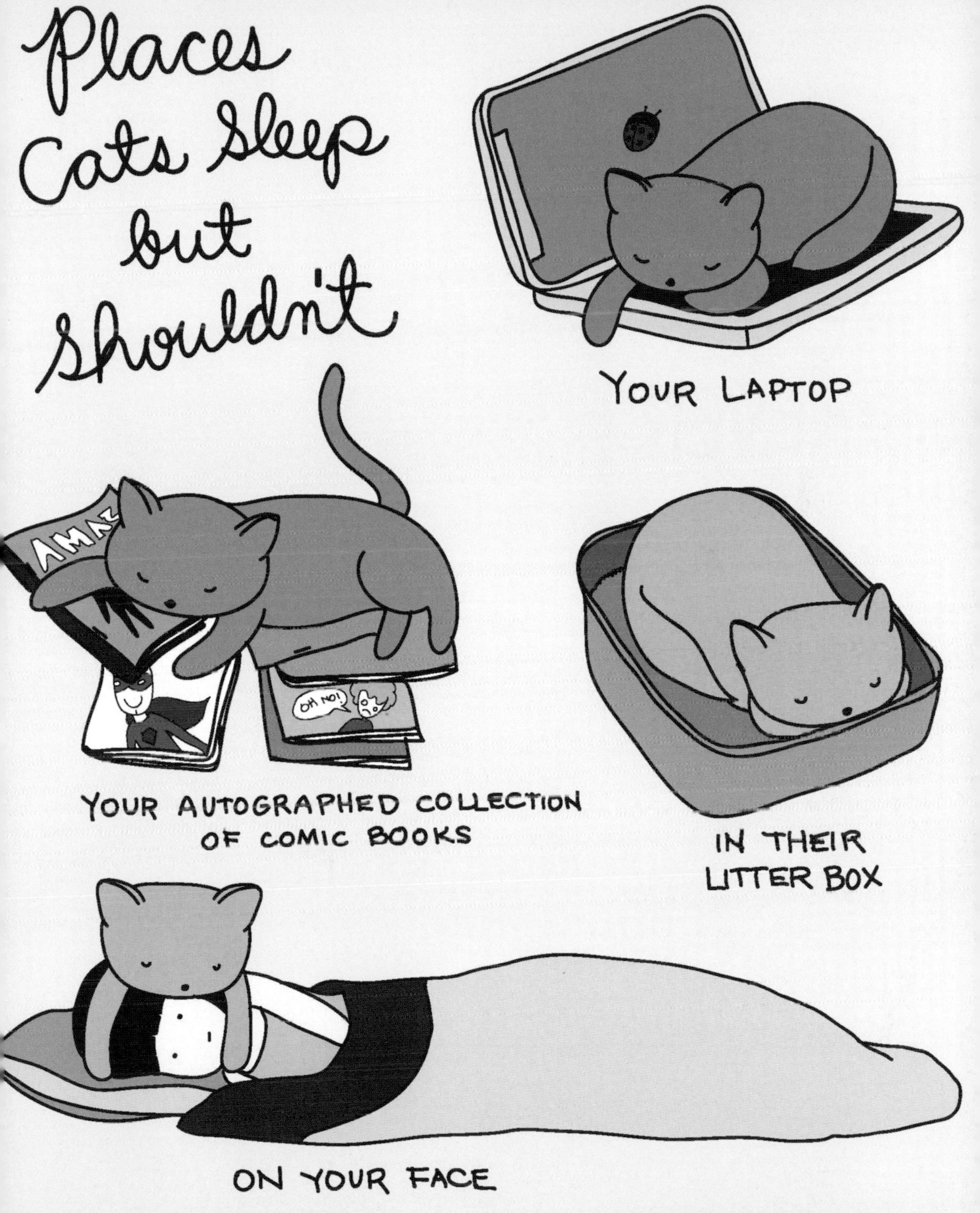

Places Cats Sleep but Shouldn't
YOUR LAPTOP
AMAZ
OH NO!
YOUR AUTOGRAPHED COLLECTION OF COMIC BOOKS
IN THEIR LITTER BOX
ON YOUR FACE

IF THE INTERNET BREAKS-FOREVER

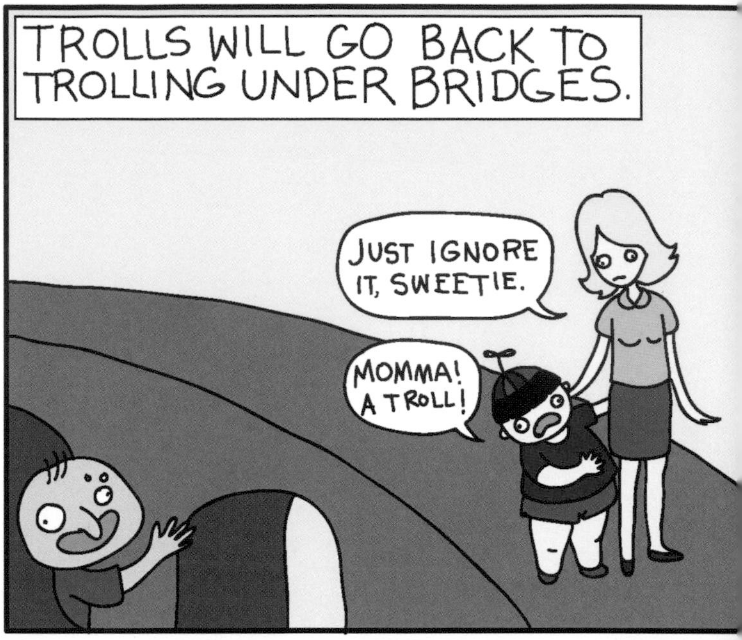
TROLLS WILL GO BACK TO TROLLING UNDER BRIDGES.
JUST IGNORE IT, SWEETIE.
MOMMA! A TROLL!

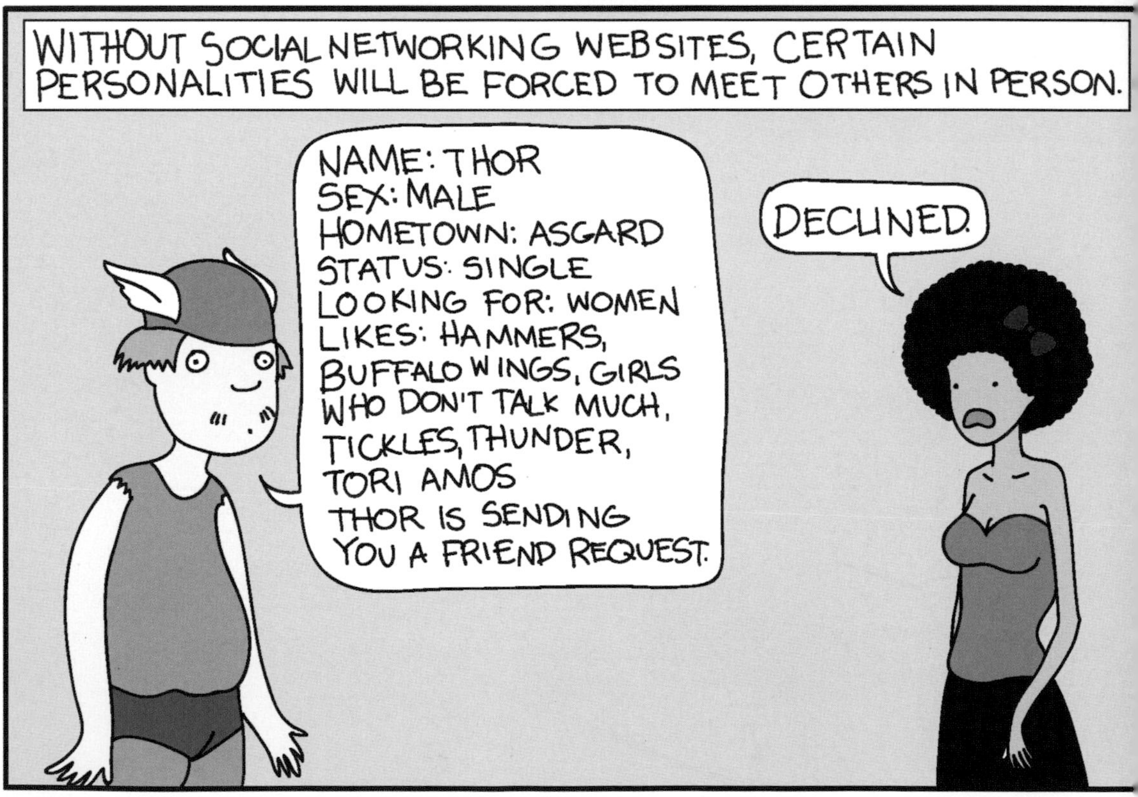
WITHOUT SOCIAL NETWORKING WEBSITES, CERTAIN PERSONALITIES WILL BE FORCED TO MEET OTHERS IN PERSON.
NAME: THOR SEX: MALE HOMETOWN: ASGARD STATUS: SINGLE LOOKING FOR: WOMEN LIKES: HAMMERS, BUFFALO WINGS, GIRLS WHO DON'T TALK MUCH, TICKLES, THUNDER, TORI AMOS THOR IS SENDING YOU A FRIEND REQUEST.
DECLINED.

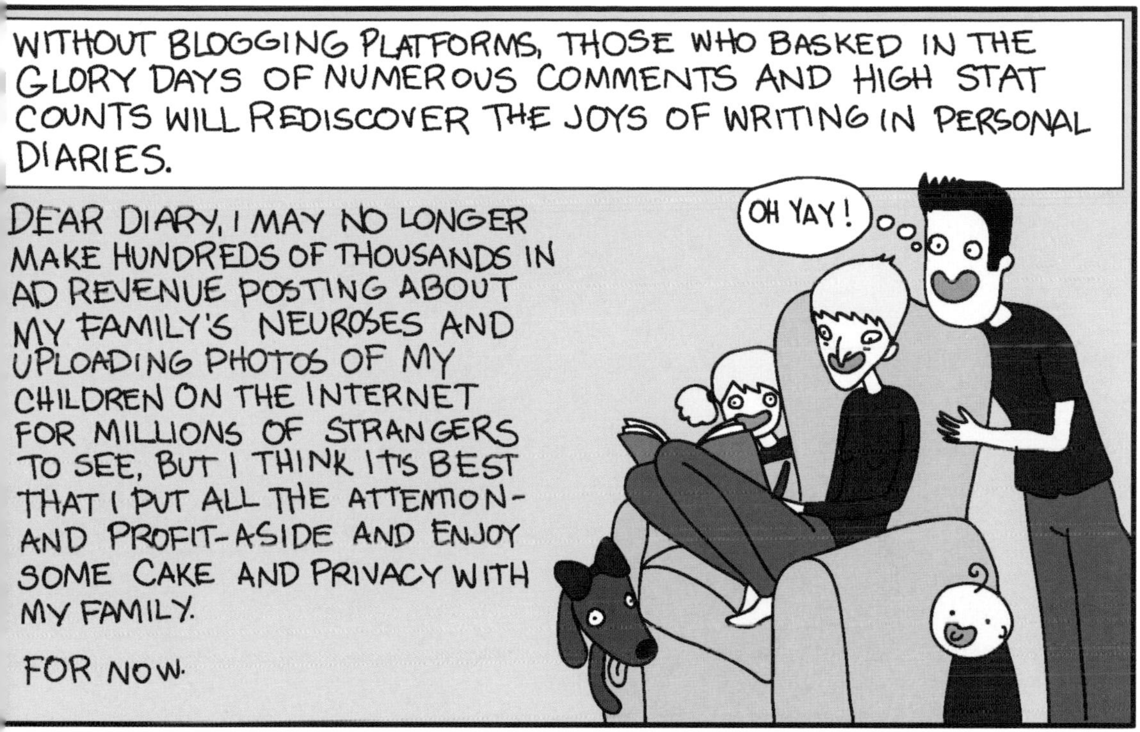
WITHOUT BLOGGING PLATFORMS, THOSE WHO BASKED IN THE GLORY DAYS OF NUMEROUS COMMENTS AND HIGH STAT COUNTS WILL REDISCOVER THE JOYS OF WRITING IN PERSONAL DIARIES.
DEAR DIARY, I MAY NO LONGER MAKE HUNDREDS OF THOUSANDS IN AD REVENUE POSTING ABOUT MY FAMILY'S NEUROSES AND UPLOADING PHOTOS OF MY CHILDREN ON THE INTERNET FOR MILLIONS OF STRANGERS TO SEE, BUT I THINK IT'S BEST THAT I PUT ALL THE ATTENTION-AND PROFIT-ASIDE AND ENJOY SOME CAKE AND PRIVACY WITH MY FAMILY.
FOR NOW.
OH YAY!

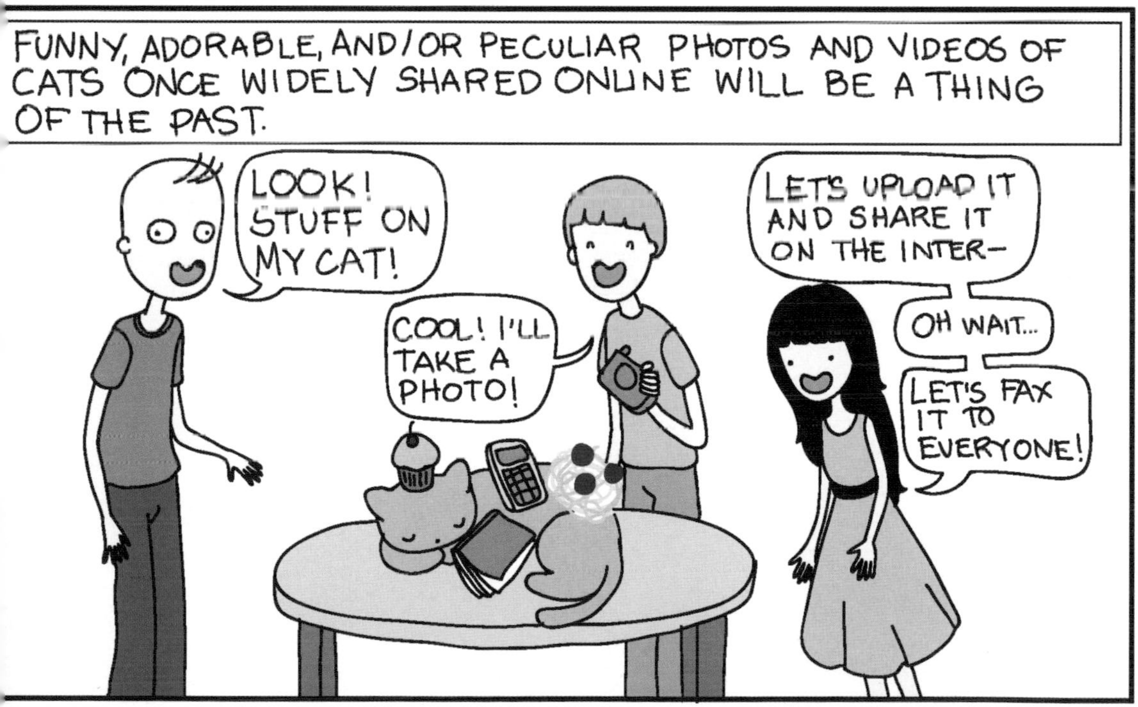
FUNNY, ADORABLE, AND/OR PECULIAR PHOTOS AND VIDEOS OF CATS ONCE WIDELY SHARED ONLINE WILL BE A THING OF THE PAST.
LOOK! STUFF ON MY CAT!
COOL! I'LL TAKE A PHOTO!
LET'S UPLOAD IT AND SHARE IT ON THE INTER–
OH WAIT...
LET'S FAX IT TO EVERYONE!

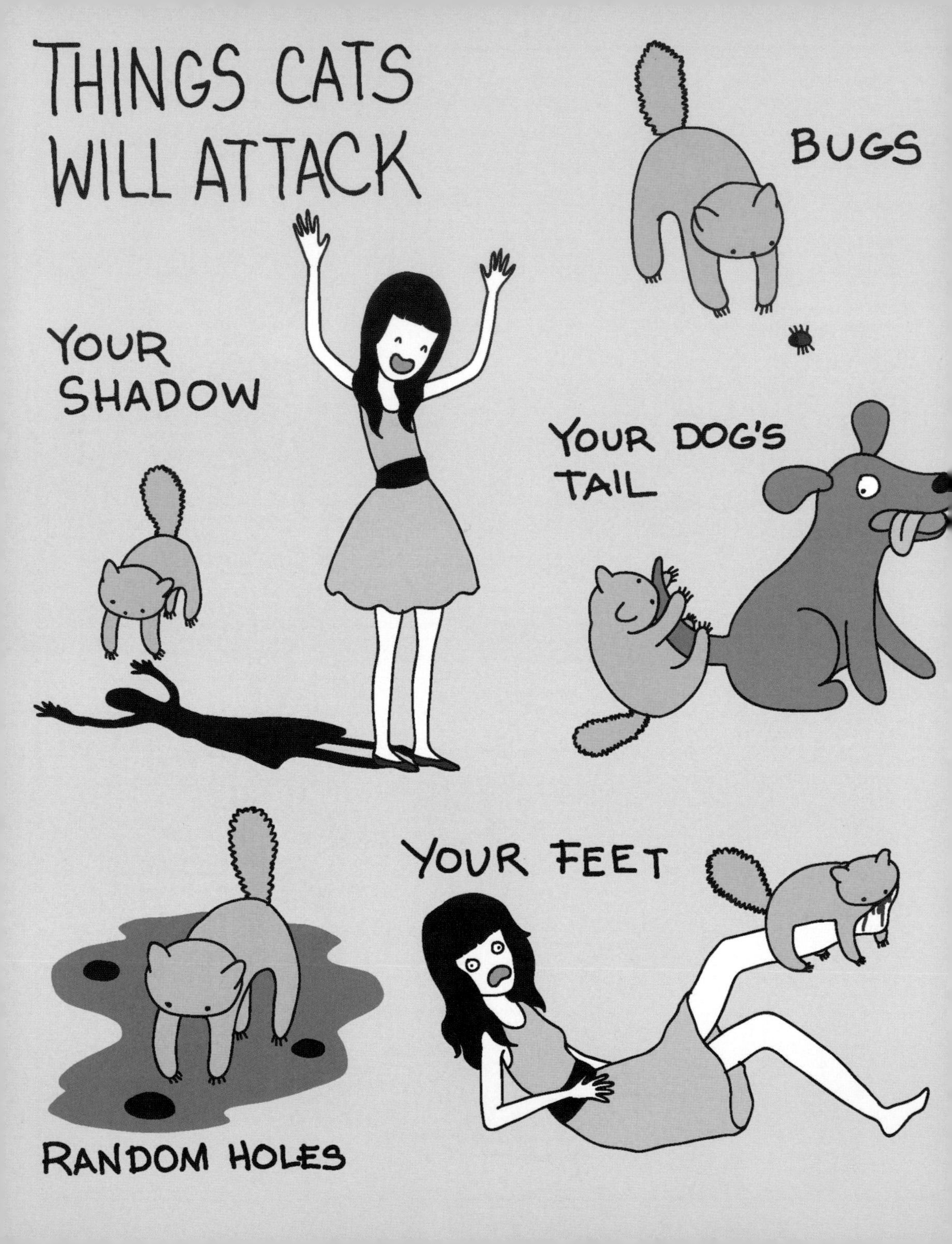
THINGS CATS WILL ATTACK
BUGS
YOUR SHADOW
YOUR DOG'S TAIL
YOUR FEET
RANDOM HOLES

Things Cats Drink Water From

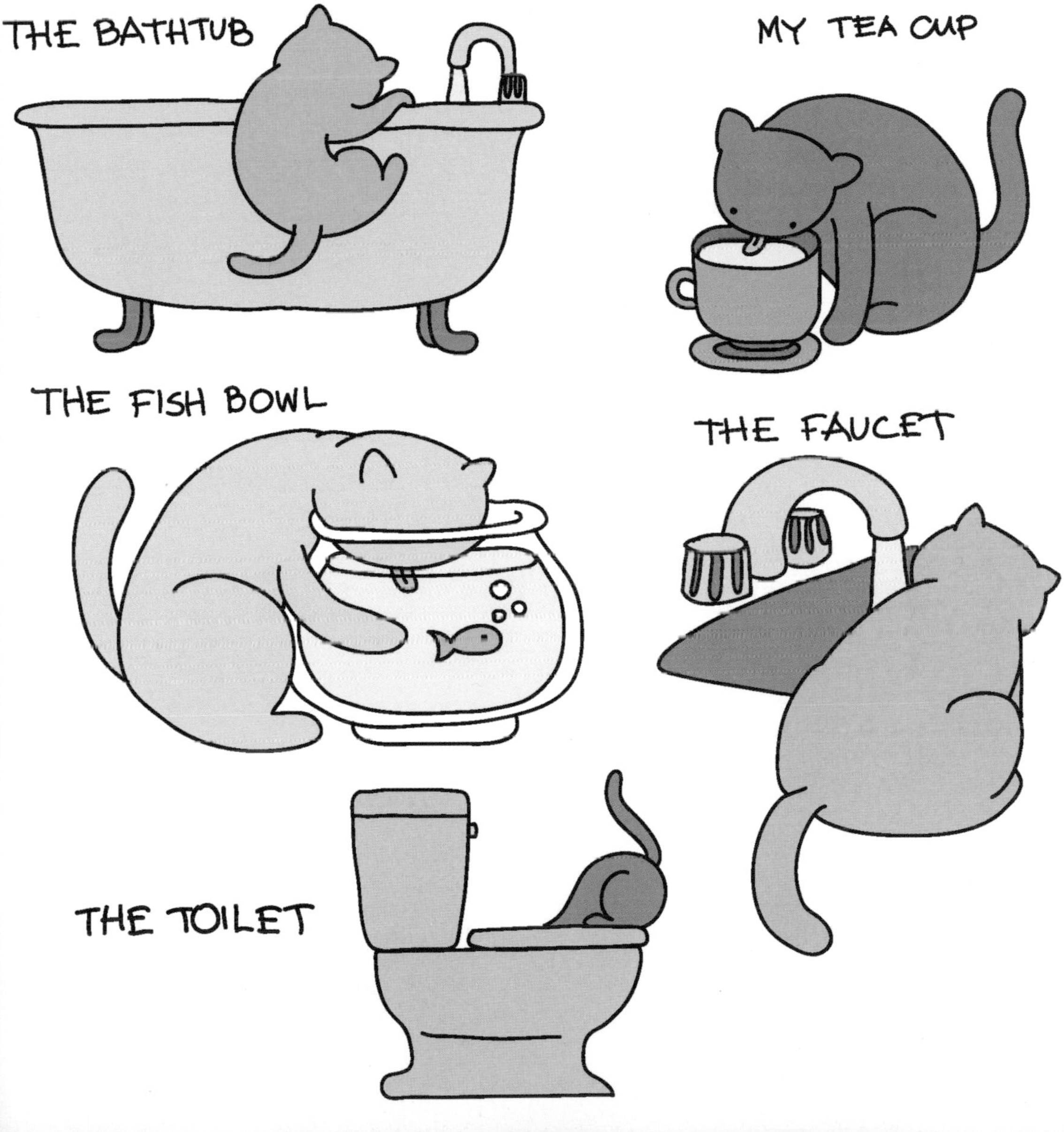
THE BATHTUB
MY TEA CUP
THE FISH BOWL
THE FAUCET
THE TOILET

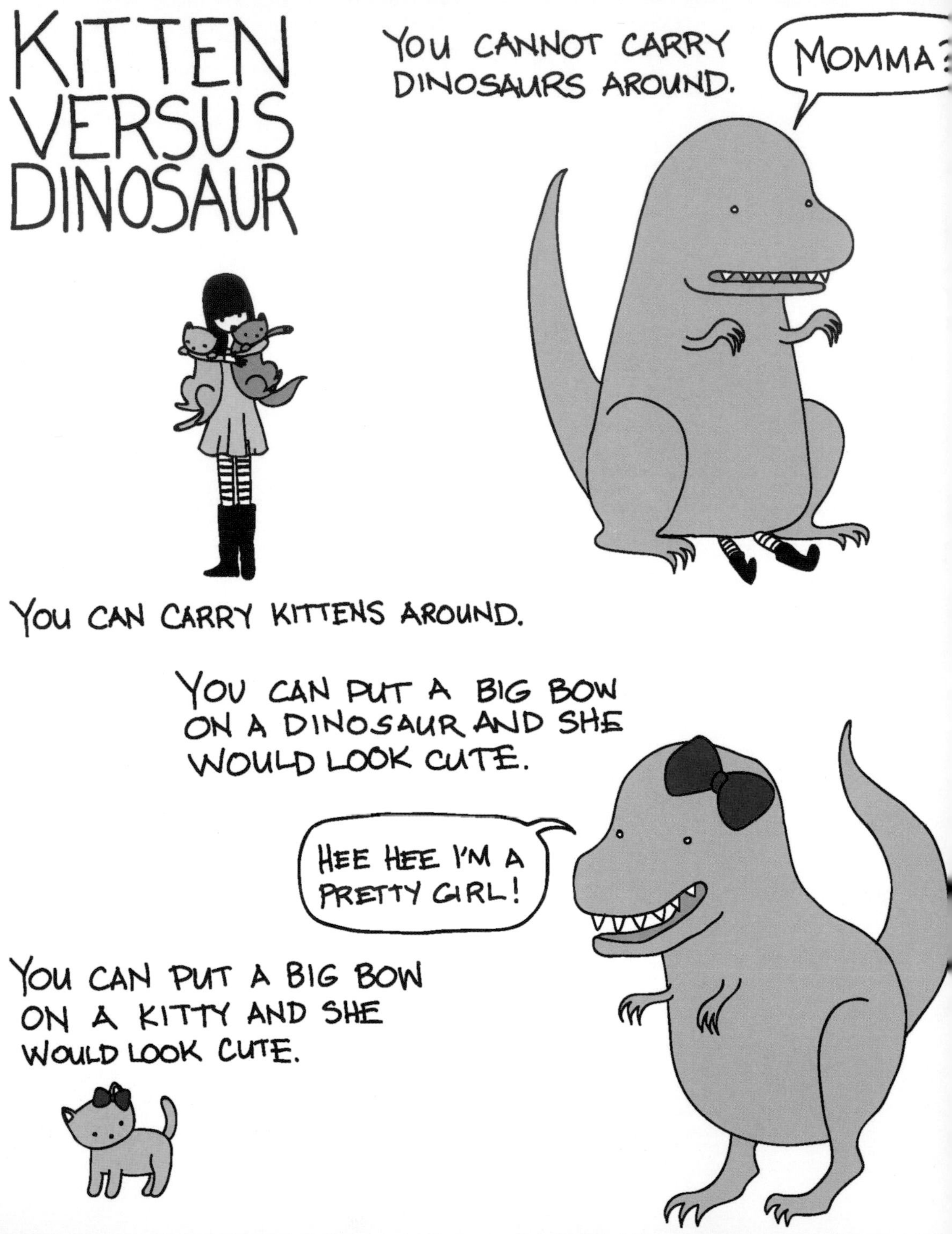
KITTEN VERSUS DINOSAUR
YOU CANNOT CARRY DINOSAURS AROUND.
MOMMA
YOU CAN CARRY KITTENS AROUND.
YOU CAN PUT A BIG BOW ON A DINOSAUR AND SHE WOULD LOOK CUTE.
HEE HEE I'M A PRETTY GIRL!
YOU CAN PUT A BIG BOW ON A KITTY AND SHE WOULD LOOK CUTE.

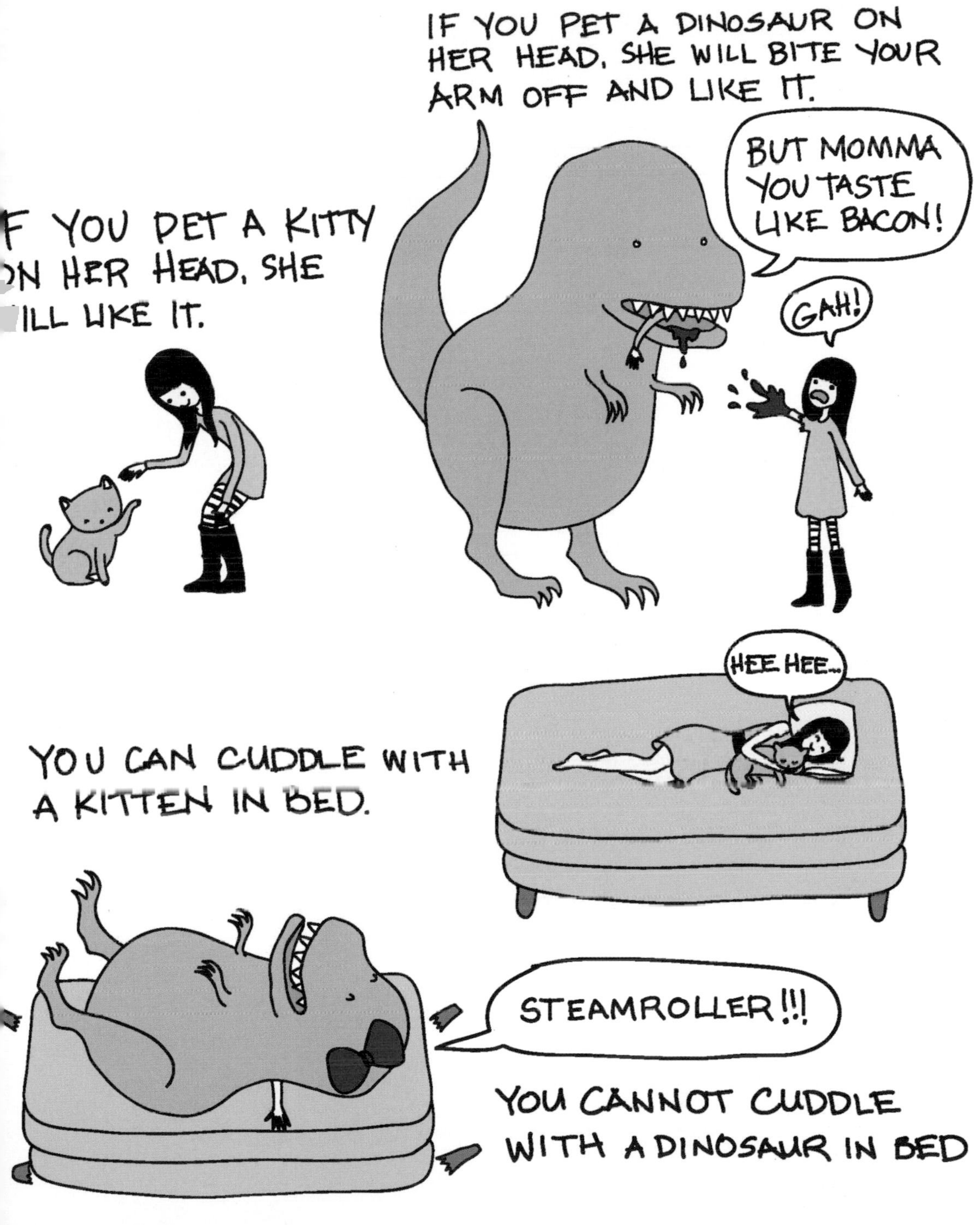
IF YOU PET A KITTY ON HER HEAD, SHE WILL LIKE IT.
IF YOU PET A DINOSAUR ON HER HEAD, SHE WILL BITE YOUR ARM OFF AND LIKE IT.
BUT MOMMA YOU TASTE LIKE BACON!
GAH!
YOU CAN CUDDLE WITH A KITTEN IN BED.
HEE HEE...
STEAMROLLER!!!
YOU CANNOT CUDDLE WITH A DINOSAUR IN BED

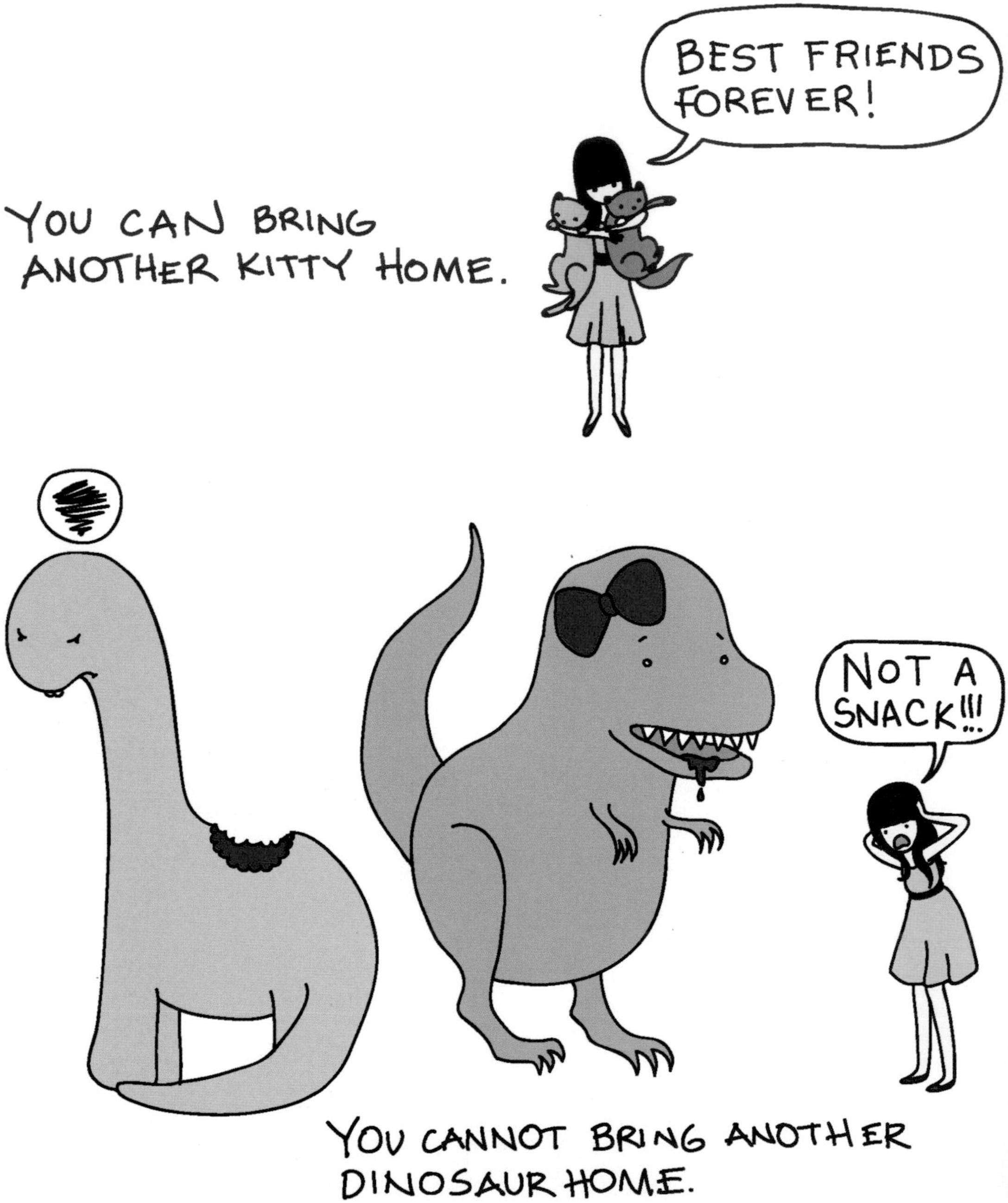
YOU CAN BRING ANOTHER KITTY HOME.
BEST FRIENDS FOREVER!
NOT A SNACK!!!
YOU CANNOT BRING ANOTHER DINOSAUR HOME.

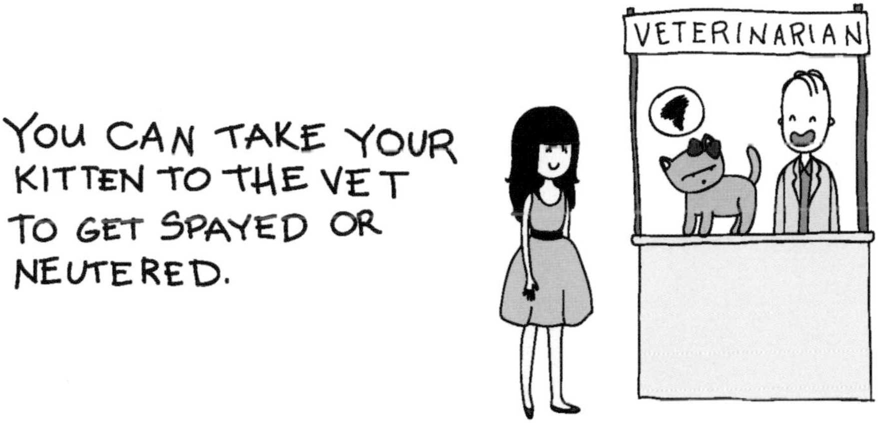
YOU CAN TAKE YOUR KITTEN TO THE VET TO GET SPAYED OR NEUTERED.
VETERINARIAN

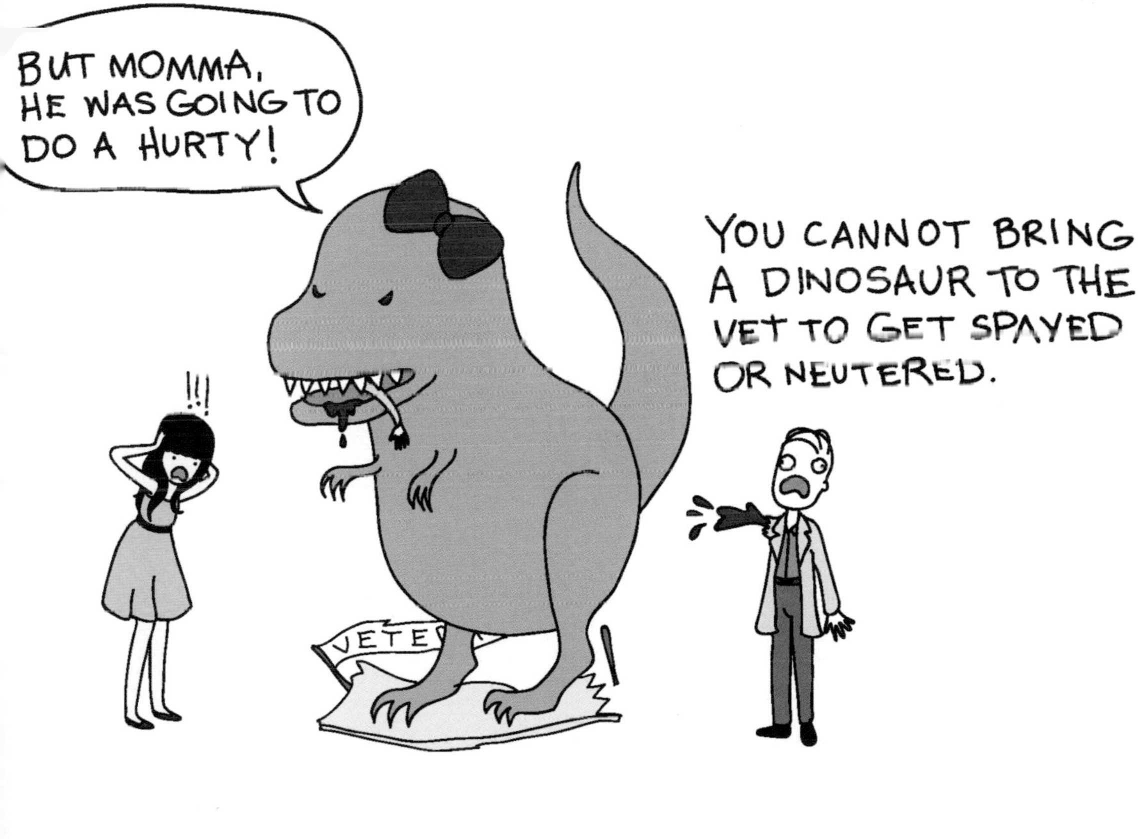
BUT MOMMA, HE WAS GOING TO DO A HURTY!
YOU CANNOT BRING A DINOSAUR TO THE VET TO GET SPAYED OR NEUTERED.
!!!
VETE

Life Without a Cat

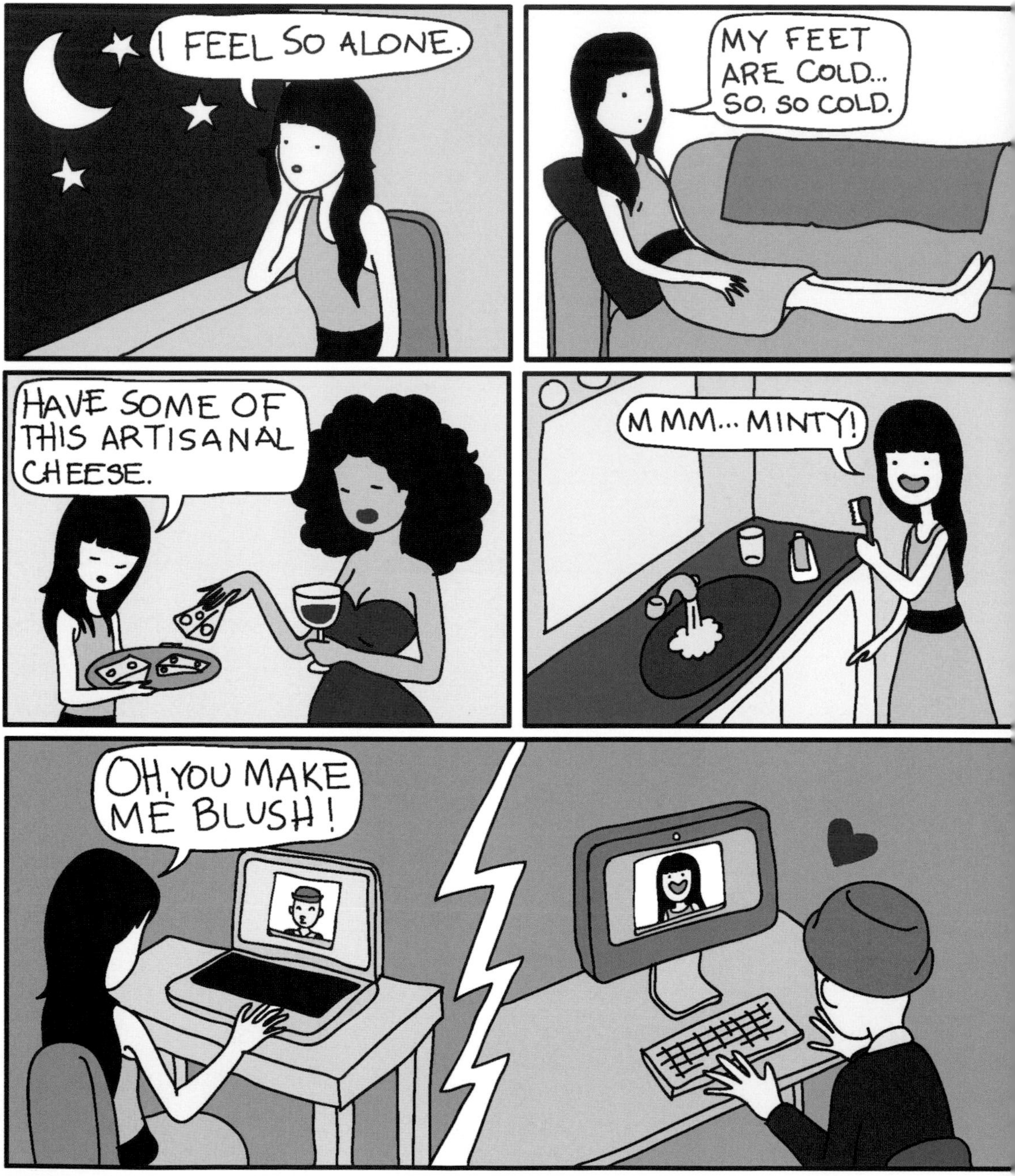

I FEEL SO ALONE.
MY FEET ARE COLD... SO, SO COLD.
HAVE SOME OF THIS ARTISANAL CHEESE.
MMM... MINTY!
OH, YOU MAKE ME BLUSH!

Life With a Cat

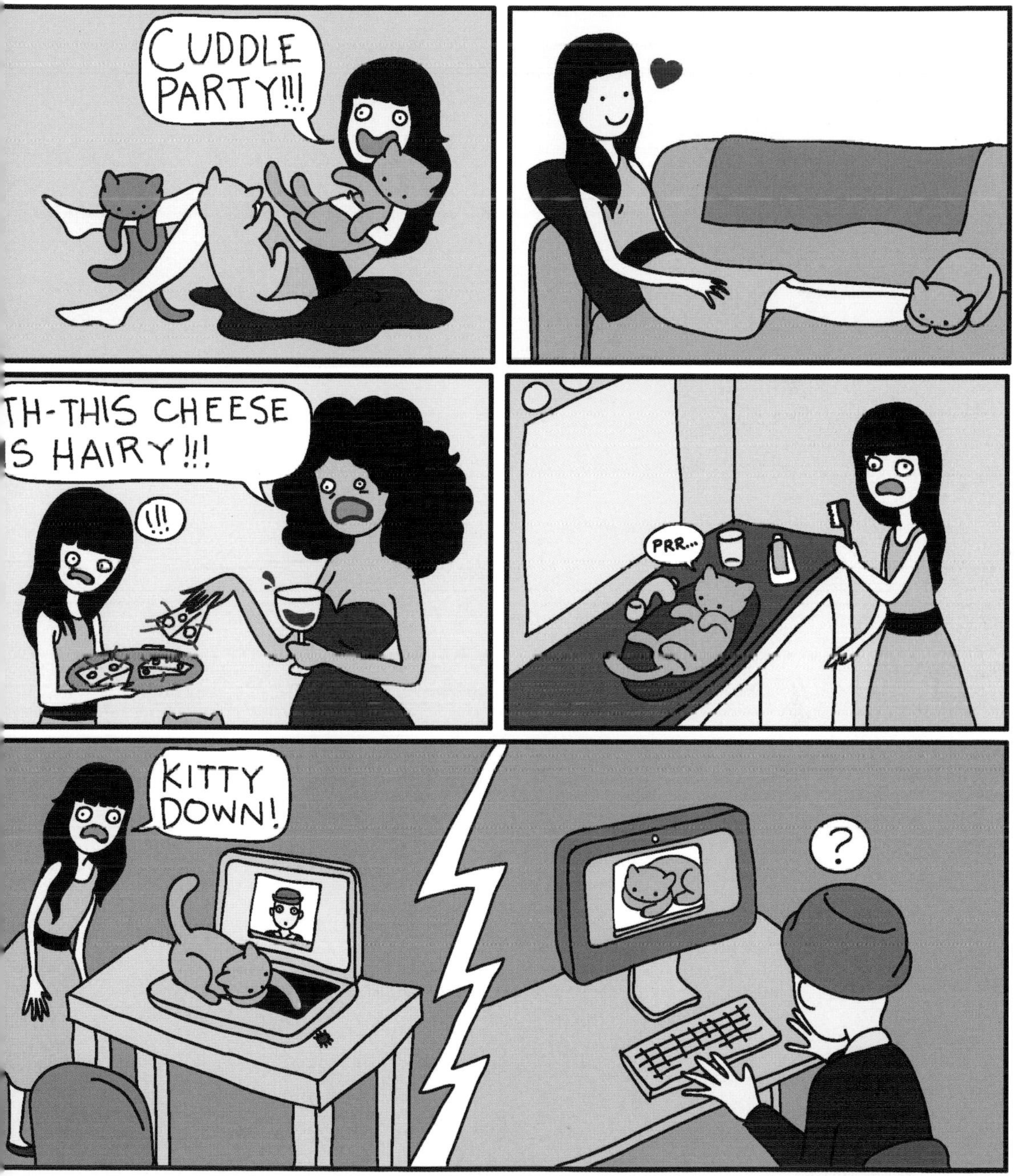

CUDDLE PARTY!!!
TH-THIS CHEESE
S HAIRY!!!
!!!
PRR...
KITTY DOWN!
?

KITTEN NIGHTMARES

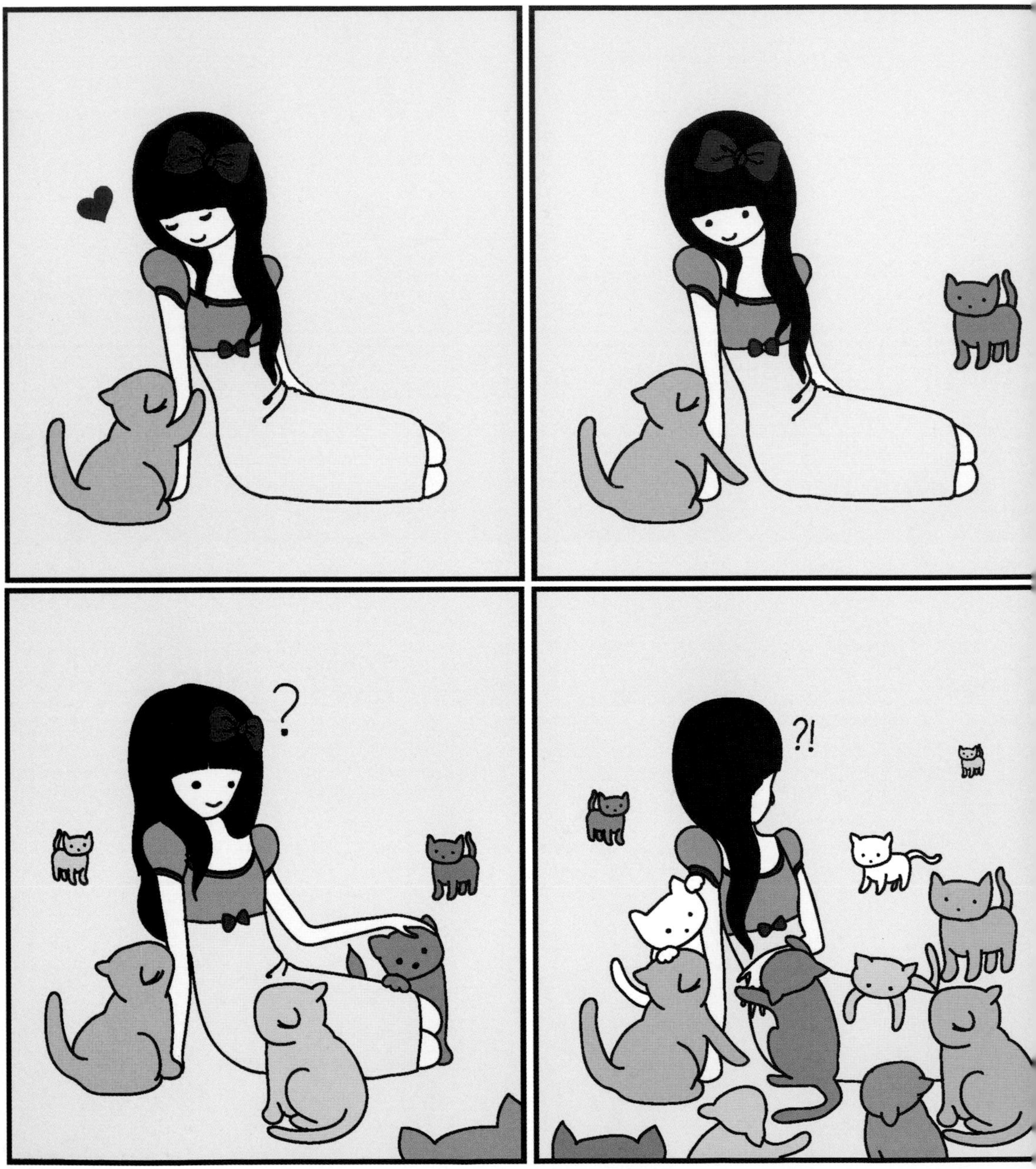
?
?!

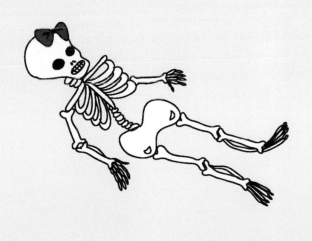

Life Without a Cat

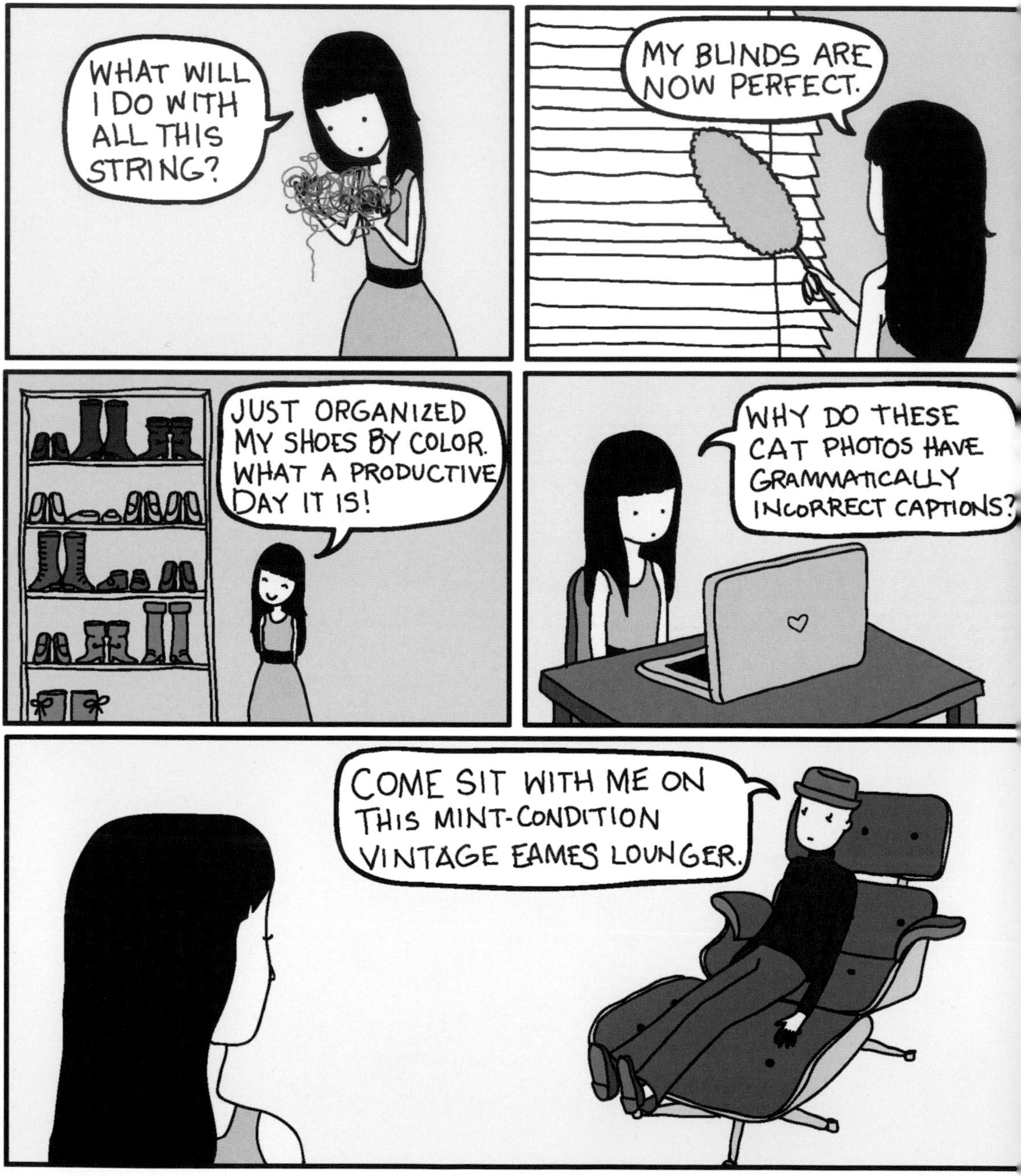

WHAT WILL I DO WITH ALL THIS STRING?
MY BLINDS ARE NOW PERFECT.
JUST ORGANIZED MY SHOES BY COLOR. WHAT A PRODUCTIVE DAY IT IS!
WHY DO THESE CAT PHOTOS HAVE GRAMMATICALLY INCORRECT CAPTIONS?
COME SIT WITH ME ON THIS MINT-CONDITION VINTAGE EAMES LOUNGER.

Life With a Cat

HACCKKK!!!
HAHA! INVISIBLE SHOPPING CART! HA HA!
THIS WOODEN BENCH NEEDS CUSHIONS.

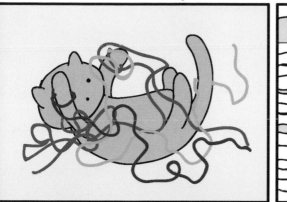

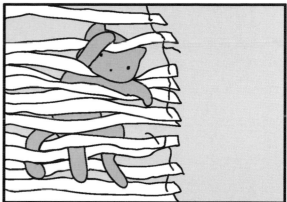

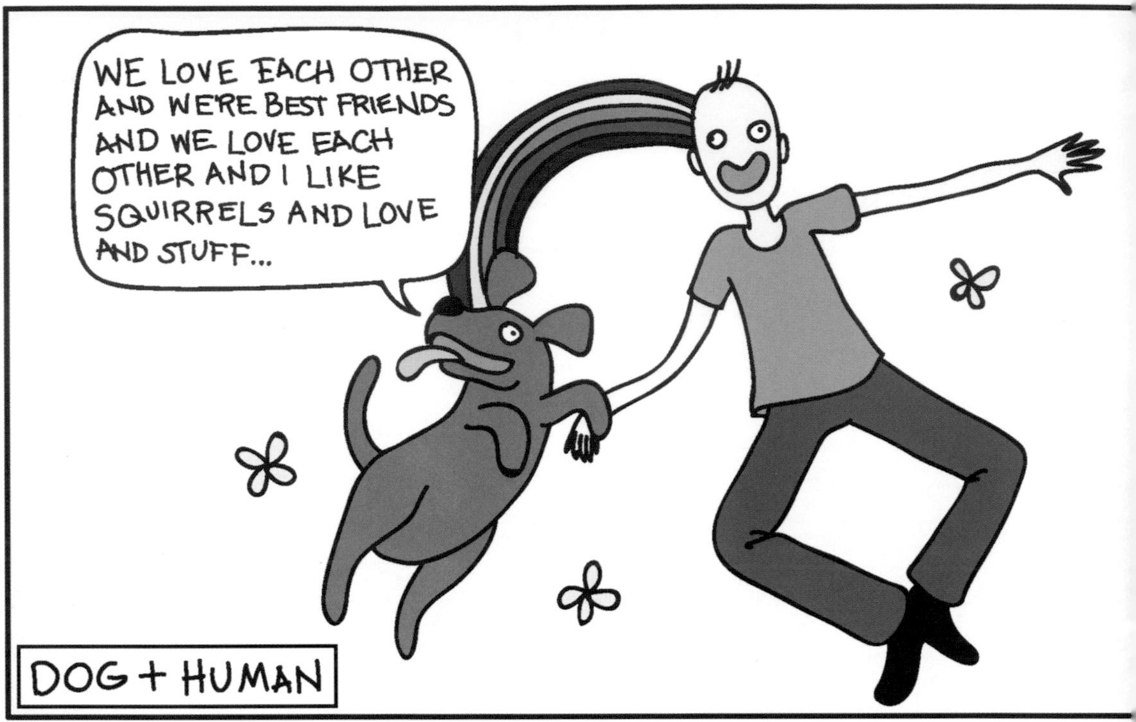
WE LOVE EACH OTHER AND WE'RE BEST FRIENDS AND WE LOVE EACH OTHER AND I LIKE SQUIRRELS AND LOVE AND STUFF...
DOG + HUMAN

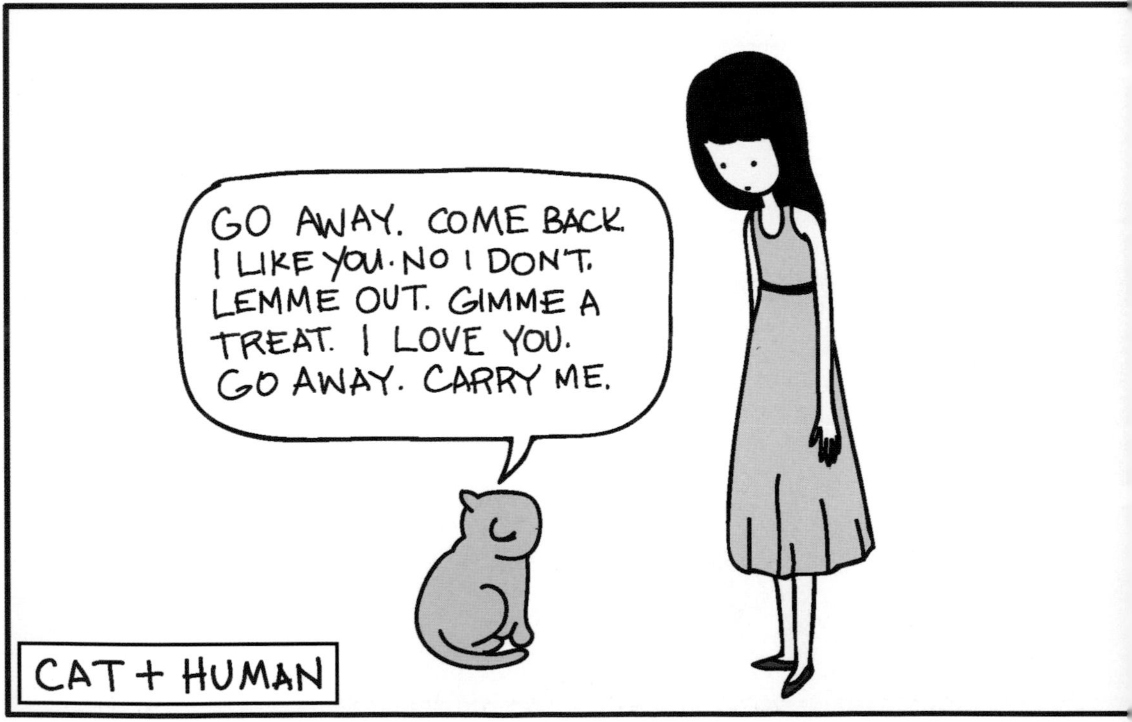
GO AWAY. COME BACK. I LIKE YOU. NO I DON'T. LEMME OUT. GIMME A TREAT. I LOVE YOU. GO AWAY. CARRY ME.
CAT + HUMAN

CATS DURING EMERGENCIES

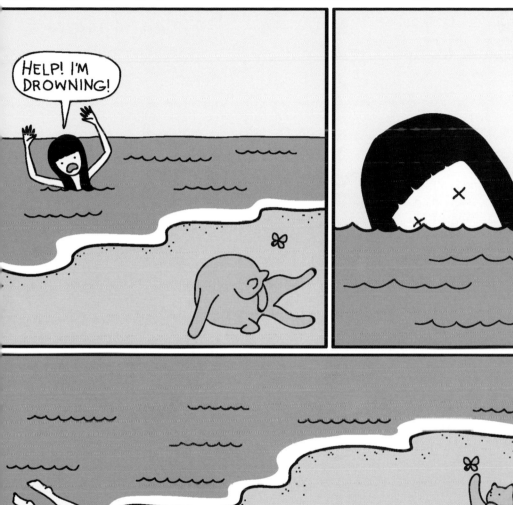

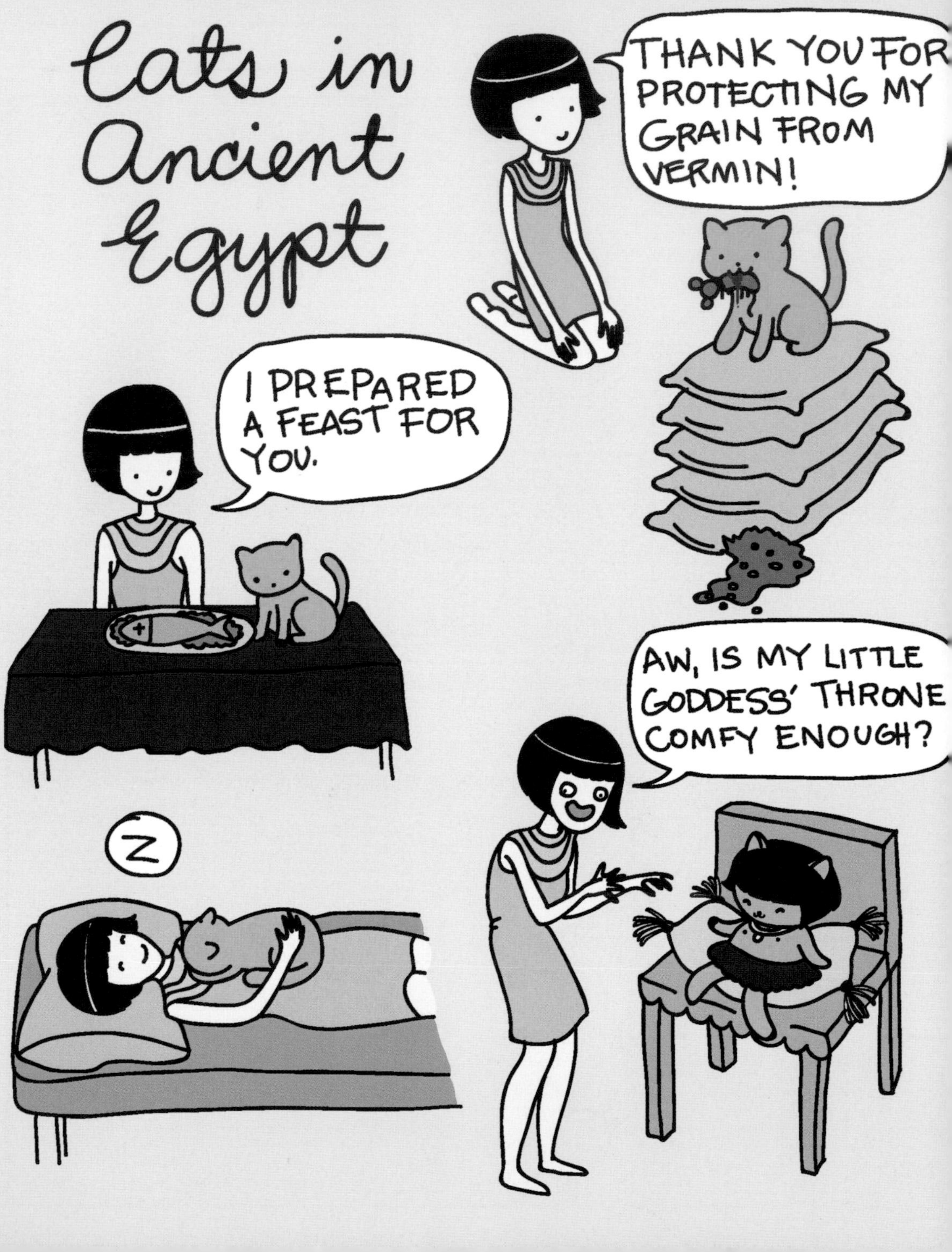
Cats in Ancient Egypt
THANK YOU FOR PROTECTING MY GRAIN FROM VERMIN!
I PREPARED A FEAST FOR YOU.
AW, IS MY LITTLE GODDESS' THRONE COMFY ENOUGH?
Z

Cats in Modern Times
I'LL HUMANELY CAPTURE THESE MICE AND RELEASE THEM IN THE WOODS!
YUM-E KIBBLE
Z
INTERNET GOLD.

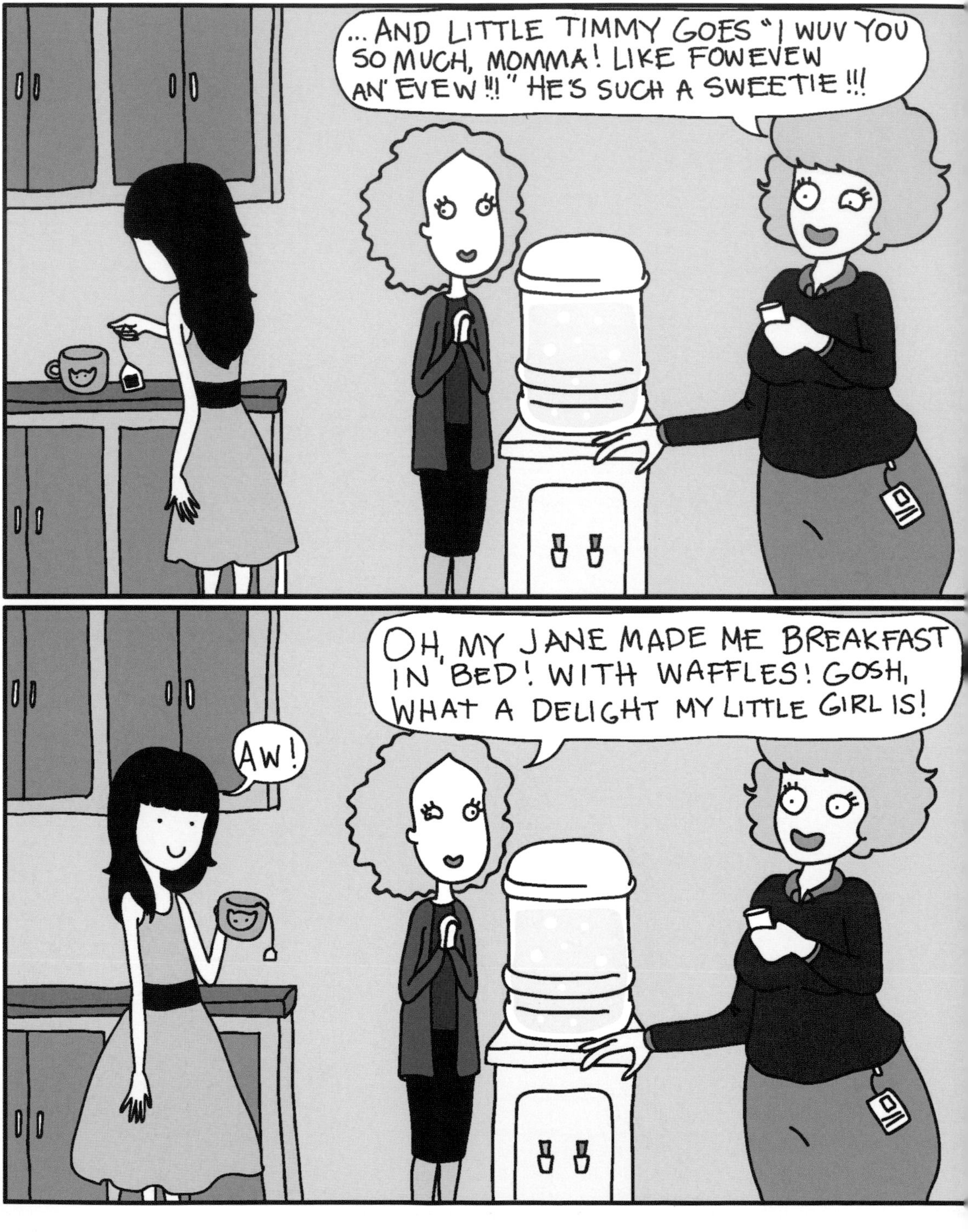
...AND LITTLE TIMMY GOES "I WUV YOU SO MUCH, MOMMA! LIKE FOWEVEW AN' EVEW!!!" HE'S SUCH A SWEETIE!!!
OH, MY JANE MADE ME BREAKFAST IN BED! WITH WAFFLES! GOSH, WHAT A DELIGHT MY LITTLE GIRL IS!
AW!

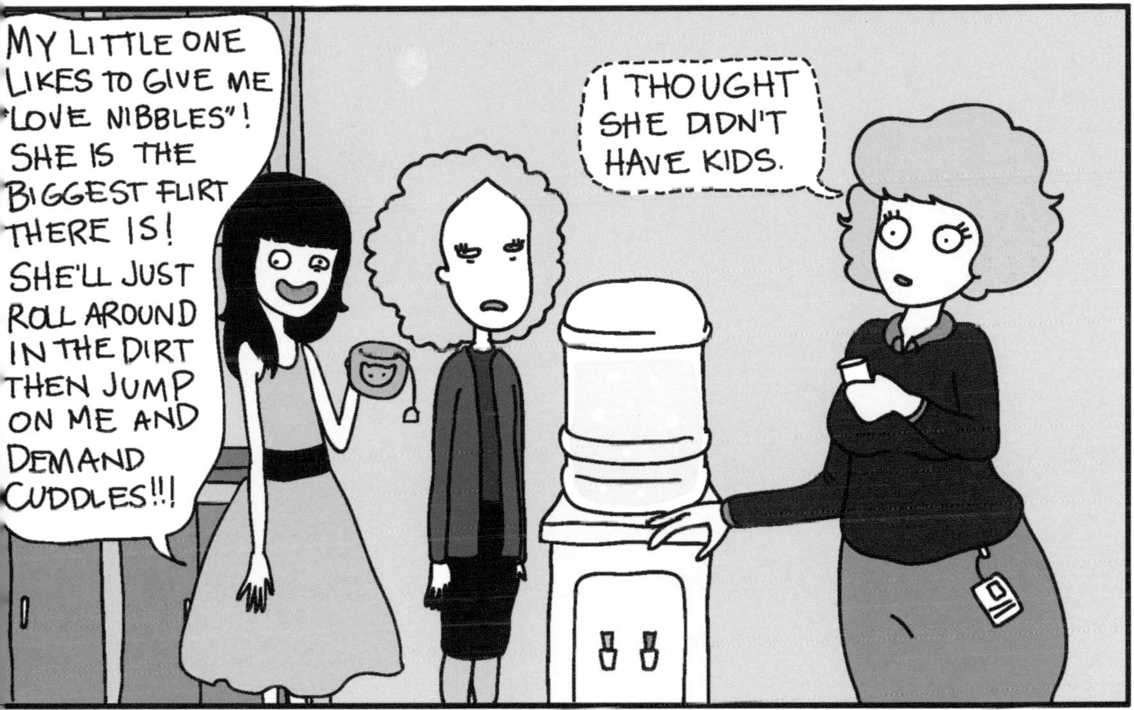
MY LITTLE ONE LIKES TO GIVE ME "LOVE NIBBLES"! SHE IS THE BIGGEST FLIRT THERE IS! SHE'LL JUST ROLL AROUND IN THE DIRT THEN JUMP ON ME AND DEMAND CUDDLES!!!
I THOUGHT SHE DIDN'T HAVE KIDS.

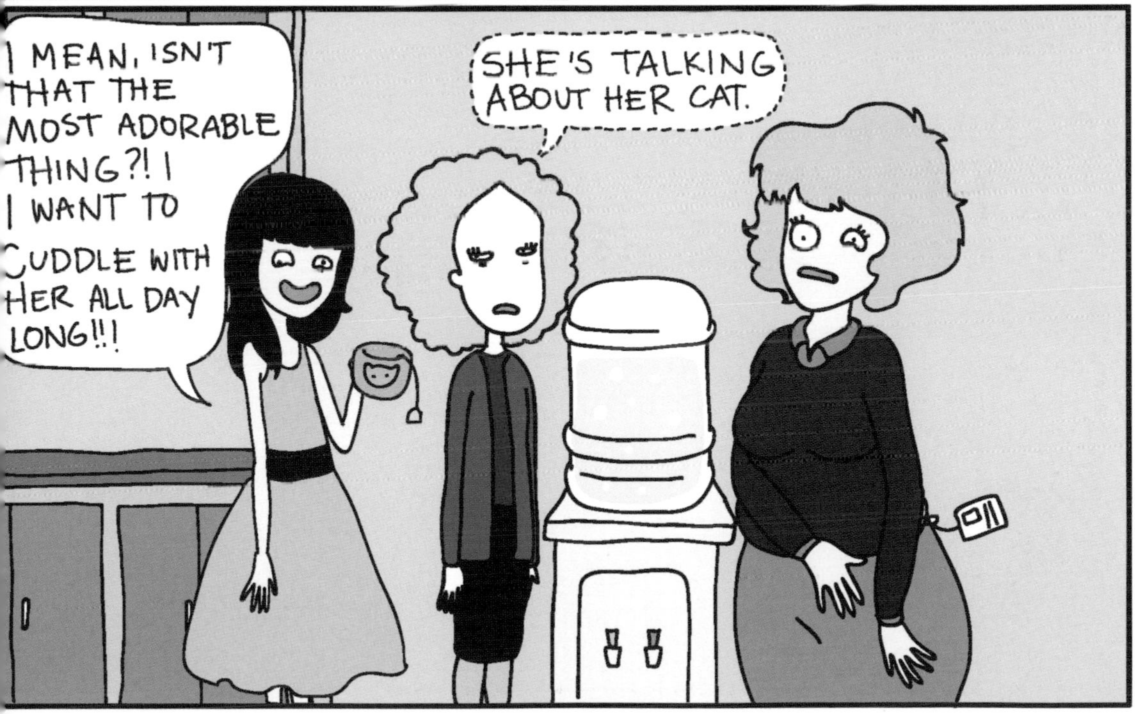
I MEAN, ISN'T THAT THE MOST ADORABLE THING?! I WANT TO CUDDLE WITH HER ALL DAY LONG!!!
SHE'S TALKING ABOUT HER CAT.

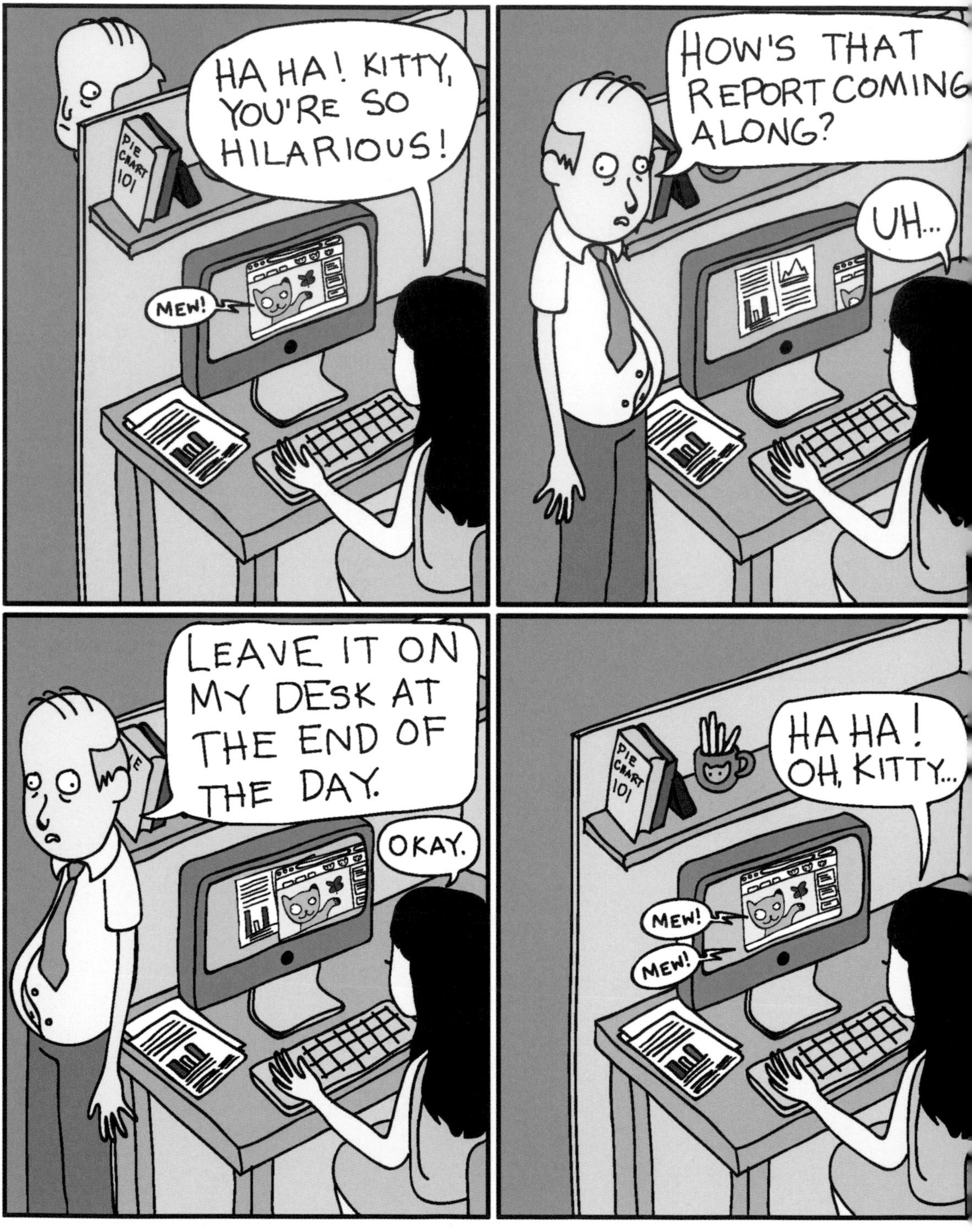
HA HA! KITTY, YOU'RE SO HILARIOUS!
MEW!
HOW'S THAT REPORT COMING ALONG?
UH...
LEAVE IT ON MY DESK AT THE END OF THE DAY.
OKAY.
PIE CHART 101
HA HA! OH, KITTY...
MEW!
MEW!

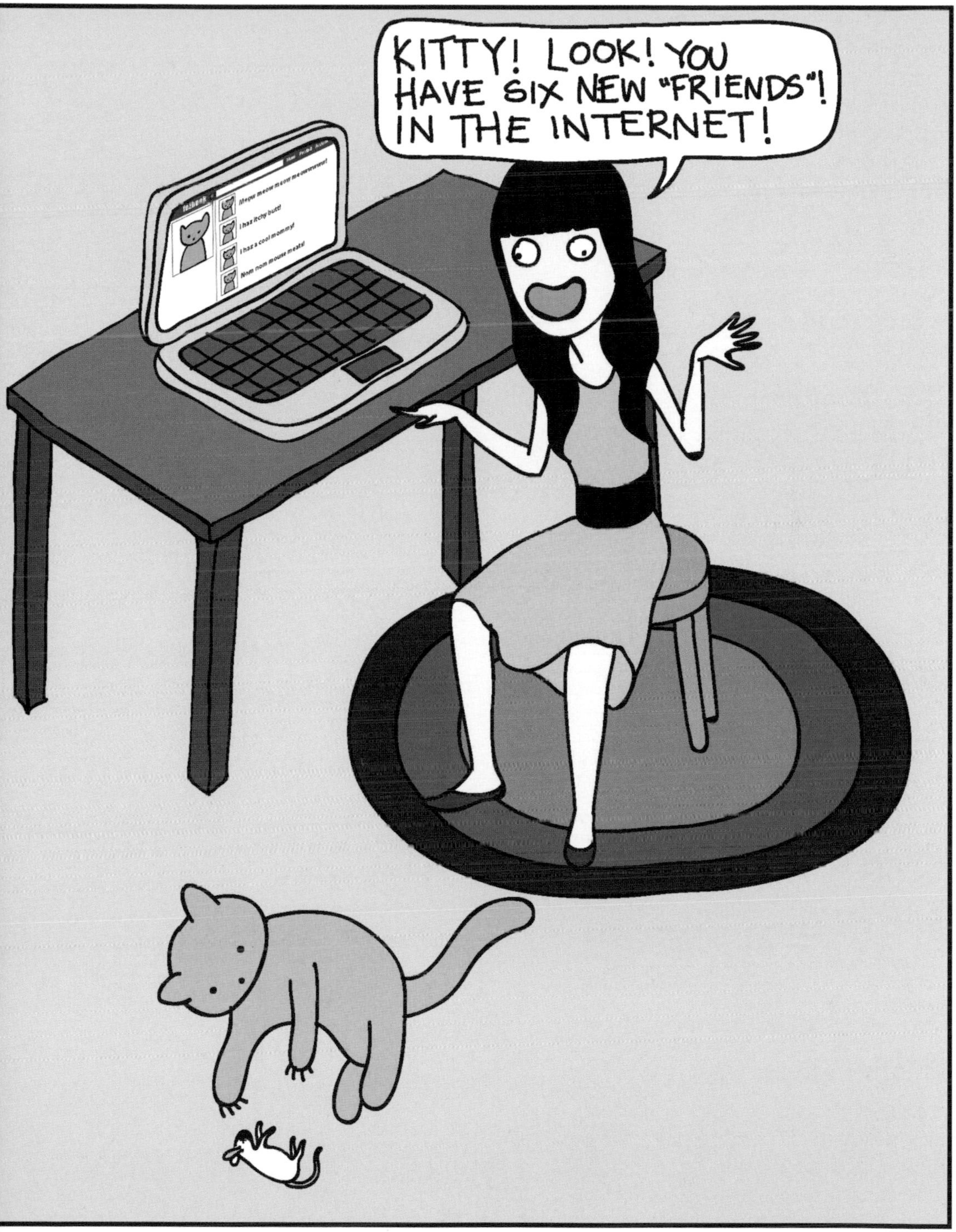
KITTY! LOOK! YOU HAVE SIX NEW "FRIENDS"! IN THE INTERNET!
I haz itchy butt!
I haz a cool mommy!
Nom nom mouse meats!

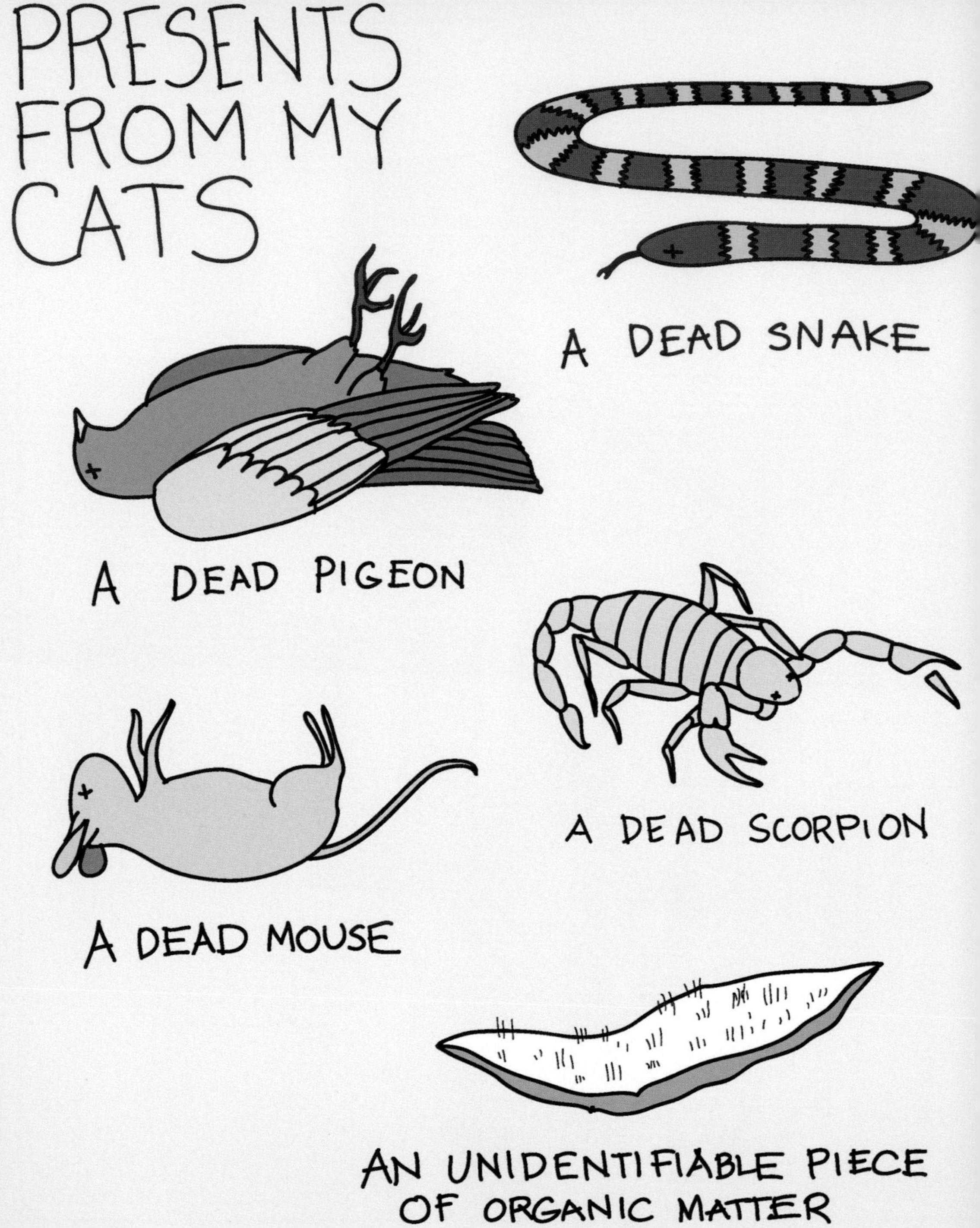

PRESENTS FROM MY CATS

A DEAD SNAKE

A DEAD PIGEON

A DEAD SCORPION

A DEAD MOUSE

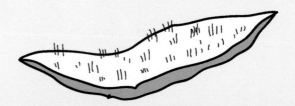

AN UNIDENTIFIABLE PIECE
OF ORGANIC MATTER

Things Cats Hate

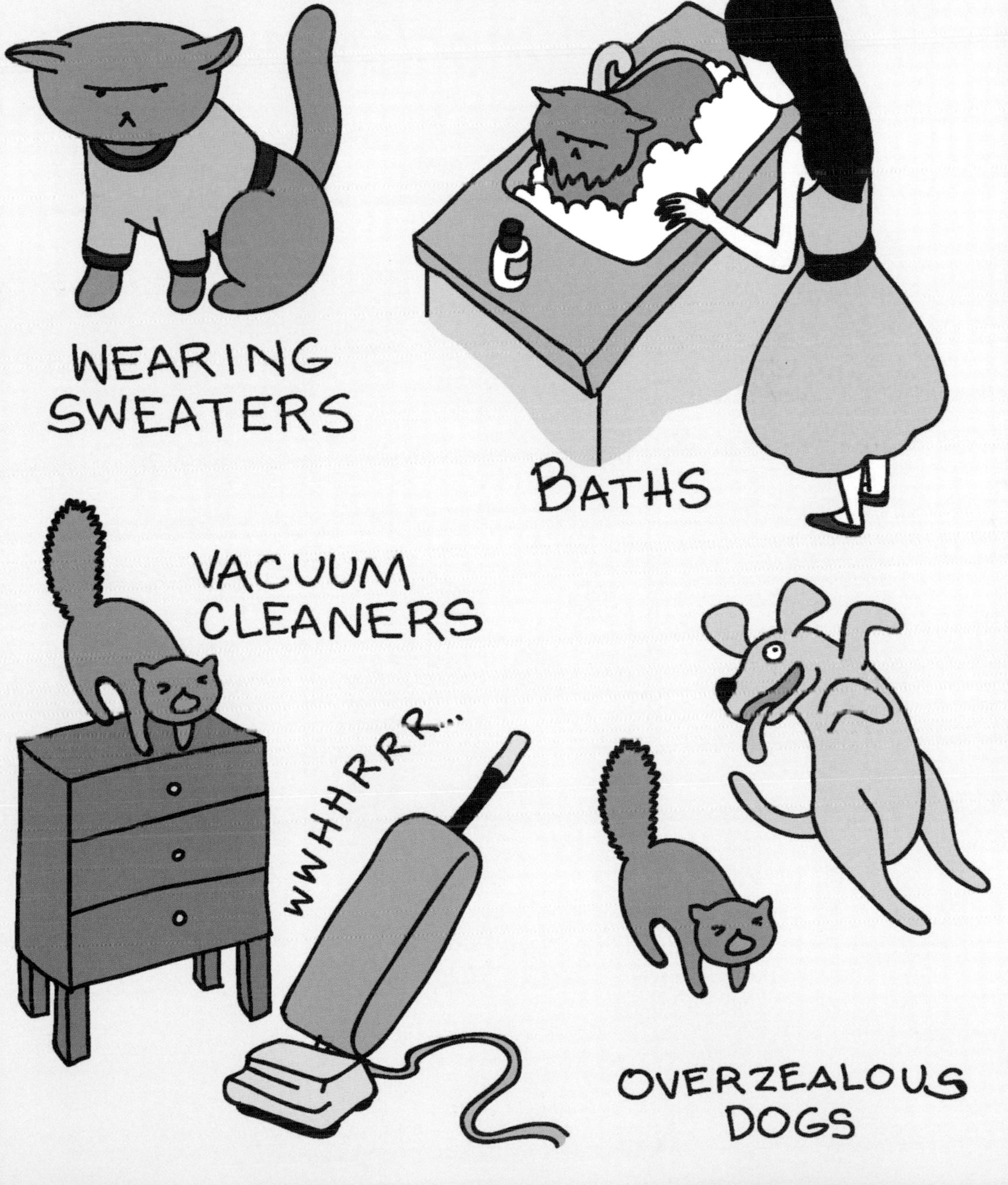
WEARING SWEATERS
BATHS
VACUUM CLEANERS
WWHHRRR...
OVERZEALOUS DOGS

The Girl Who Cried "Cute"

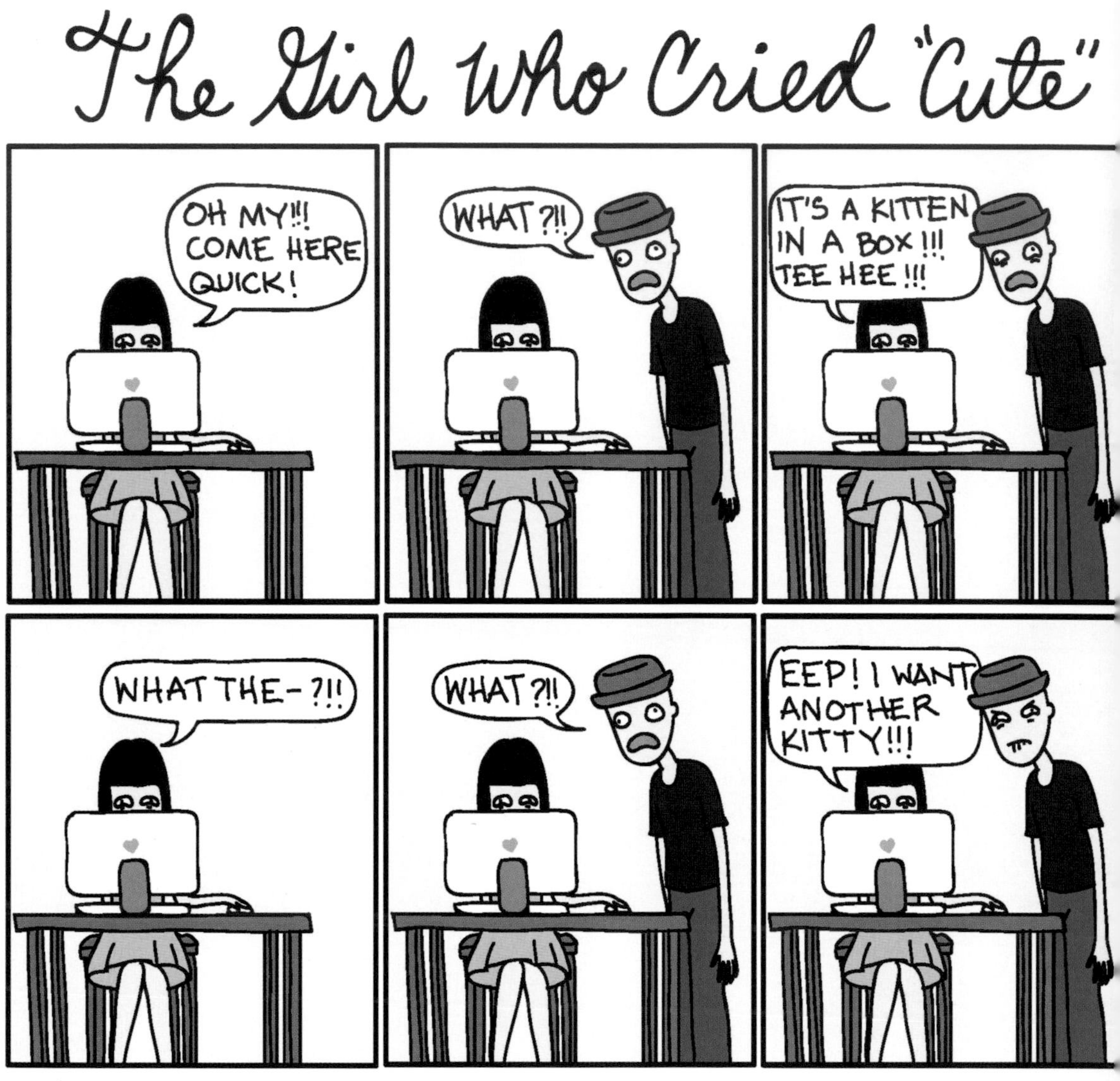
OH MY!!! COME HERE QUICK!
WHAT?!!
IT'S A KITTEN IN A BOX!!! TEE HEE!!!
WHAT THE-?!!
WHAT?!!
EEP! I WANT ANOTHER KITTY!!!

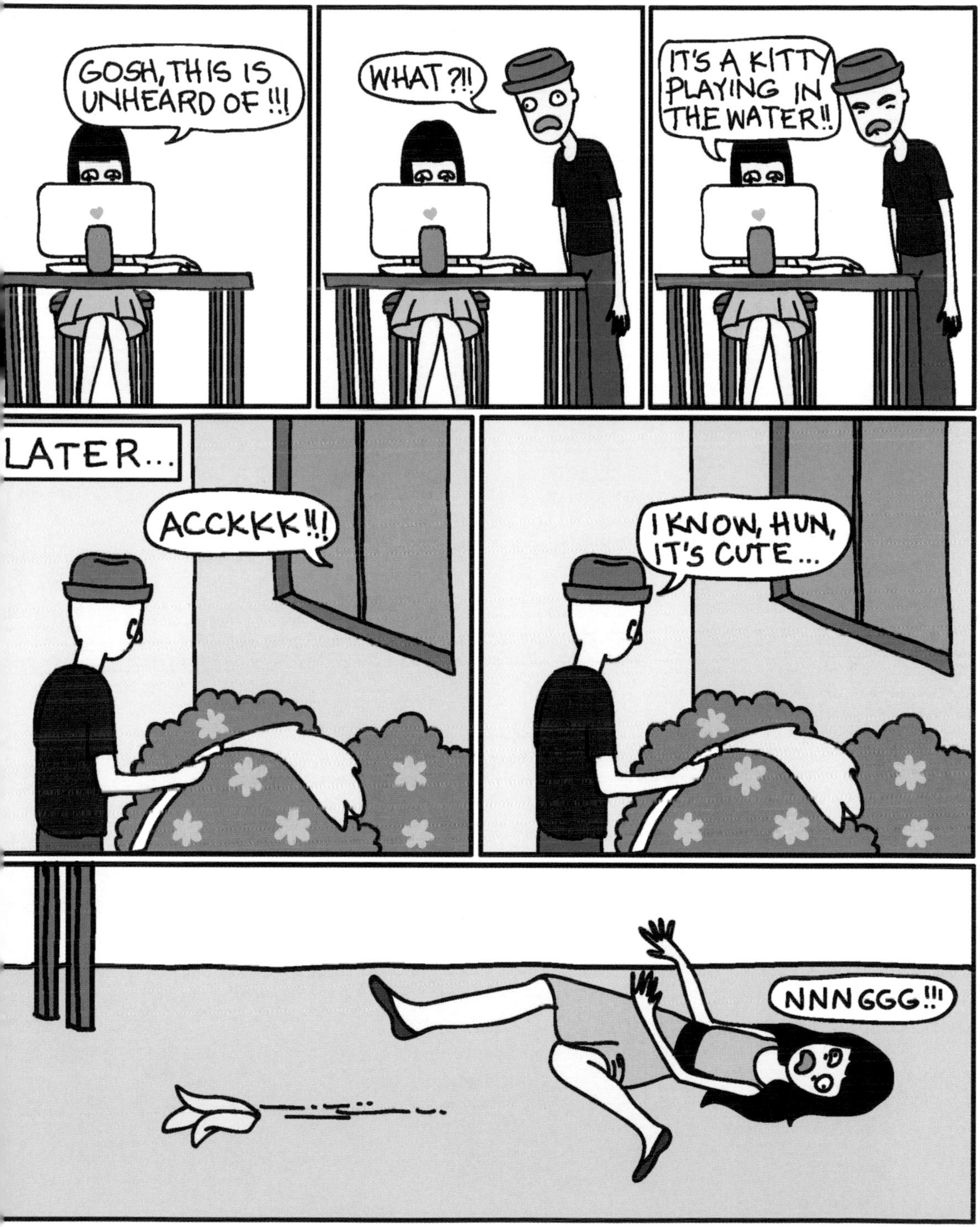
GOSH, THIS IS UNHEARD OF !!!
WHAT ?!!
IT'S A KITTY PLAYING IN THE WATER!!
LATER...
ACCKKK!!!
I KNOW, HUN, IT'S CUTE...
NNNGGG!!!

CATS > GIRL FRIENDS

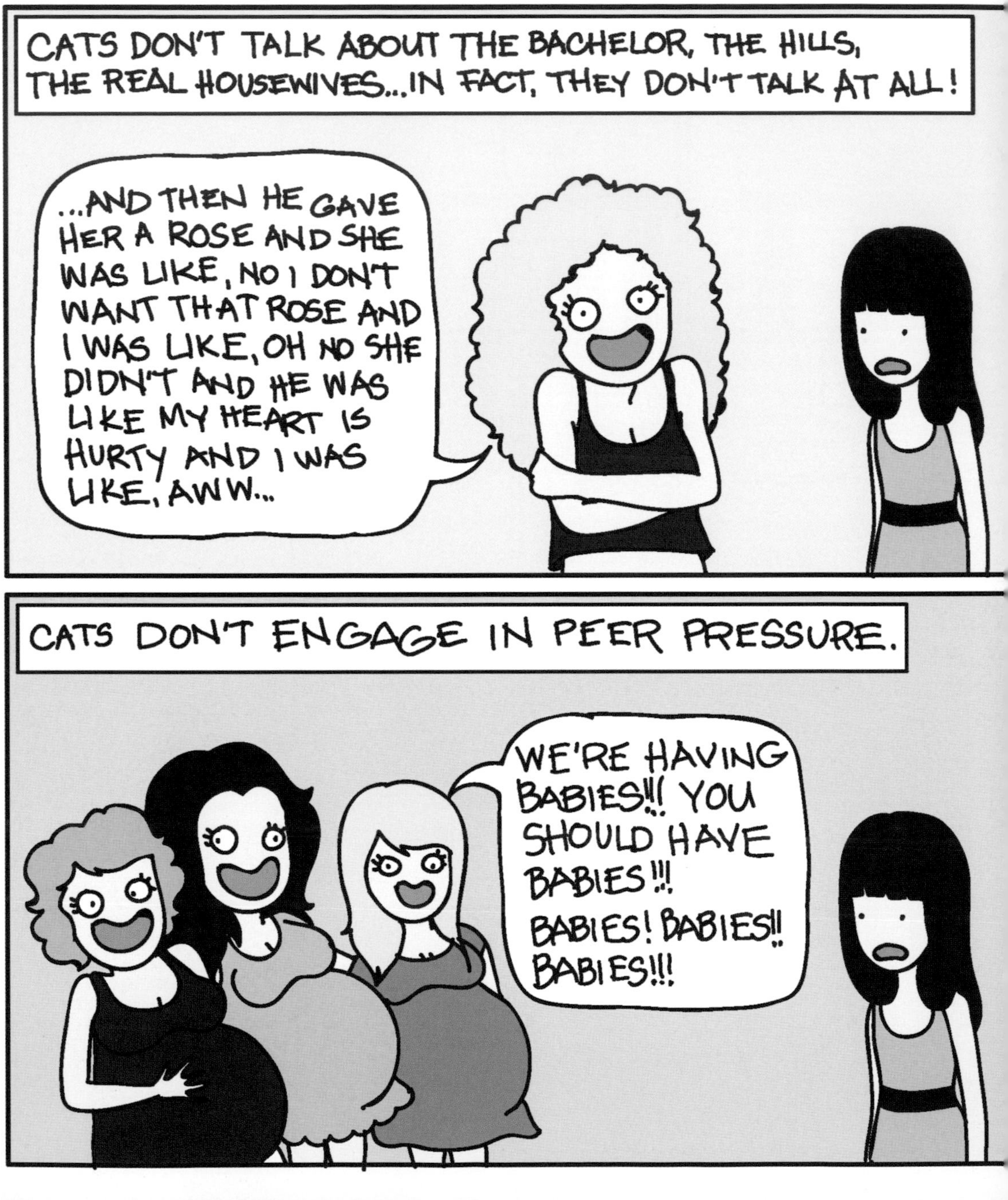
CATS DON'T TALK ABOUT THE BACHELOR, THE HILLS, THE REAL HOUSEWIVES...IN FACT, THEY DON'T TALK AT ALL!
...AND THEN HE GAVE HER A ROSE AND SHE WAS LIKE, NO I DON'T WANT THAT ROSE AND I WAS LIKE, OH NO SHE DIDN'T AND HE WAS LIKE MY HEART IS HURTY AND I WAS LIKE, AWW...
CATS DON'T ENGAGE IN PEER PRESSURE.
WE'RE HAVING BABIES!!! YOU SHOULD HAVE BABIES!!! BABIES! BABIES!! BABIES!!!

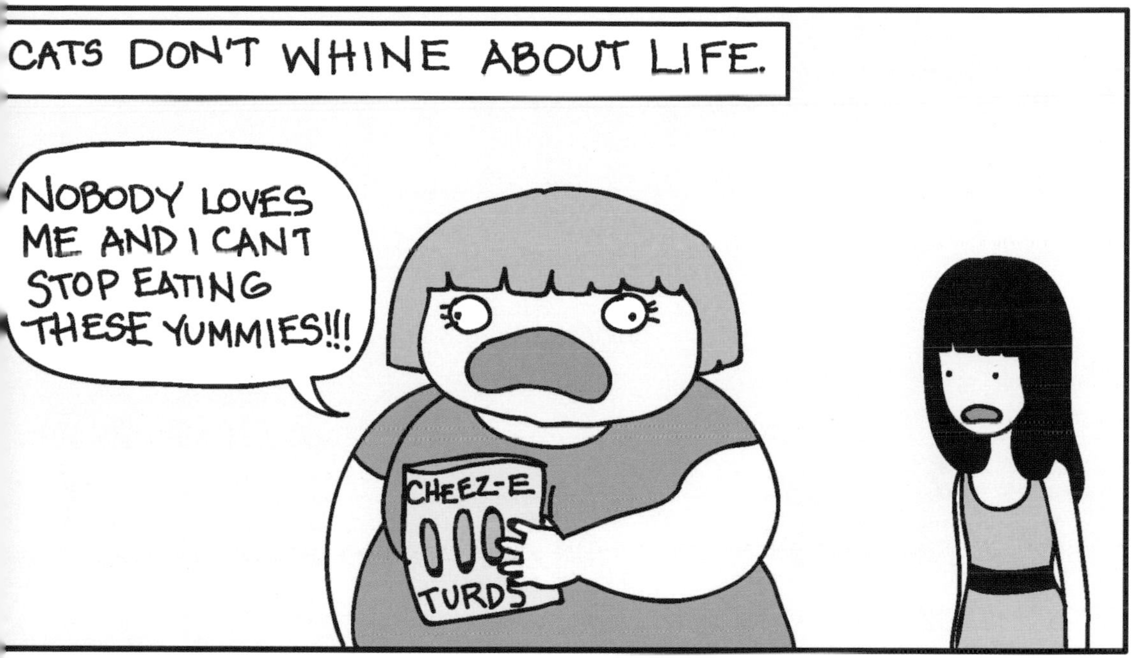
CATS DON'T WHINE ABOUT LIFE.
NOBODY LOVES ME AND I CAN'T STOP EATING THESE YUMMIES!!!
CHEEZ-E TURDS

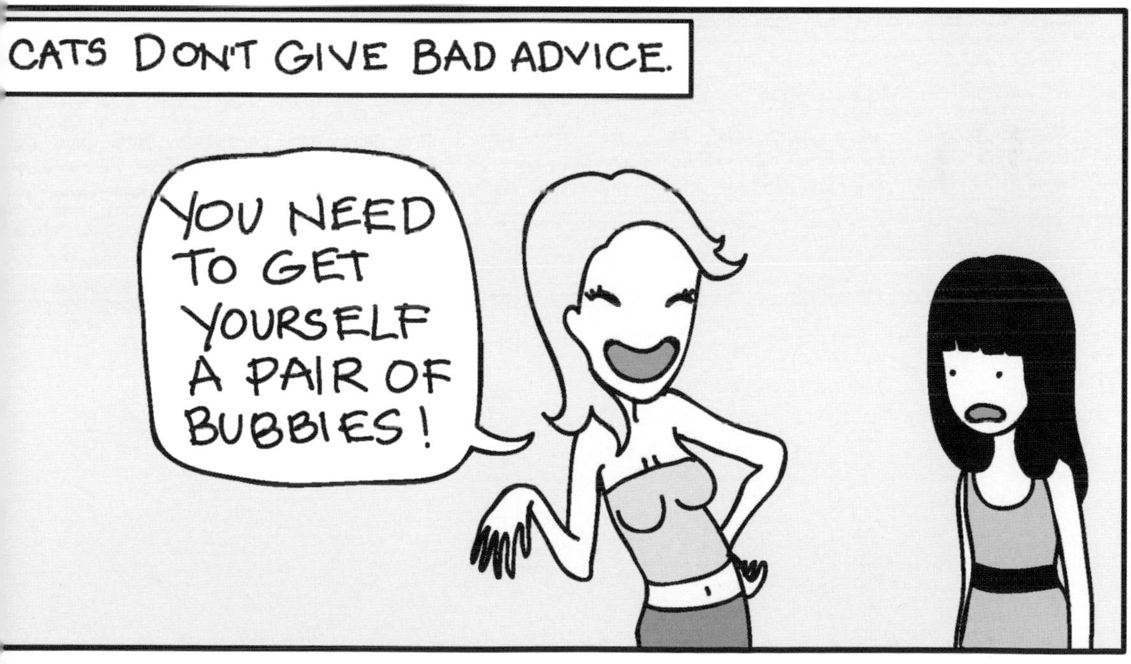
CATS DON'T GIVE BAD ADVICE.
YOU NEED TO GET YOURSELF A PAIR OF BUBBIES!

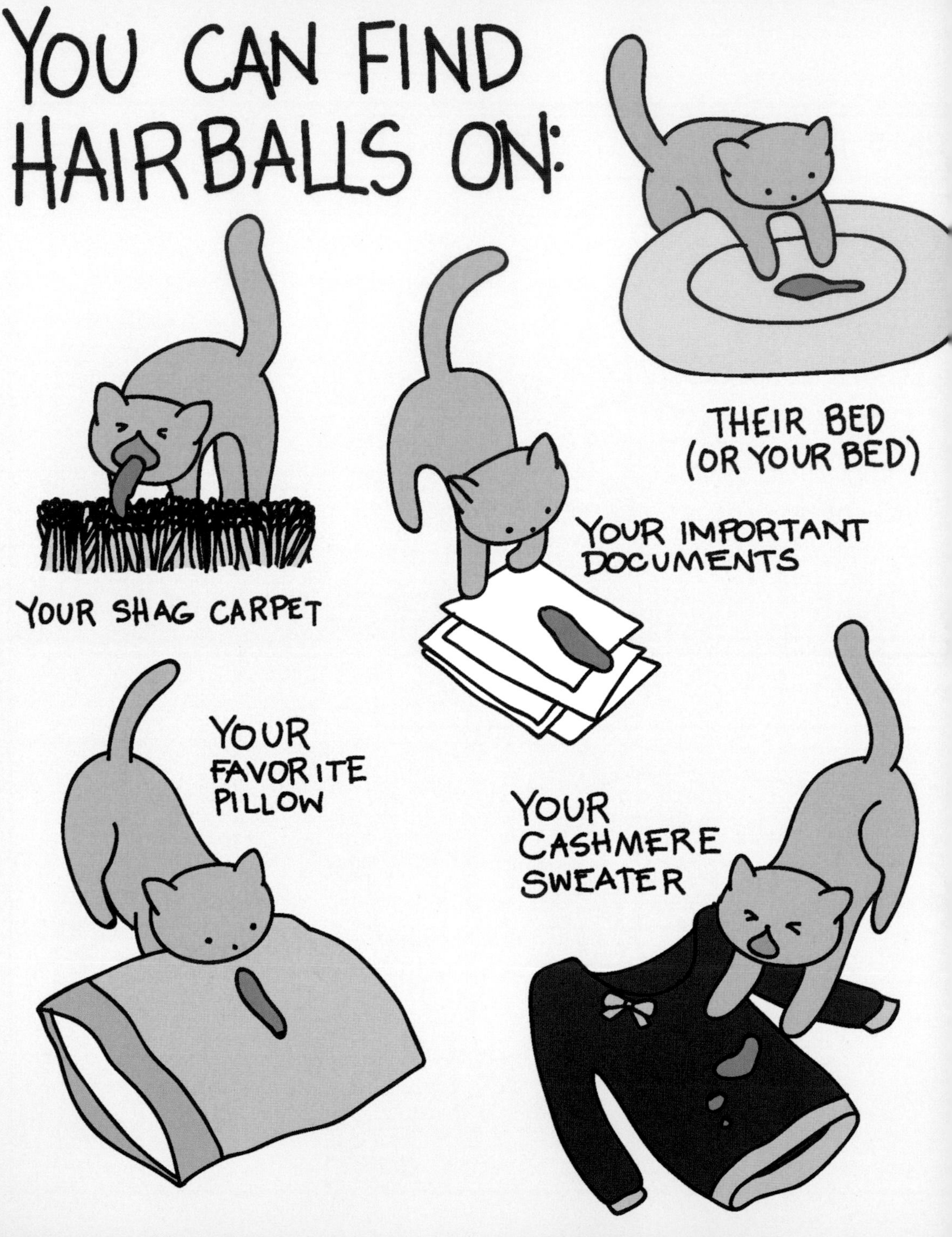
YOU CAN FIND HAIRBALLS ON:
THEIR BED (OR YOUR BED)
YOUR SHAG CARPET
YOUR IMPORTANT DOCUMENTS
YOUR FAVORITE PILLOW
YOUR CASHMERE SWEATER

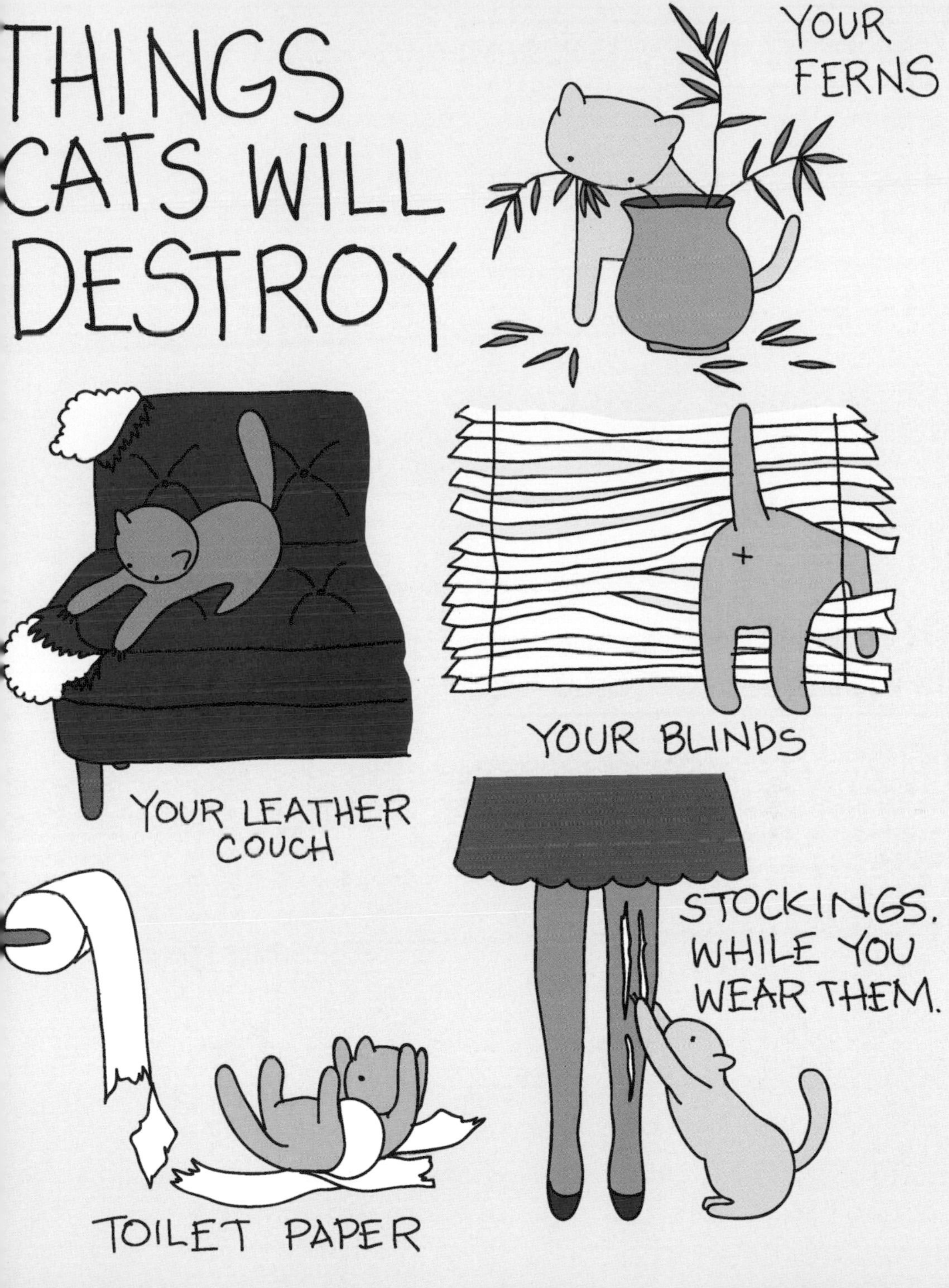
THINGS CATS WILL DESTROY
YOUR FERNS
YOUR BLINDS
YOUR LEATHER COUCH
STOCKINGS. WHILE YOU WEAR THEM.
TOILET PAPER

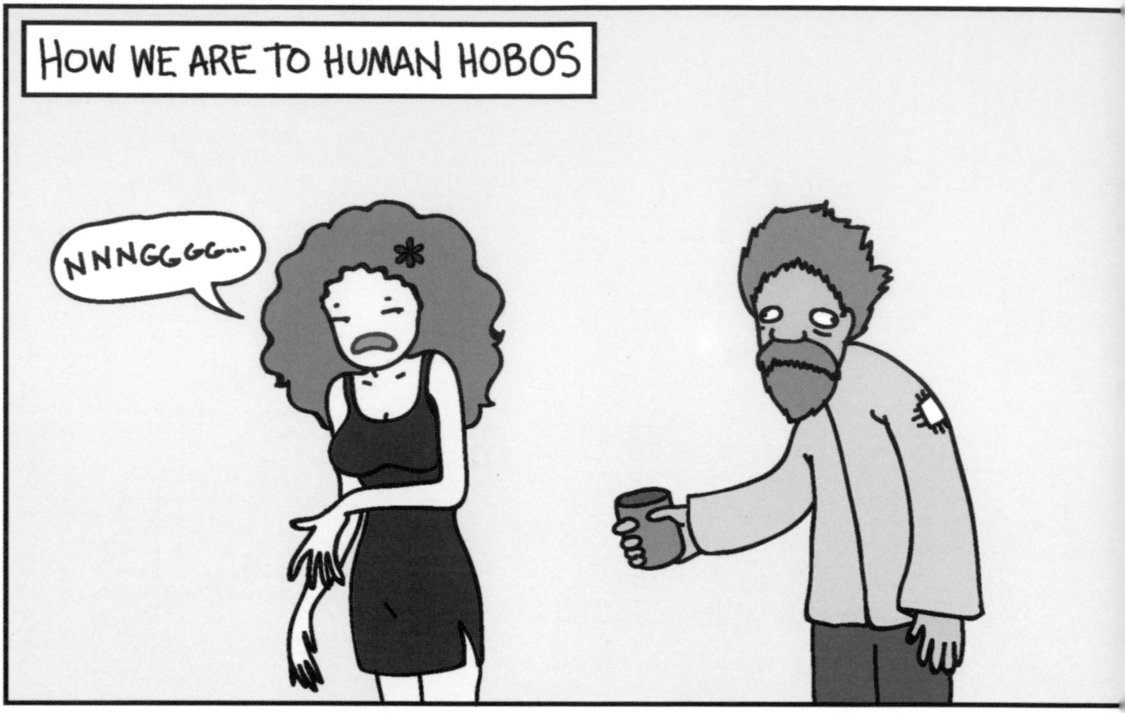
HOW WE ARE TO HUMAN HOBOS
NNNGGGG...

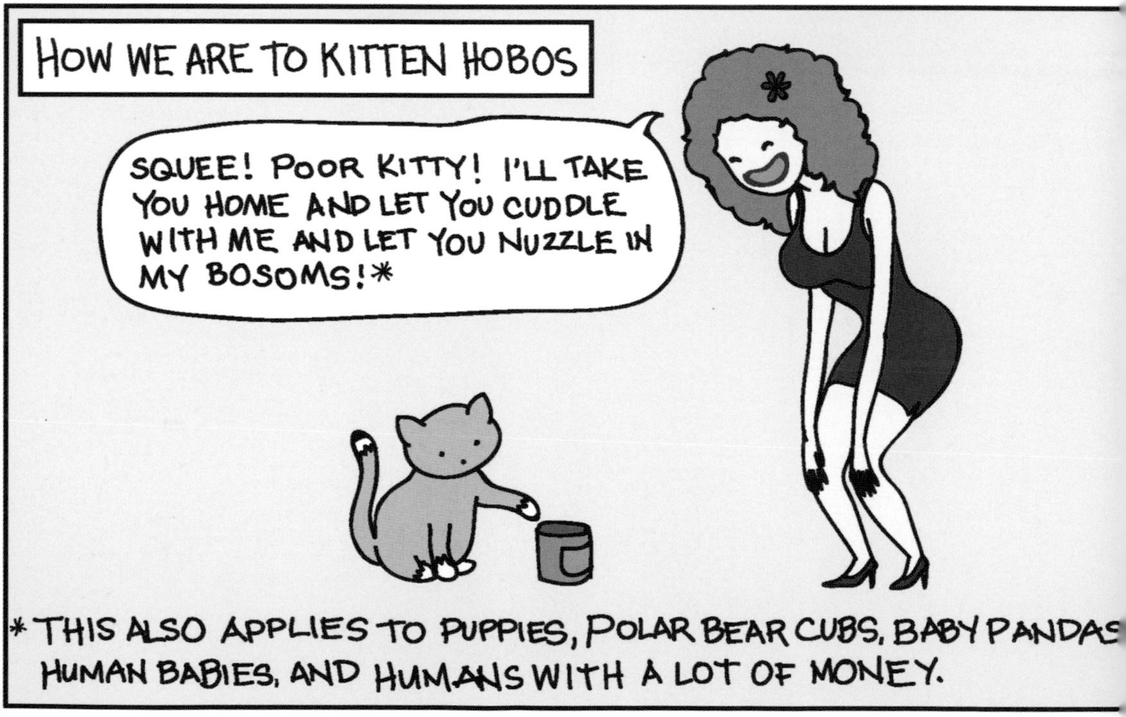
HOW WE ARE TO KITTEN HOBOS
SQUEE! POOR KITTY! I'LL TAKE YOU HOME AND LET YOU CUDDLE WITH ME AND LET YOU NUZZLE IN MY BOSOMS!*
* THIS ALSO APPLIES TO PUPPIES, POLAR BEAR CUBS, BABY PANDAS HUMAN BABIES, AND HUMANS WITH A LOT OF MONEY.

If Cats Could Talk

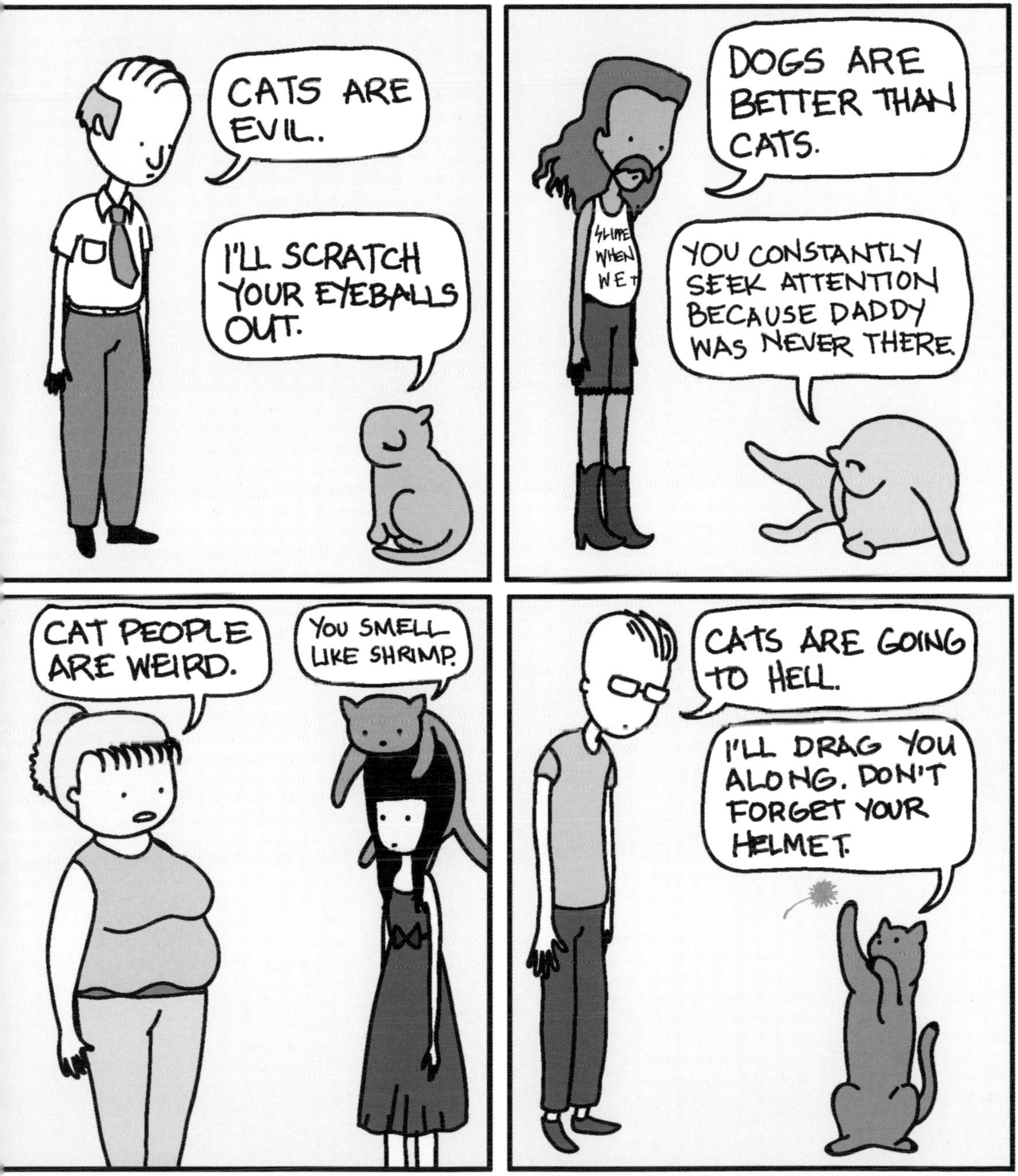
CATS ARE EVIL.
I'LL SCRATCH YOUR EYEBALLS OUT.
DOGS ARE BETTER THAN CATS.
SLIPPERY WHEN WET
YOU CONSTANTLY SEEK ATTENTION BECAUSE DADDY WAS NEVER THERE.
CAT PEOPLE ARE WEIRD.
YOU SMELL LIKE SHRIMP.
CATS ARE GOING TO HELL.
I'LL DRAG YOU ALONG. DON'T FORGET YOUR HELMET.

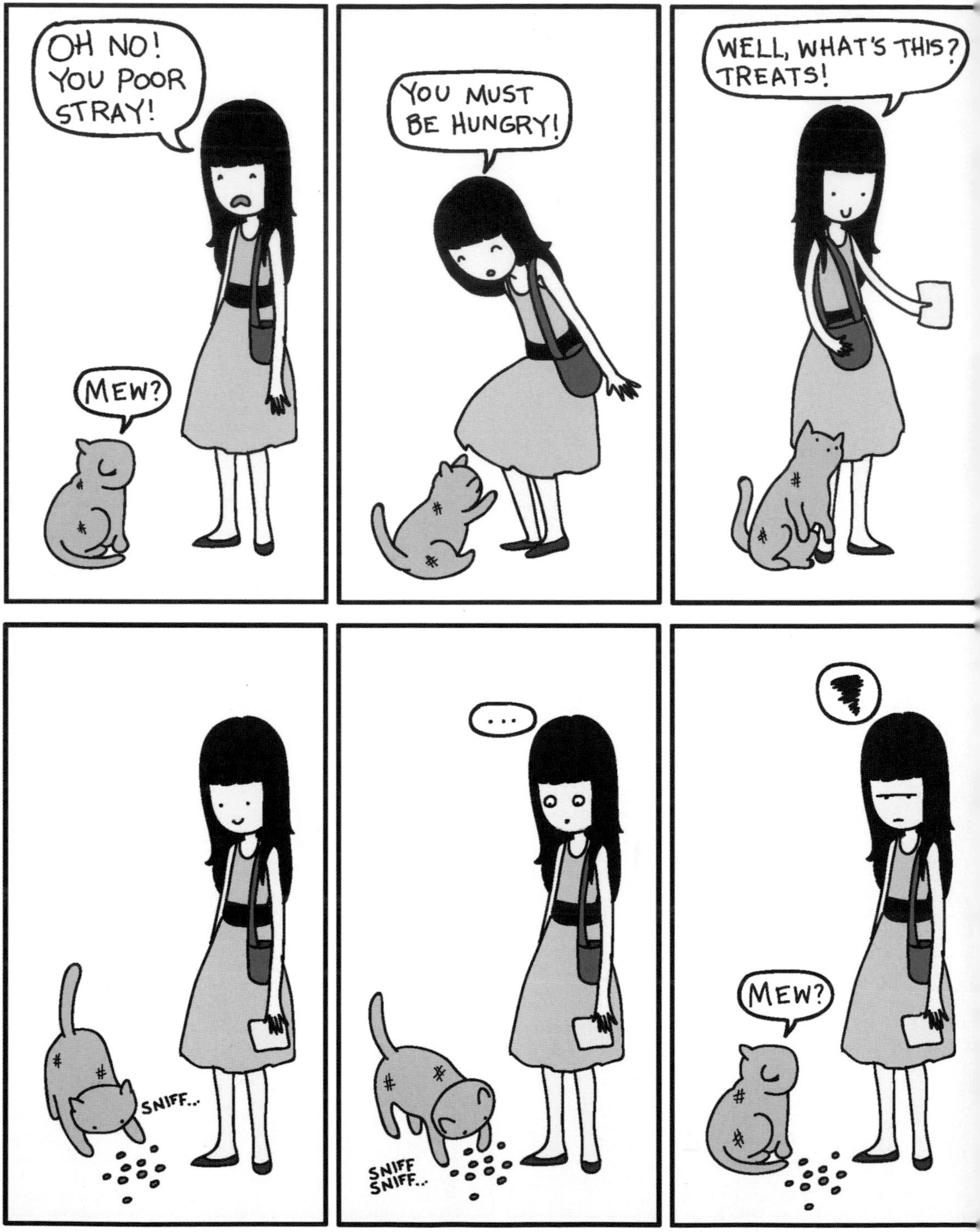
OH NO! YOU POOR STRAY!
MEW?
YOU MUST BE HUNGRY!
WELL, WHAT'S THIS? TREATS!
SNIFF...
SNIFF SNIFF...
...
MEW?

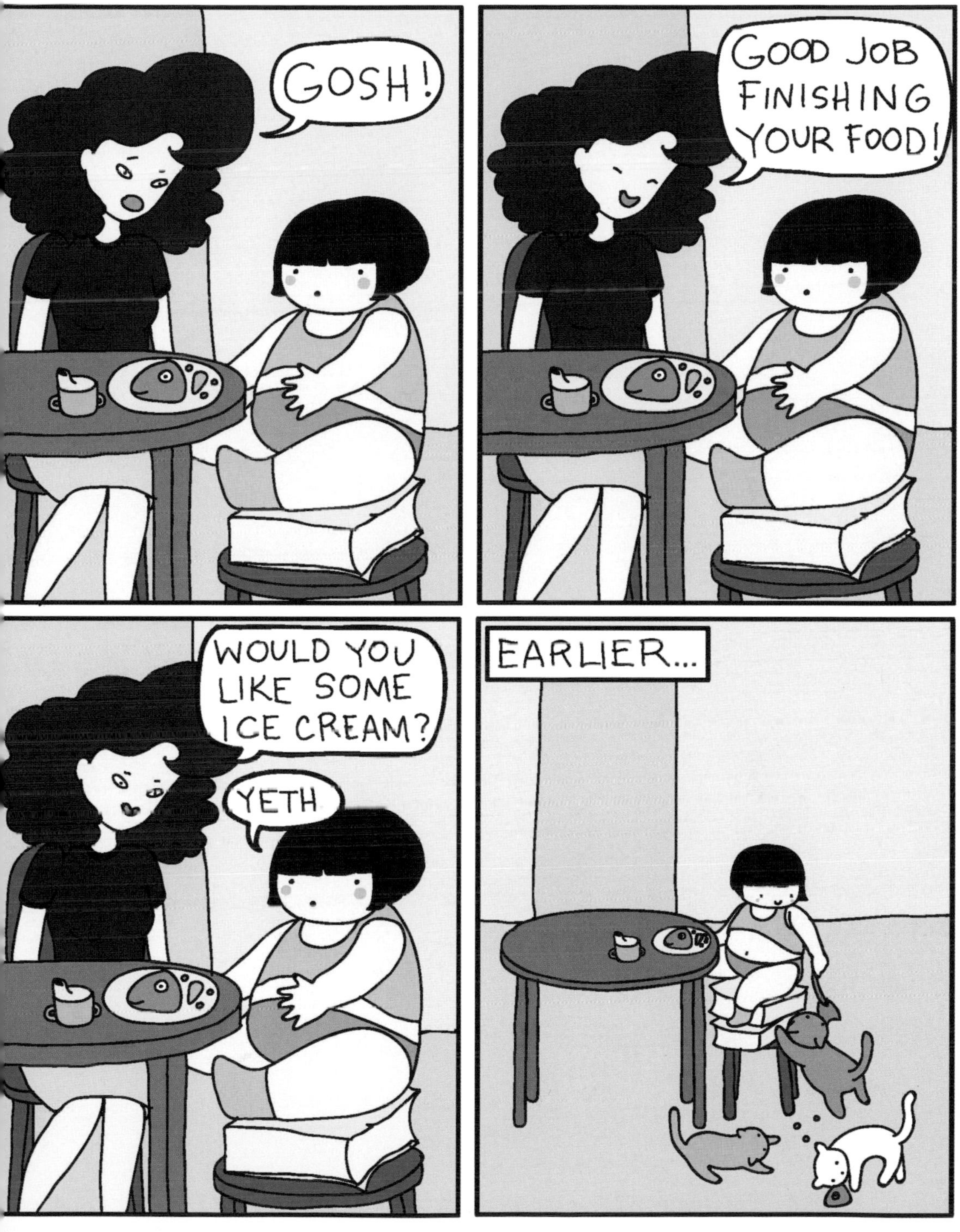
GOSH!
GOOD JOB FINISHING YOUR FOOD!
WOULD YOU LIKE SOME ICE CREAM?
YETH
EARLIER...

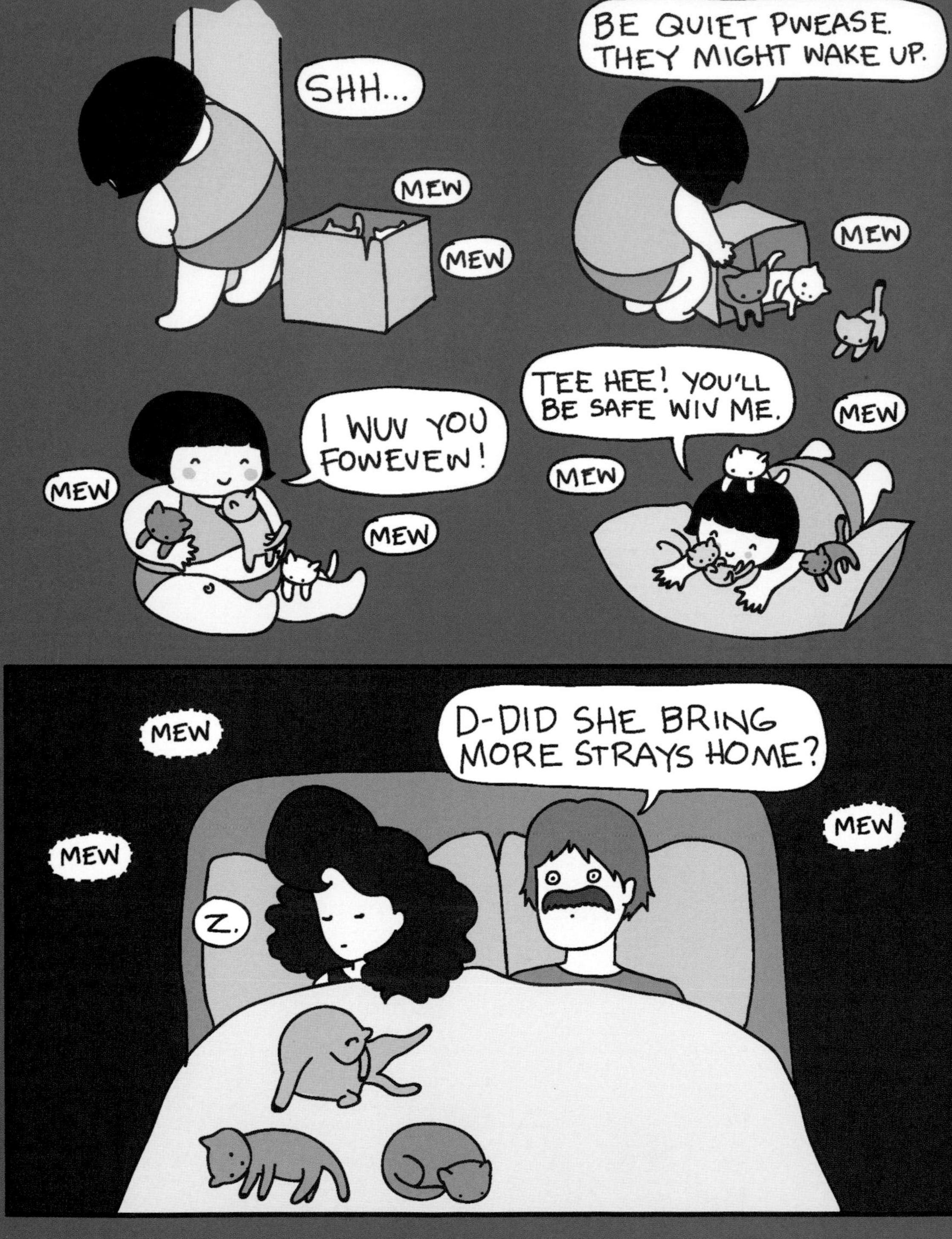
SHH...
MEW
MEW
BE QUIET PWEASE. THEY MIGHT WAKE UP.
MEW
MEW
I WUV YOU FOWEVEW!
MEW
TEE HEE! YOU'LL BE SAFE WIV ME.
MEW
MEW
MEW
D-DID SHE BRING MORE STRAYS HOME?
MEW
MEW
Z.

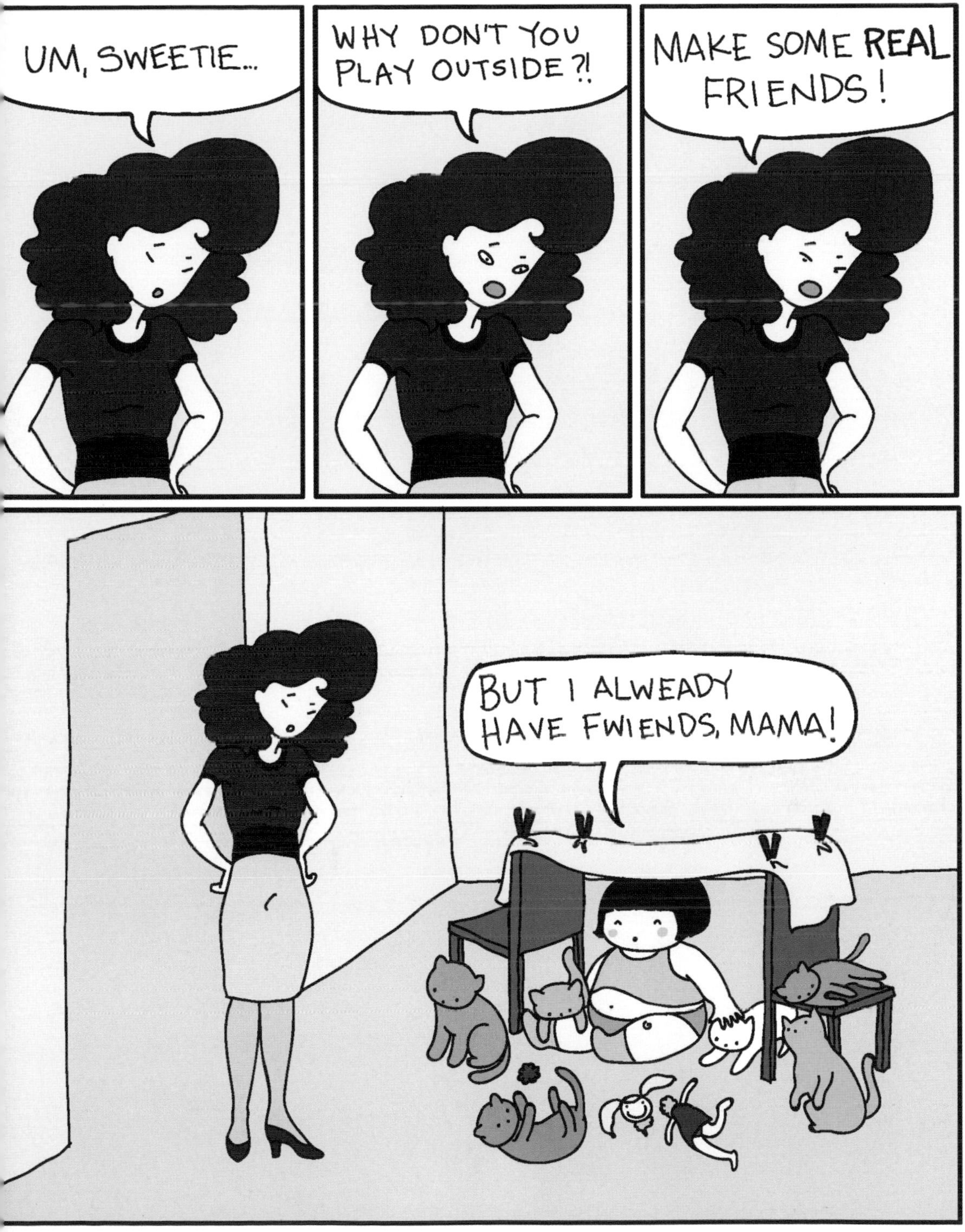
UM, SWEETIE...
WHY DON'T YOU PLAY OUTSIDE?!
MAKE SOME **REAL** FRIENDS!
BUT I ALWEADY HAVE FWIENDS, MAMA!

Mood KILLER

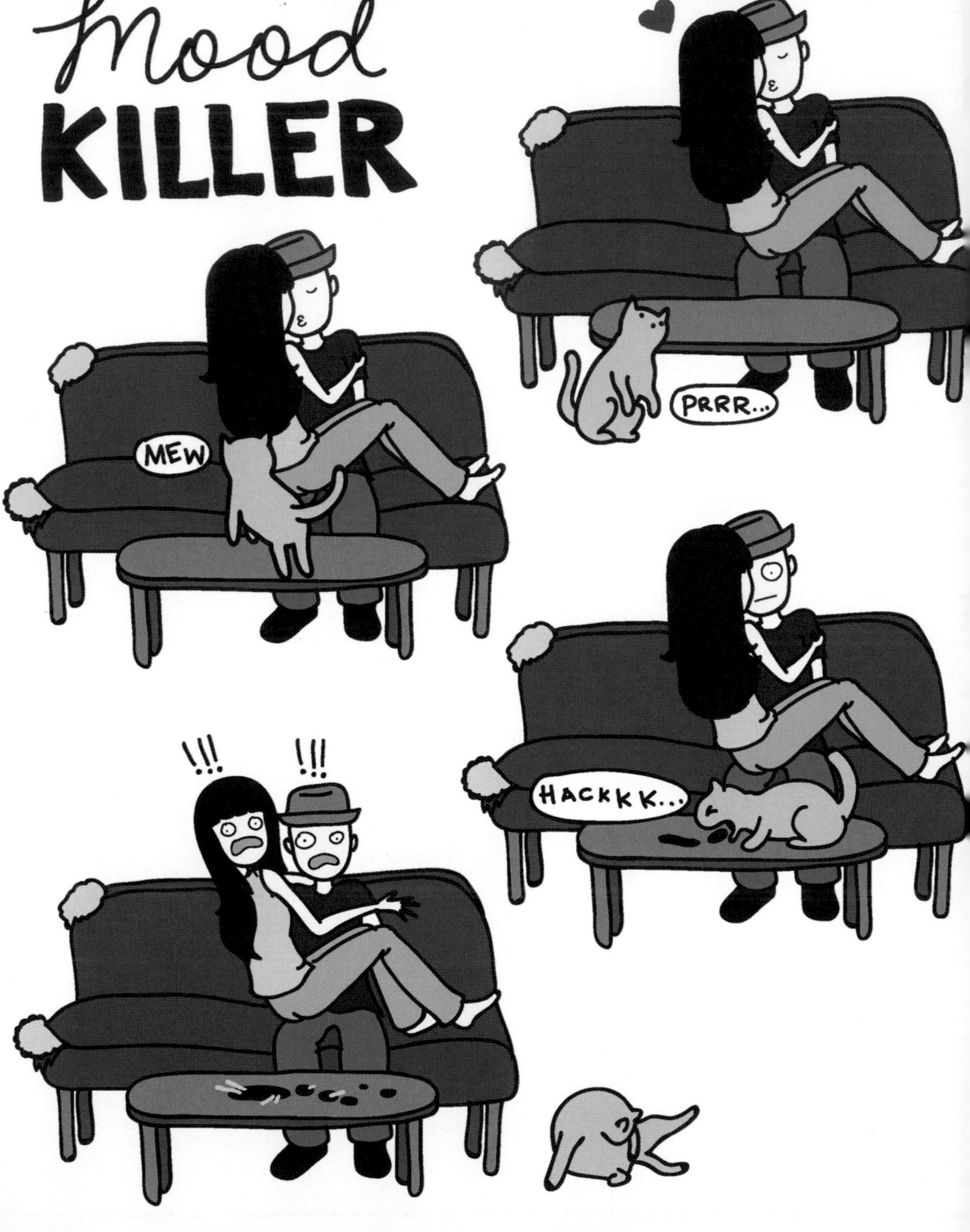

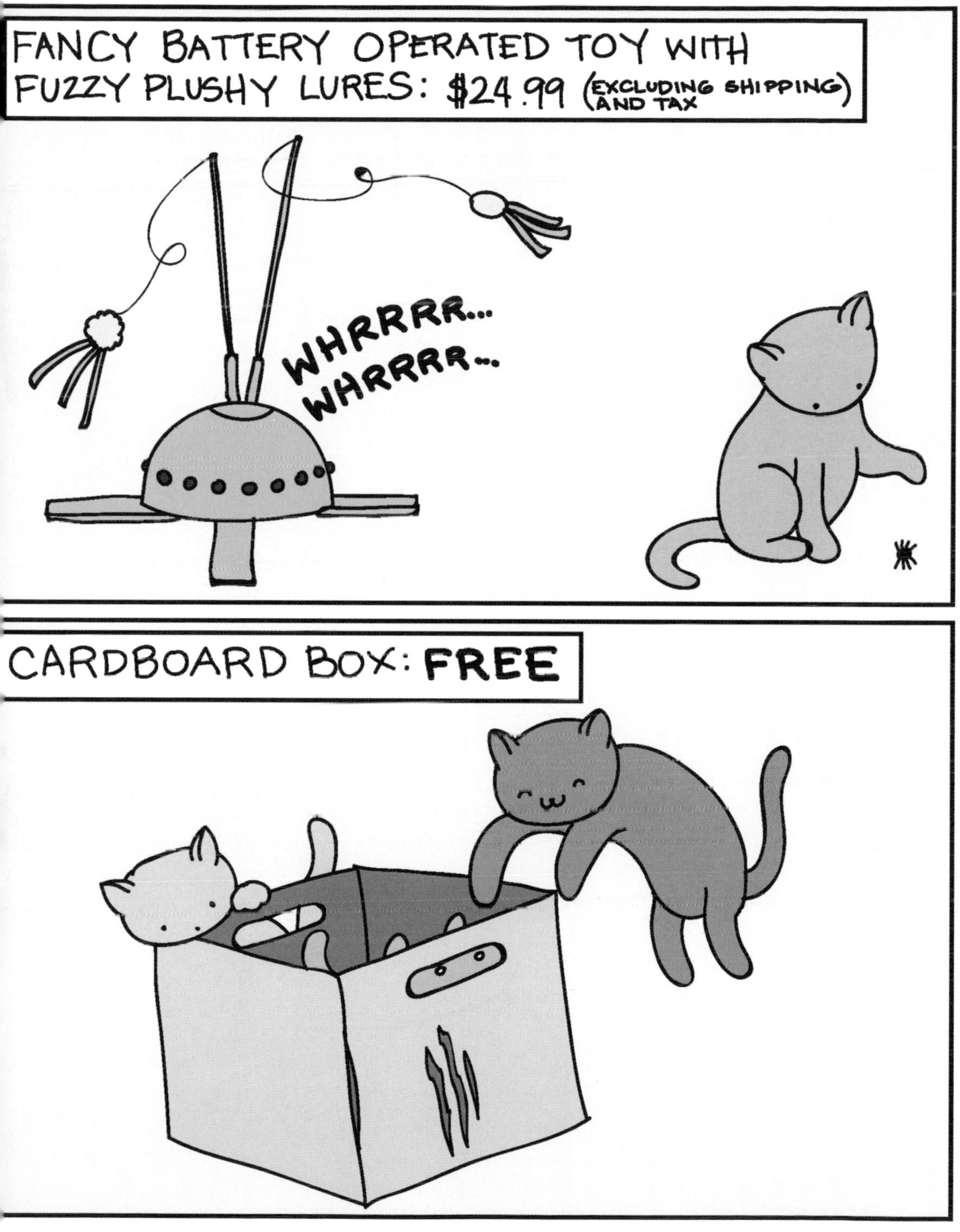
FANCY BATTERY OPERATED TOY WITH FUZZY PLUSHY LURES: $24.99 (EXCLUDING SHIPPING AND TAX)
WHRRRR... WHRRRR...
CARDBOARD BOX: FREE

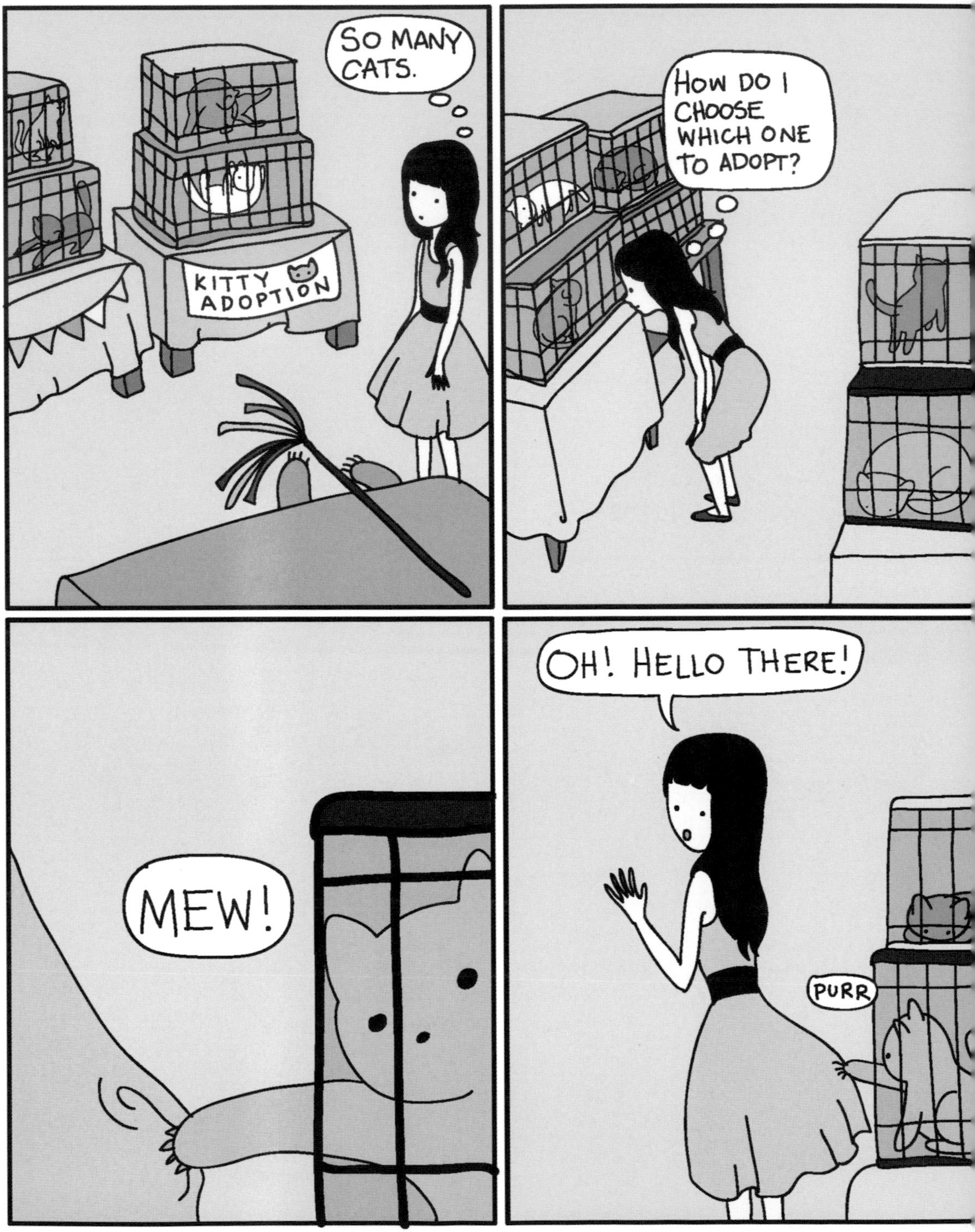
SO MANY CATS.
KITTY ADOPTION
HOW DO I CHOOSE WHICH ONE TO ADOPT?
MEW!
OH! HELLO THERE!
PURR

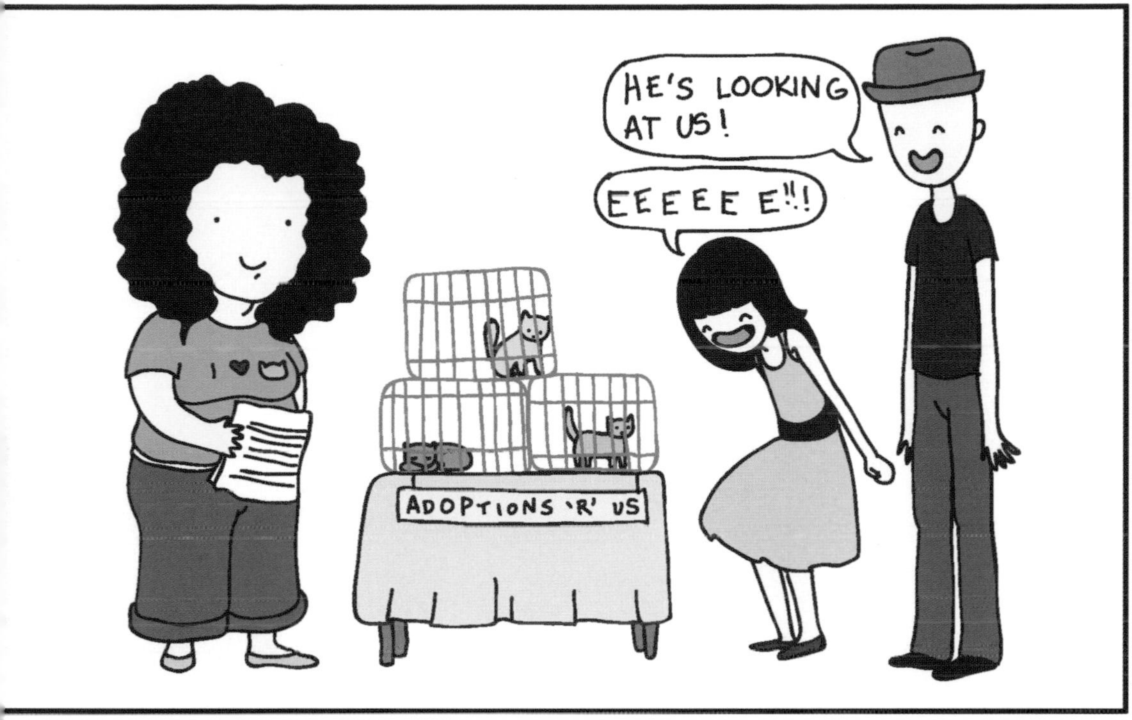
HE'S LOOKING AT US!
EEEEE E!!!
ADOPTIONS 'R' US

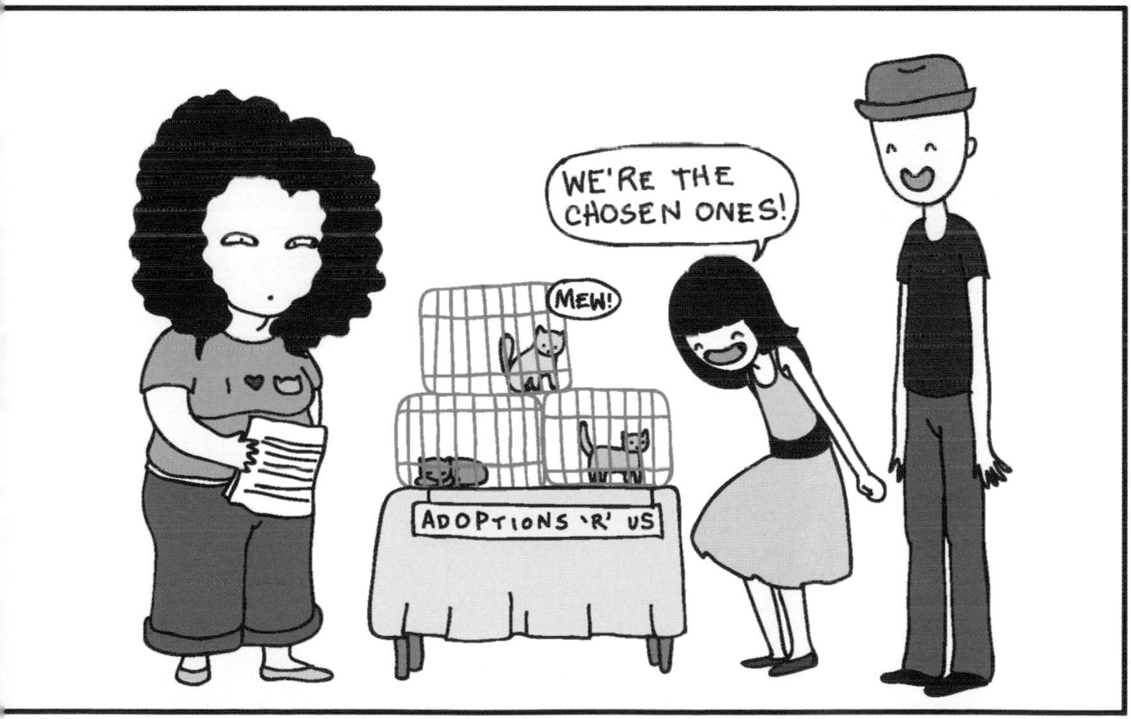
WE'RE THE CHOSEN ONES!
MEW!
ADOPTIONS 'R' US

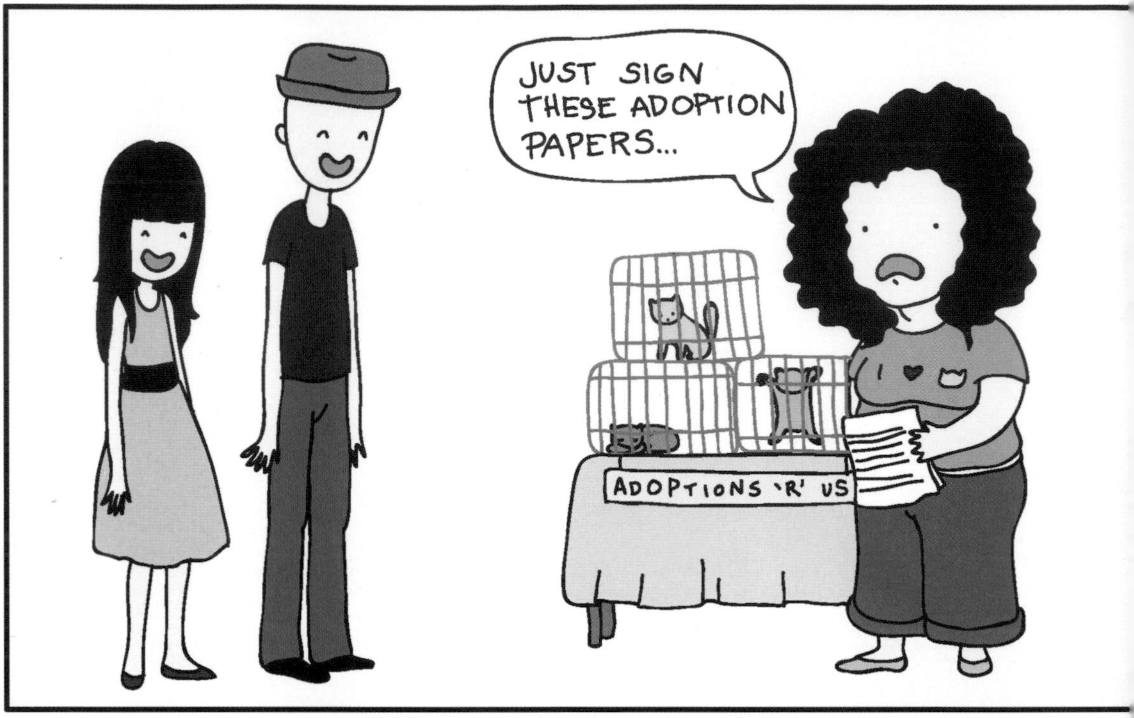
JUST SIGN THESE ADOPTION PAPERS...
ADOPTIONS 'R' US

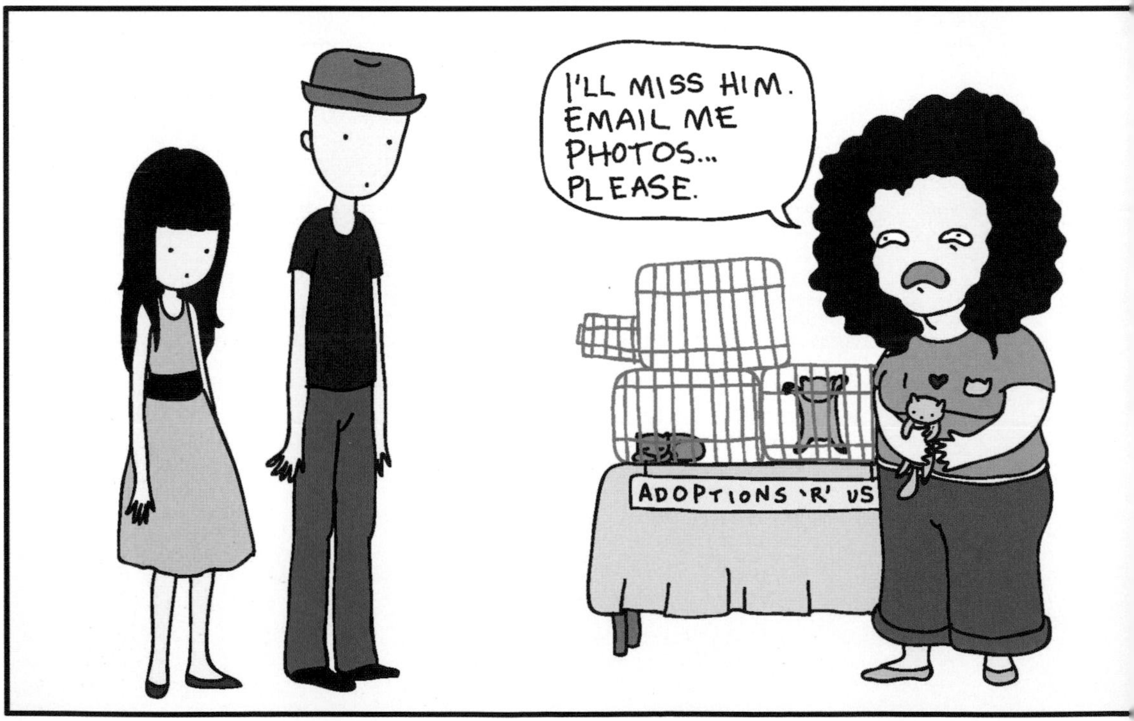
I'LL MISS HIM. EMAIL ME PHOTOS... PLEASE.
ADOPTIONS 'R' US

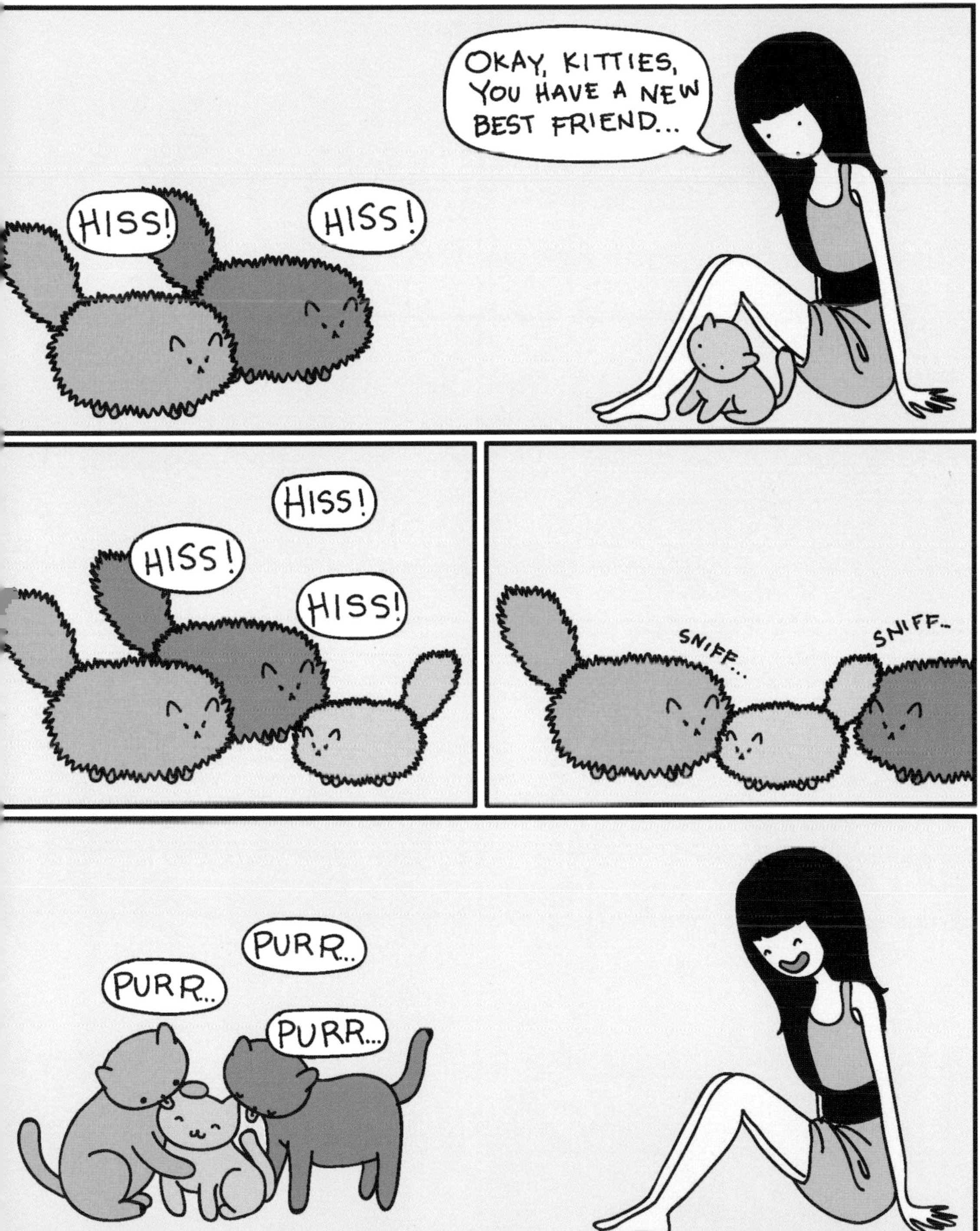

OKAY, KITTIES, YOU HAVE A NEW BEST FRIEND...
HISS!
HISS!
HISS!
HISS!
HISS!
SNIFF...
SNIFF..
PURR..
PURR...
PURR...

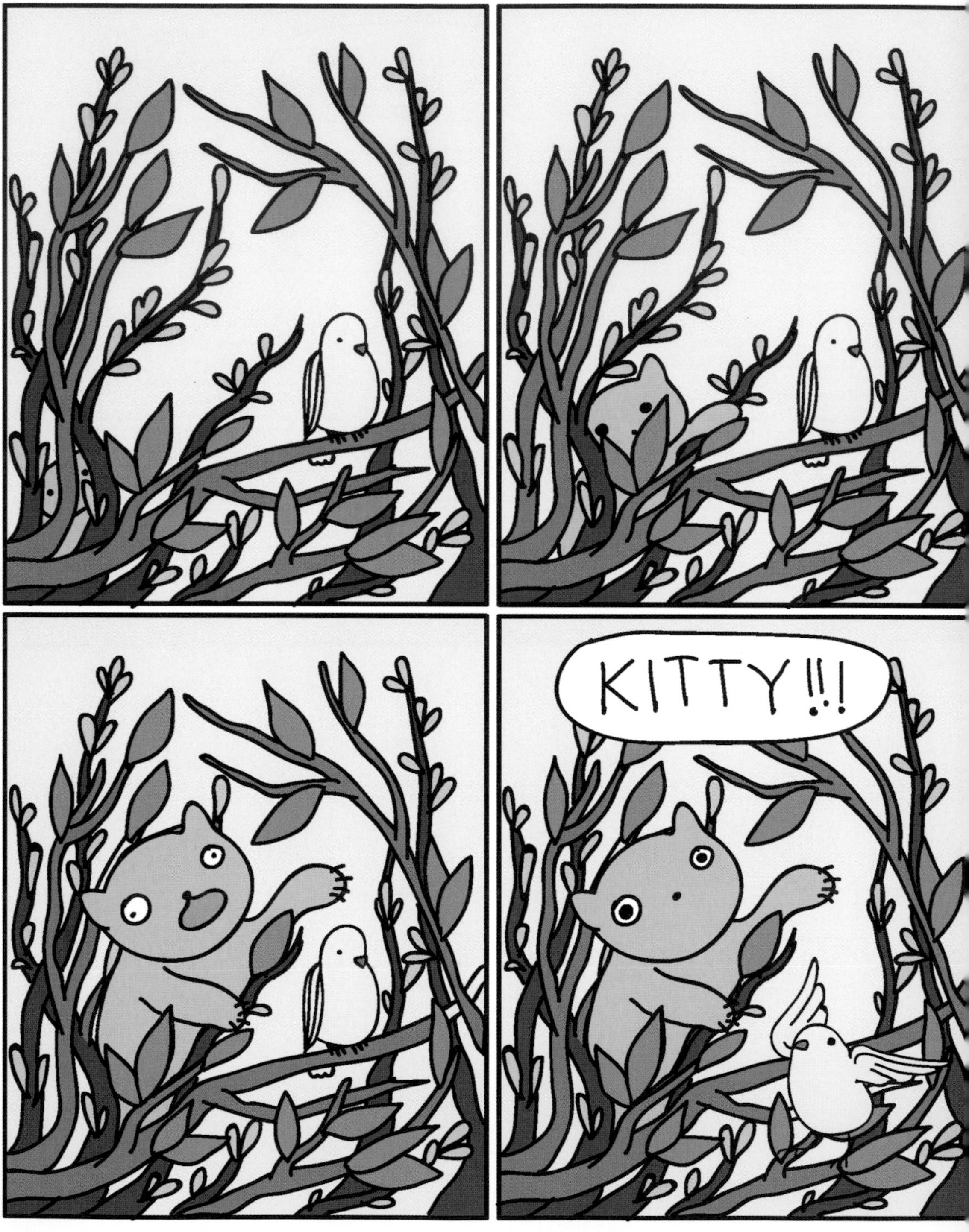
KITTY!!!

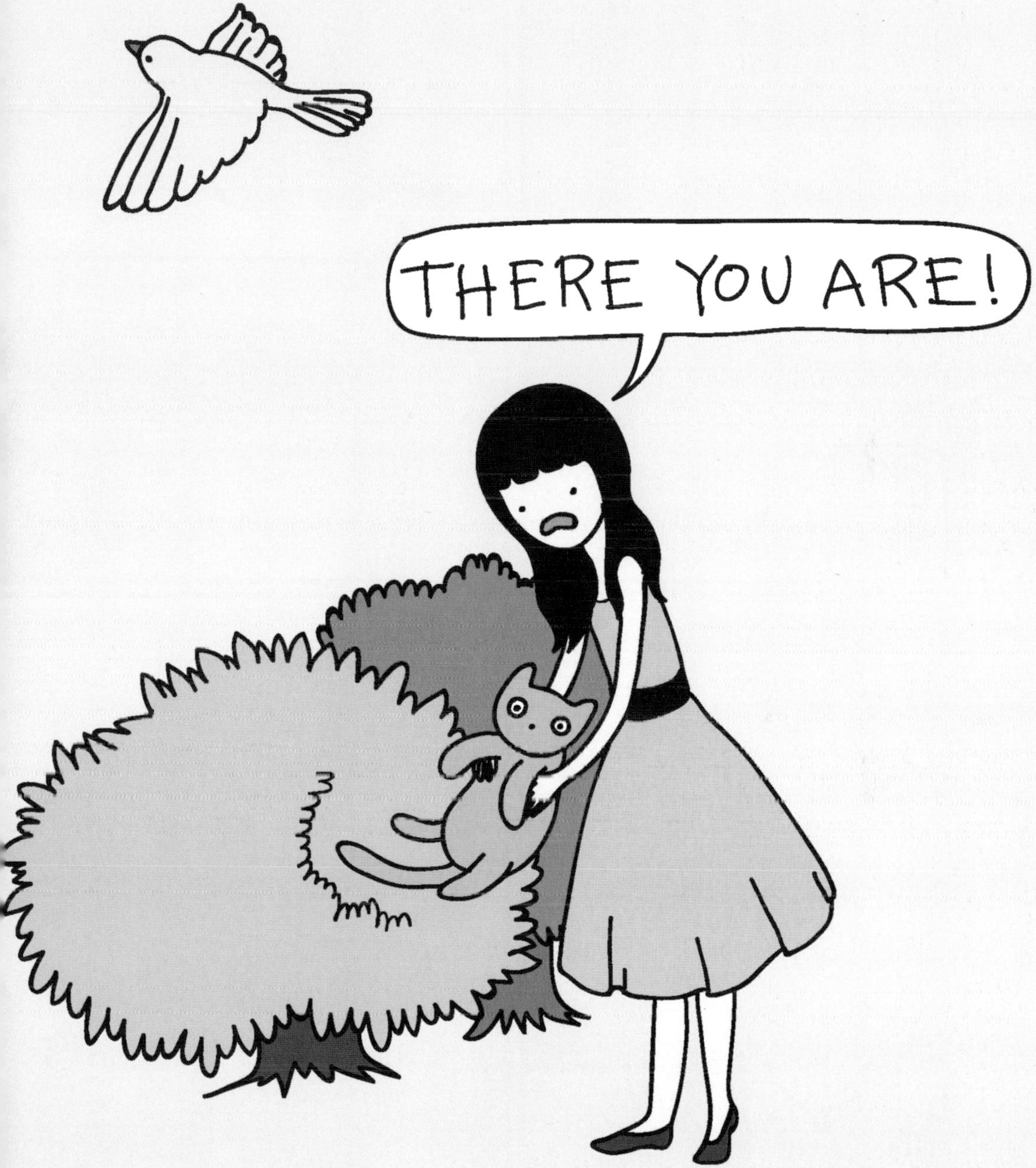
THERE YOU ARE!

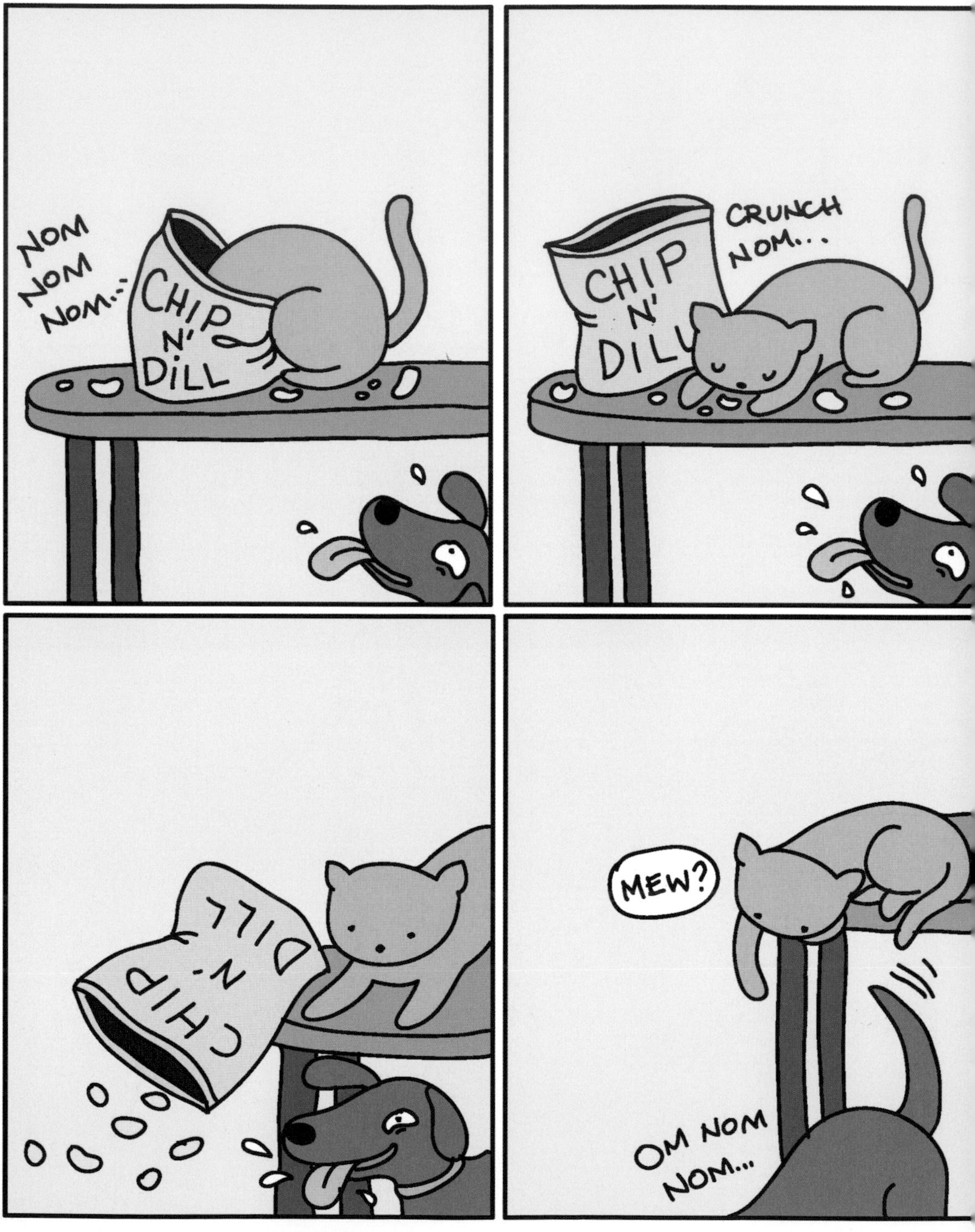
NOM NOM NOM...
CHIP N' DILL
CRUNCH NOM...
CHIP N' DILL
CHIP N' DILL
MEW?
OM NOM NOM...

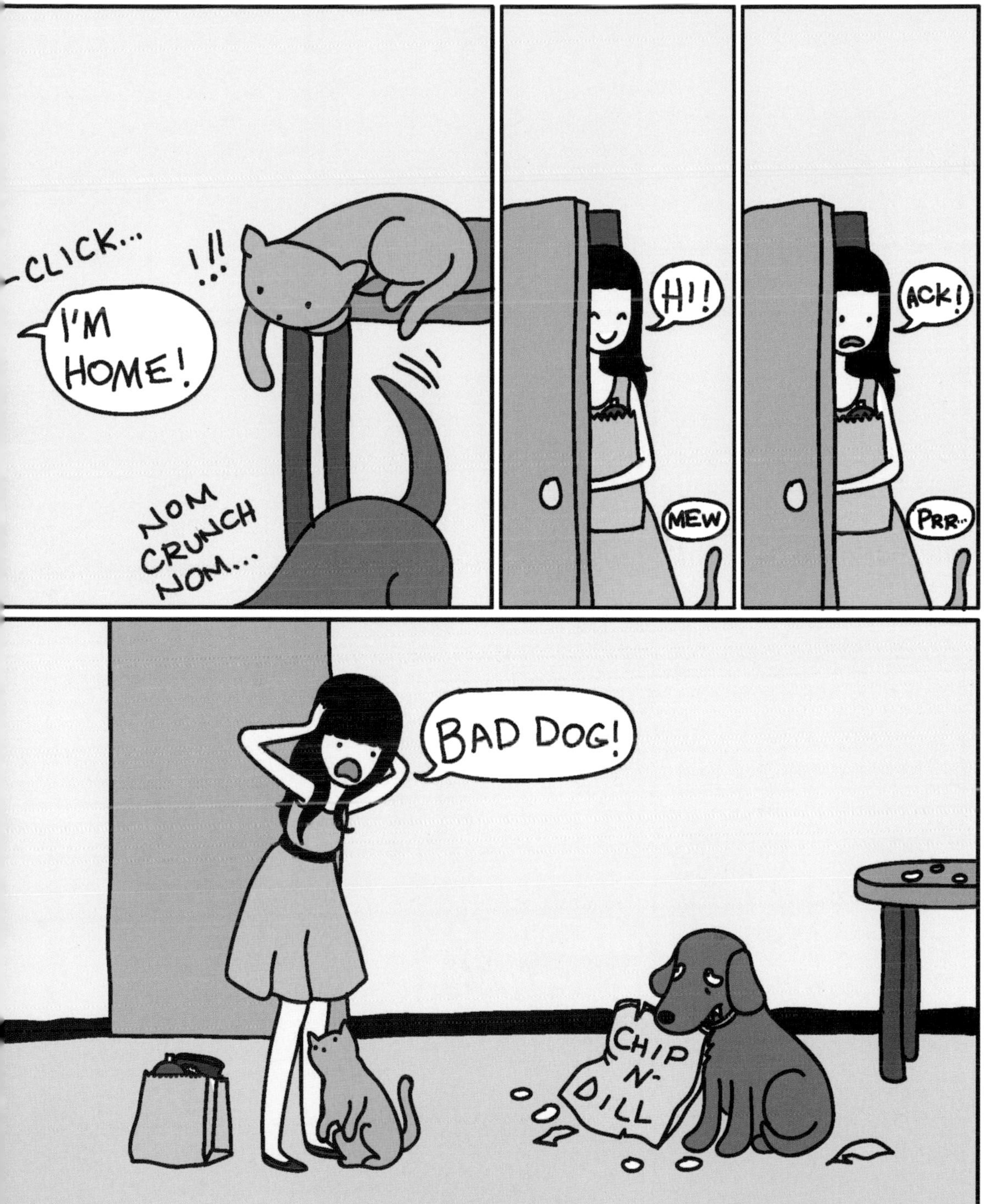

-CLICK...
I'M HOME!
!!!
NOM CRUNCH NOM...
HI!
MEW
ACK!
PRR...
BAD DOG!
CHIP N- DILL

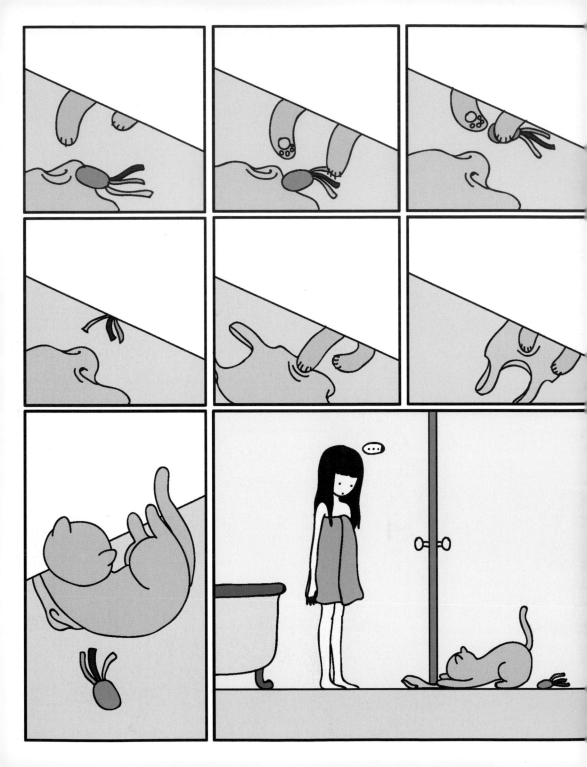

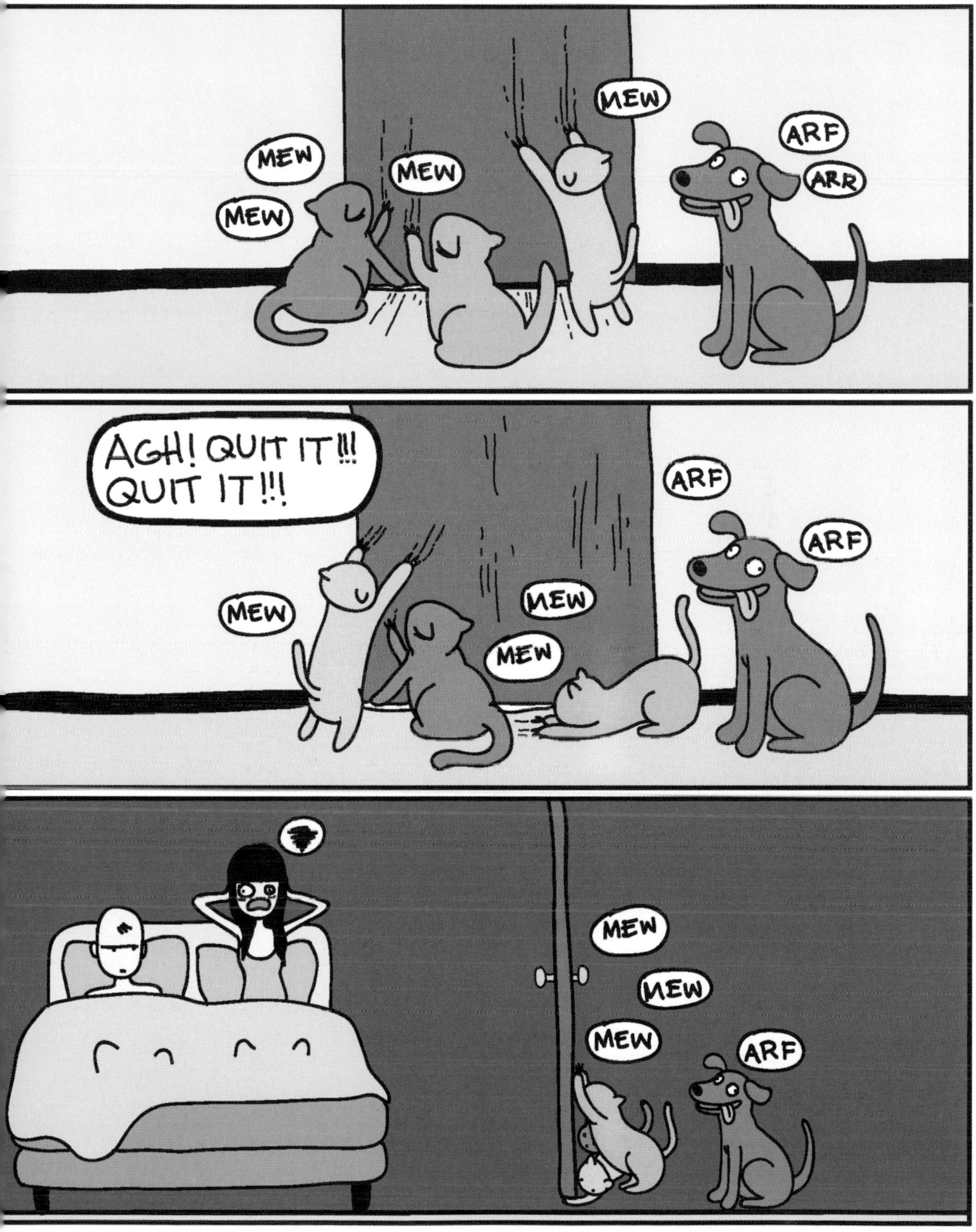
MEW
MEW
MEW
MEW
ARF
ARR
AGH! QUIT IT!!!
QUIT IT!!!
MEW
MEW
MEW
ARF
ARF
MEW
MEW
MEW
ARF

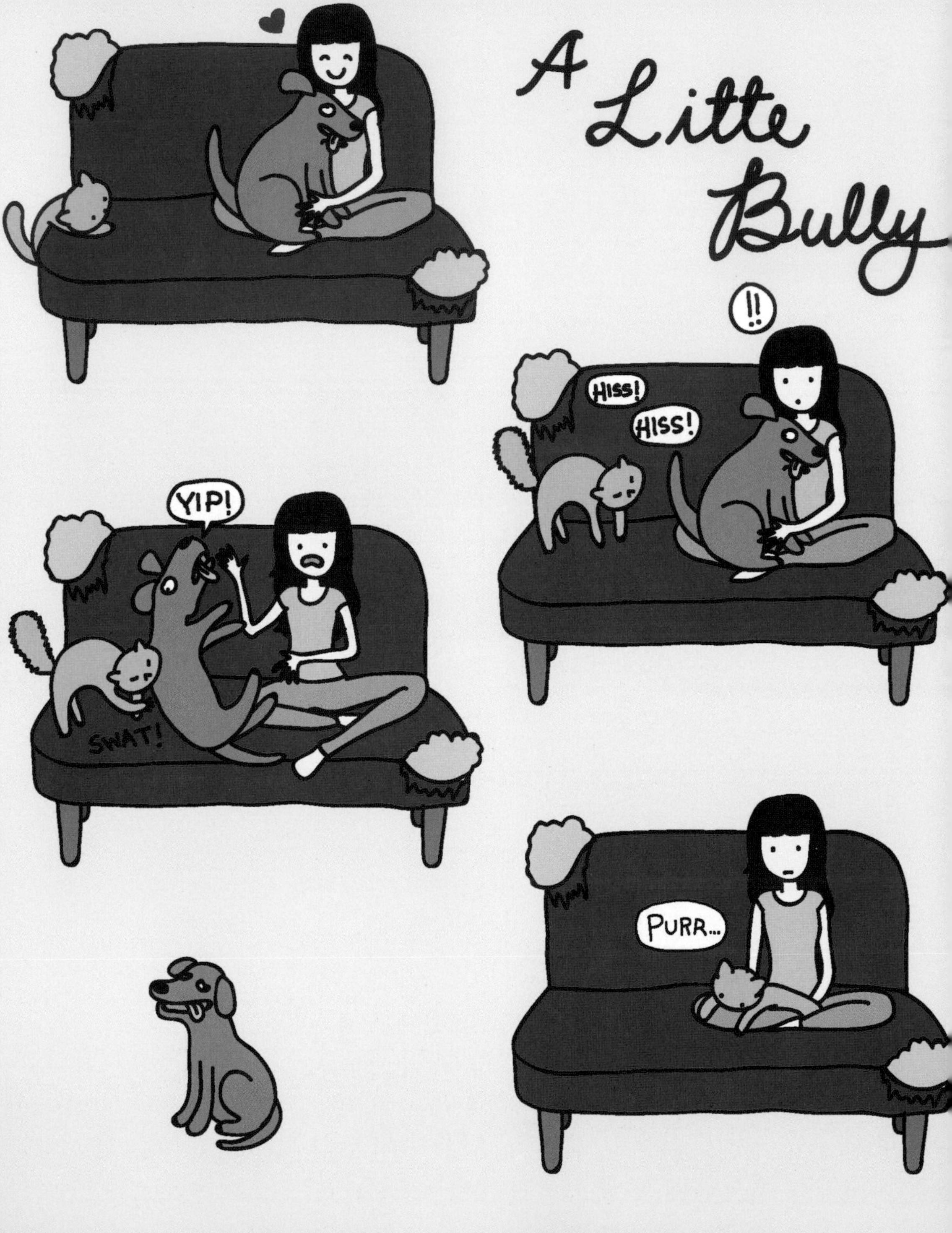

A Litte Bully
HISS!
HISS!
YIP!
SWAT!
PURR...

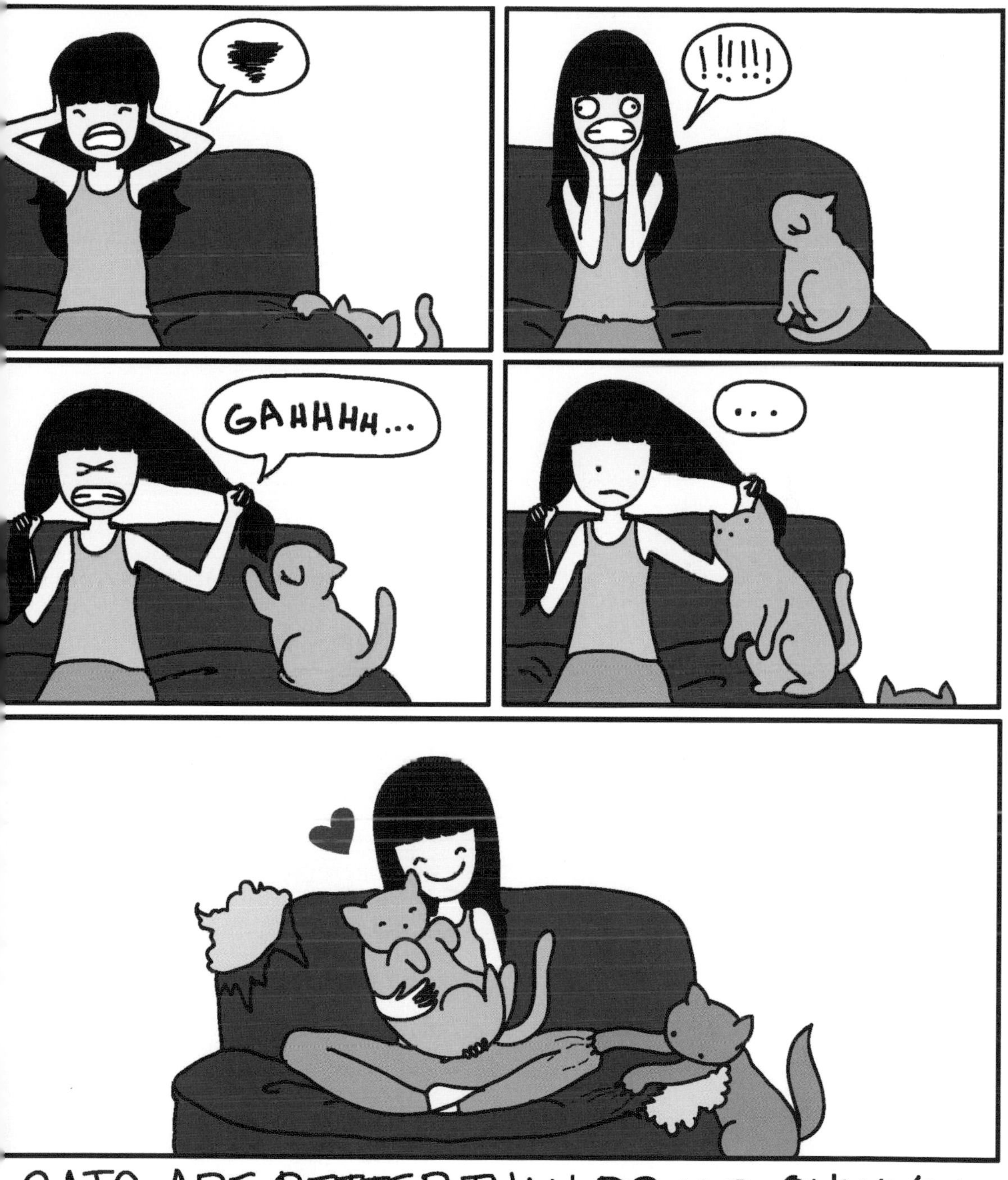
!!!!!!
GAHHHH...
...

CATS ARE BETTER THAN DRUGS. ONLY YOU CAN'T SNORT THEM IF YOU HAVE ALLERGIES.

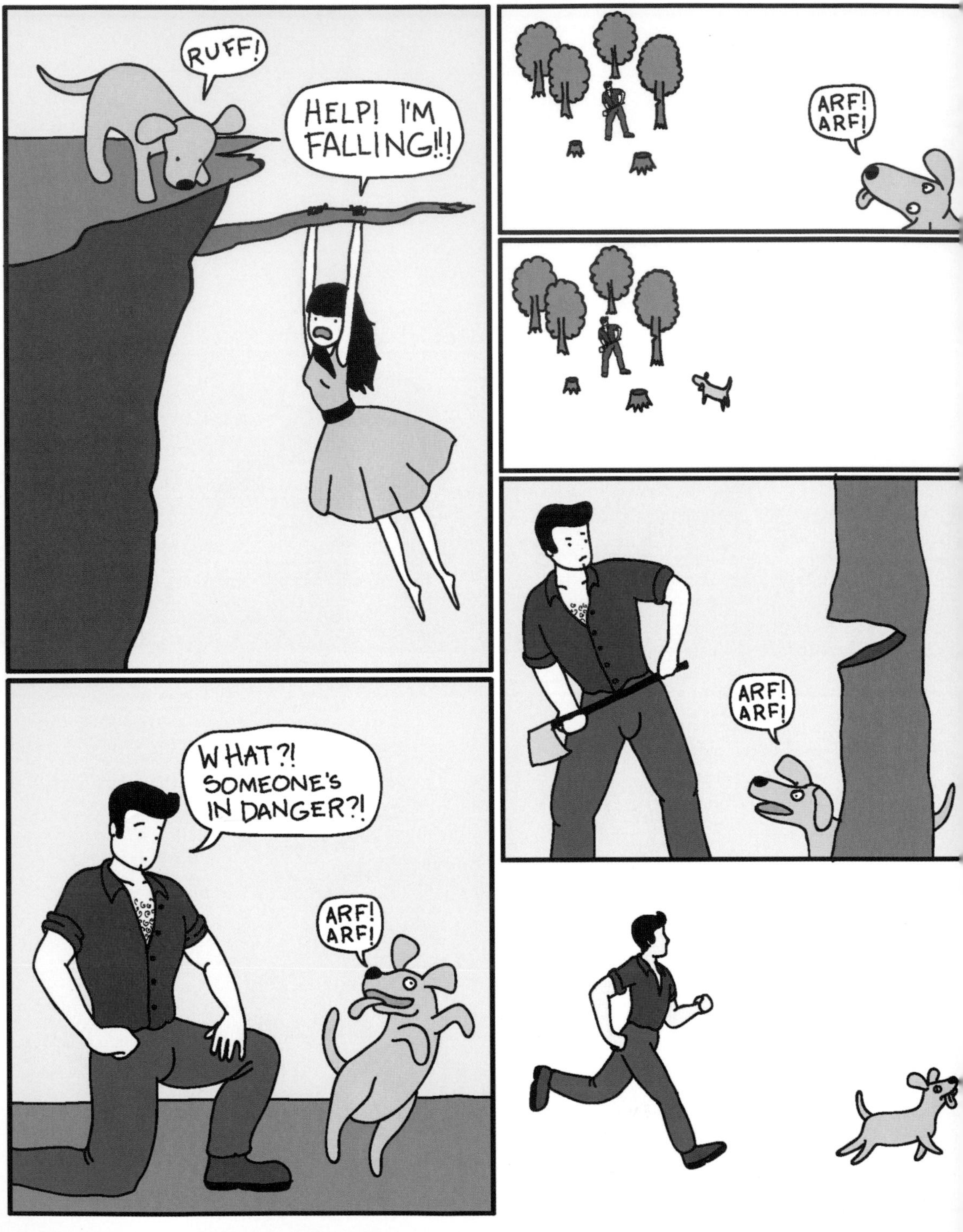
RUFF!
HELP! I'M FALLING!!!
ARF! ARF!
ARF! ARF!
WHAT?! SOMEONE'S IN DANGER?!
ARF! ARF!

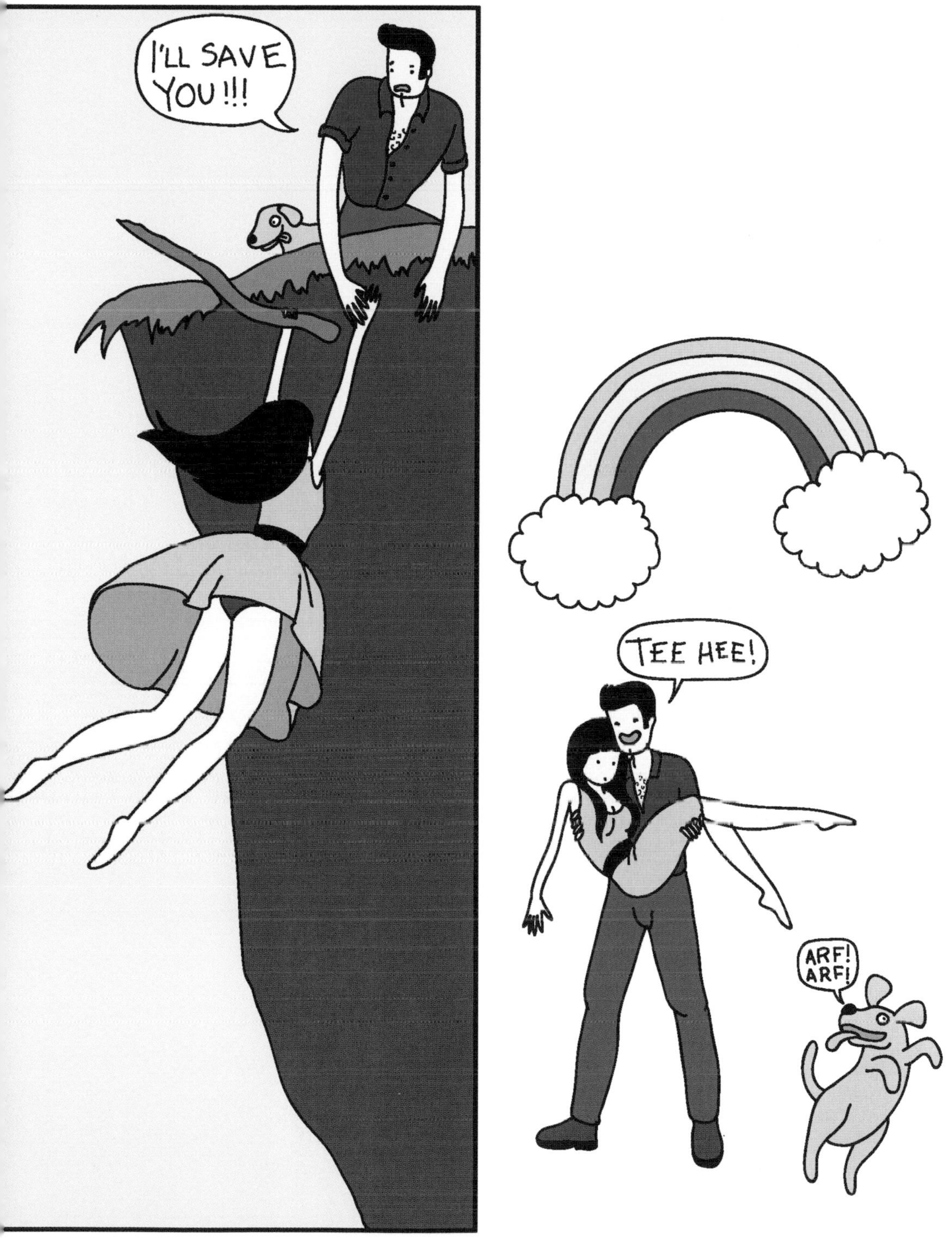
I'LL SAVE YOU!!!
TEE HEE!
ARF! ARF!

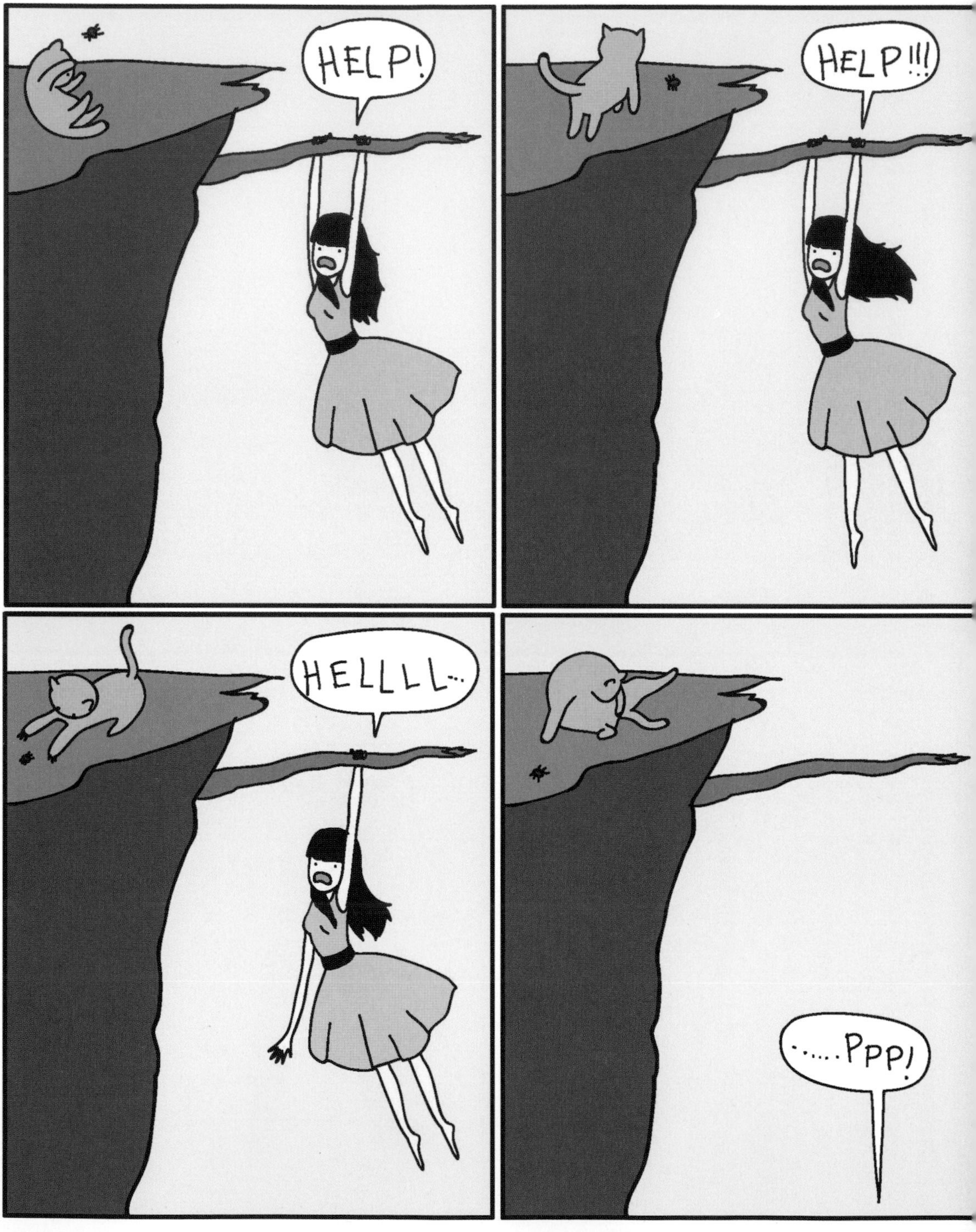
HELP!
HELP!!!
HELLLL...
.......PPP!

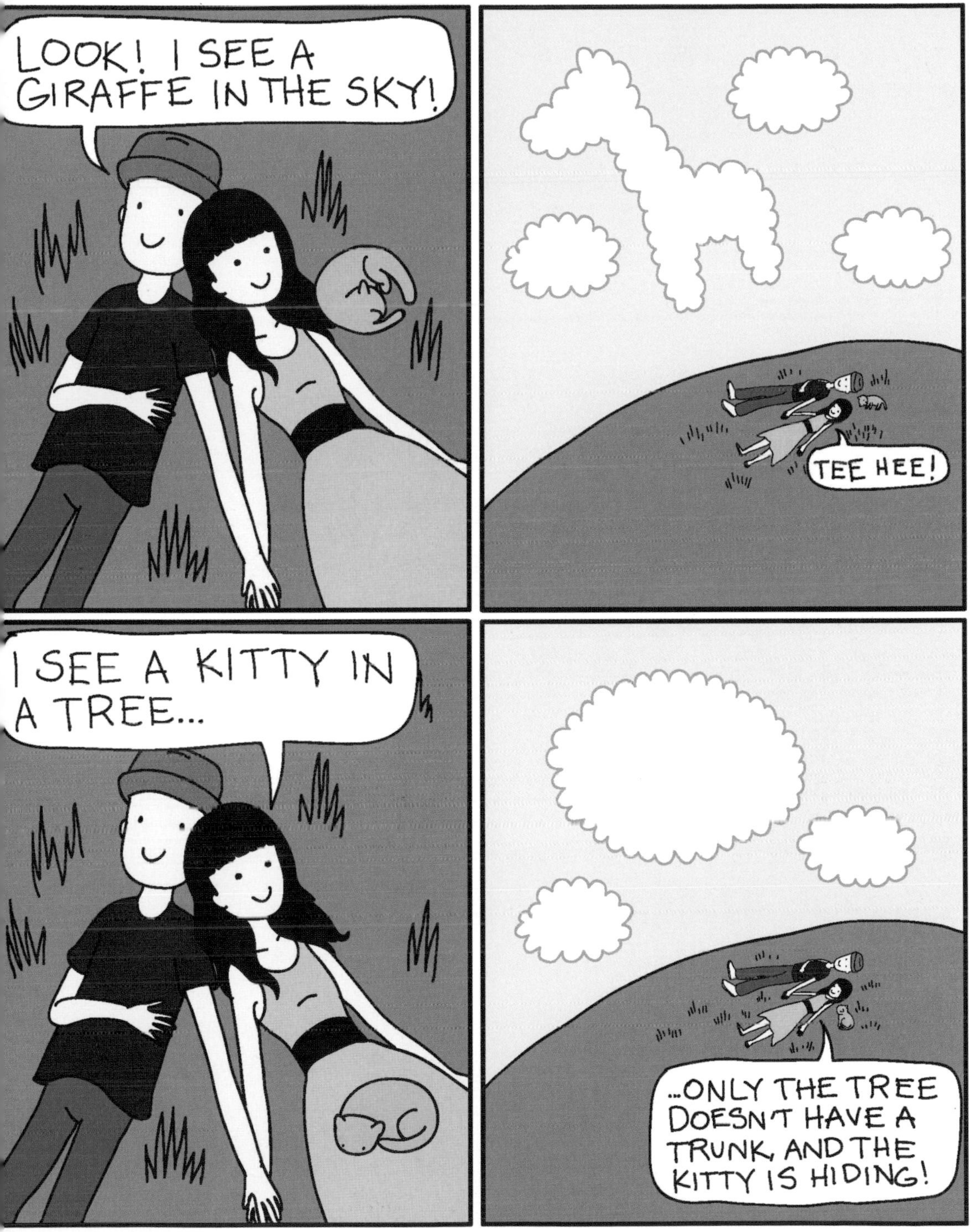
LOOK! I SEE A GIRAFFE IN THE SKY!
TEE HEE!
I SEE A KITTY IN A TREE...
..ONLY THE TREE DOESN'T HAVE A TRUNK, AND THE KITTY IS HIDING!

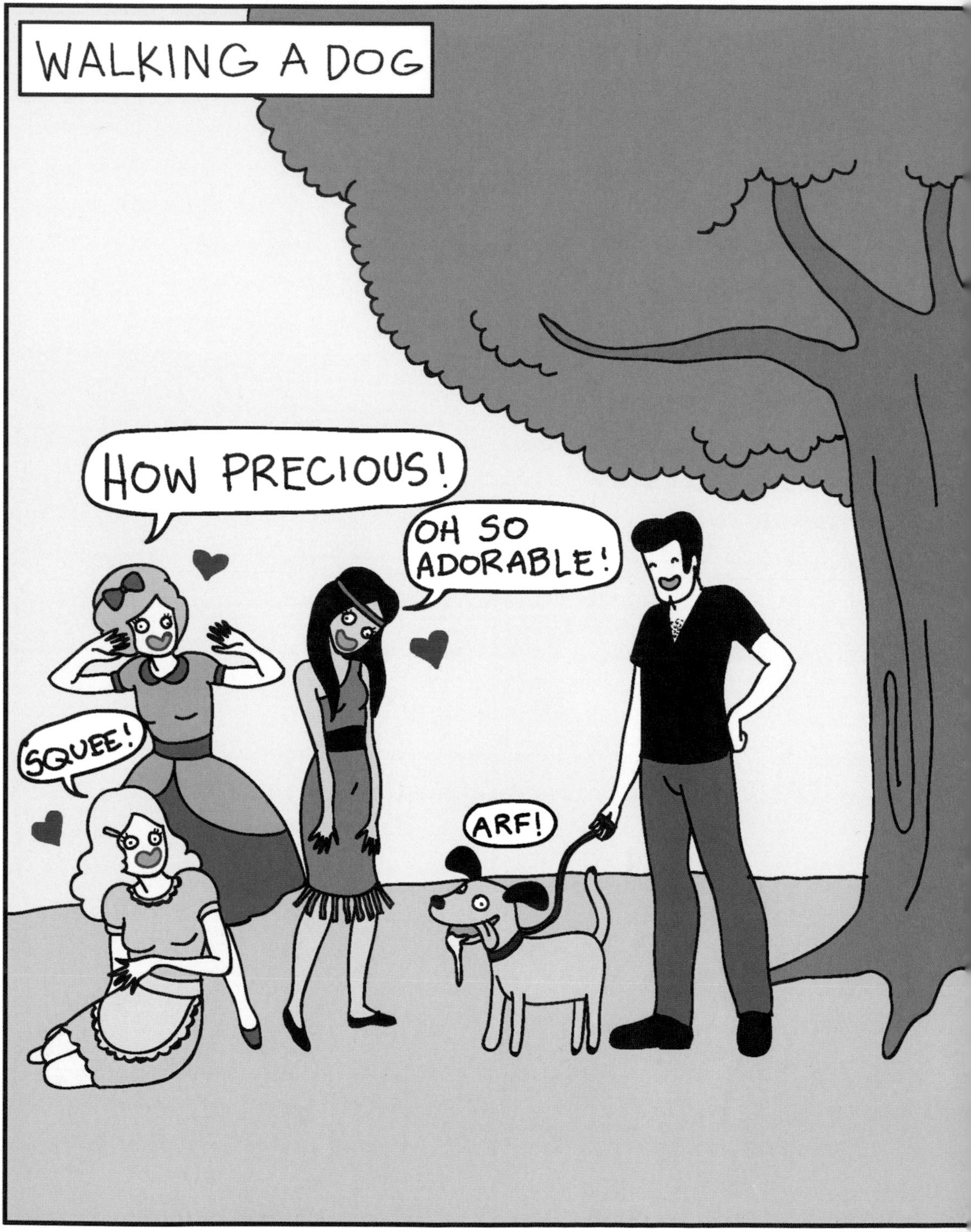
WALKING A DOG
HOW PRECIOUS!
OH SO ADORABLE!
SQUEE!
ARF!

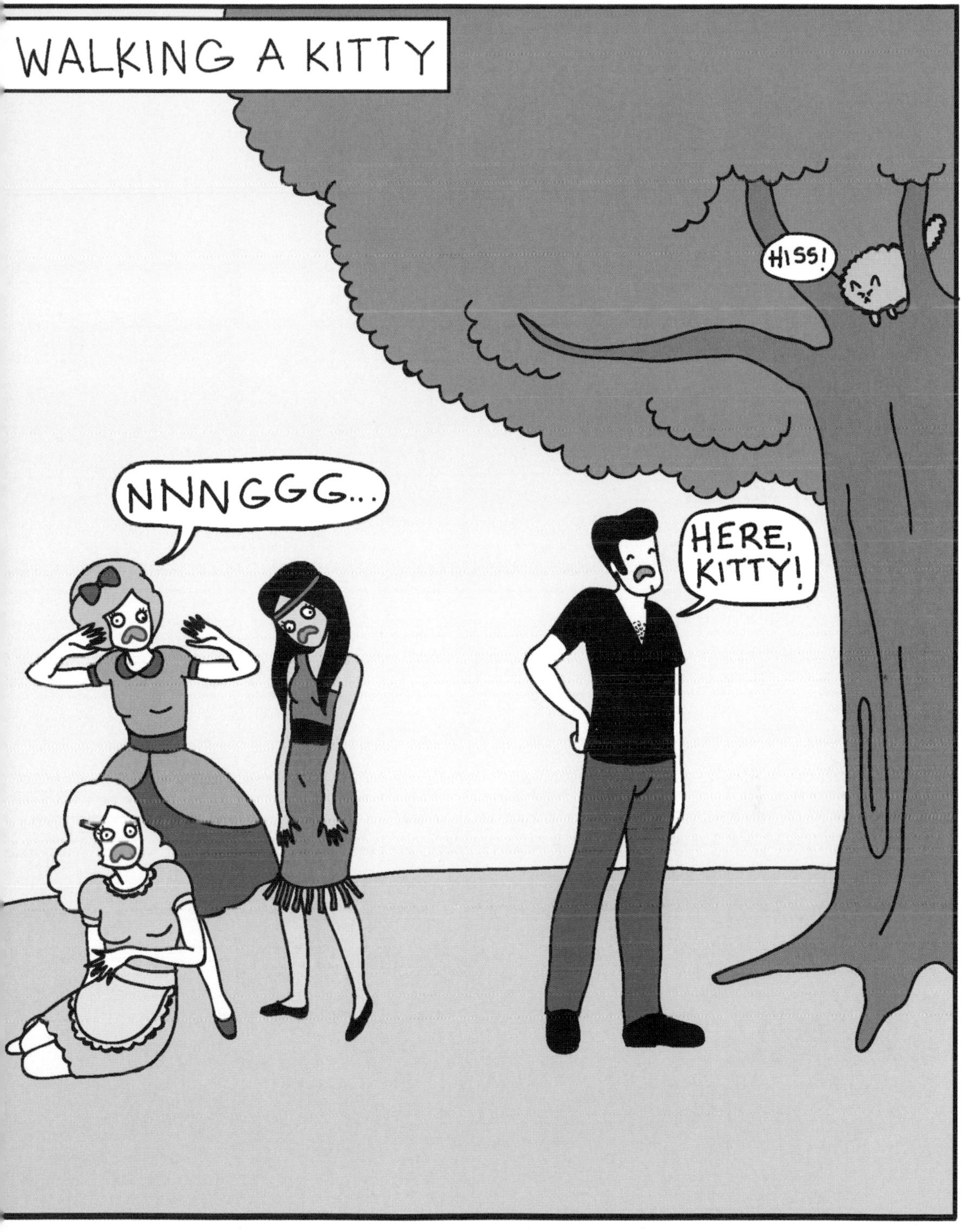
WALKING A KITTY
HISS!
NNNGGG...
HERE, KITTY!

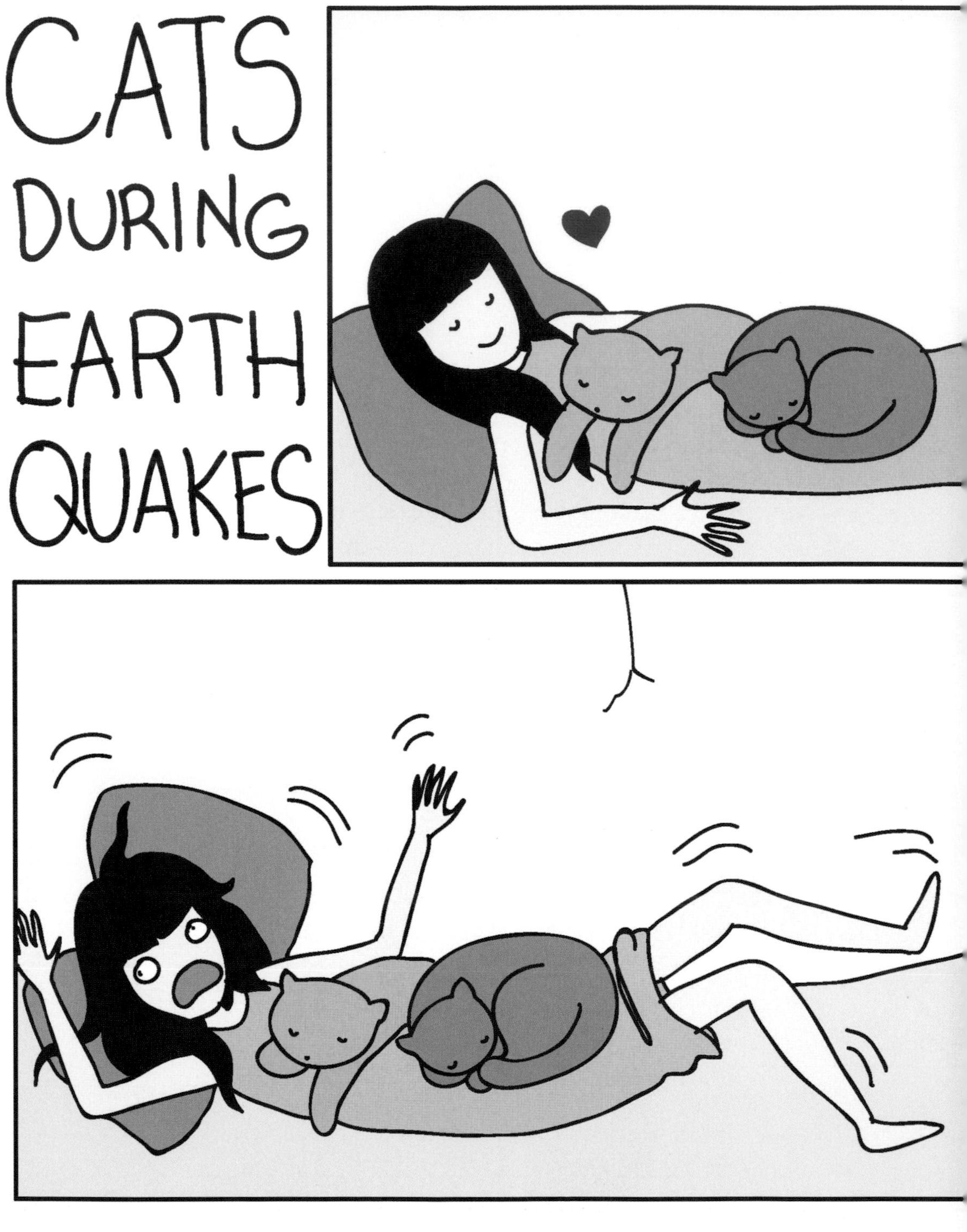
CATS DURING EARTH QUAKES

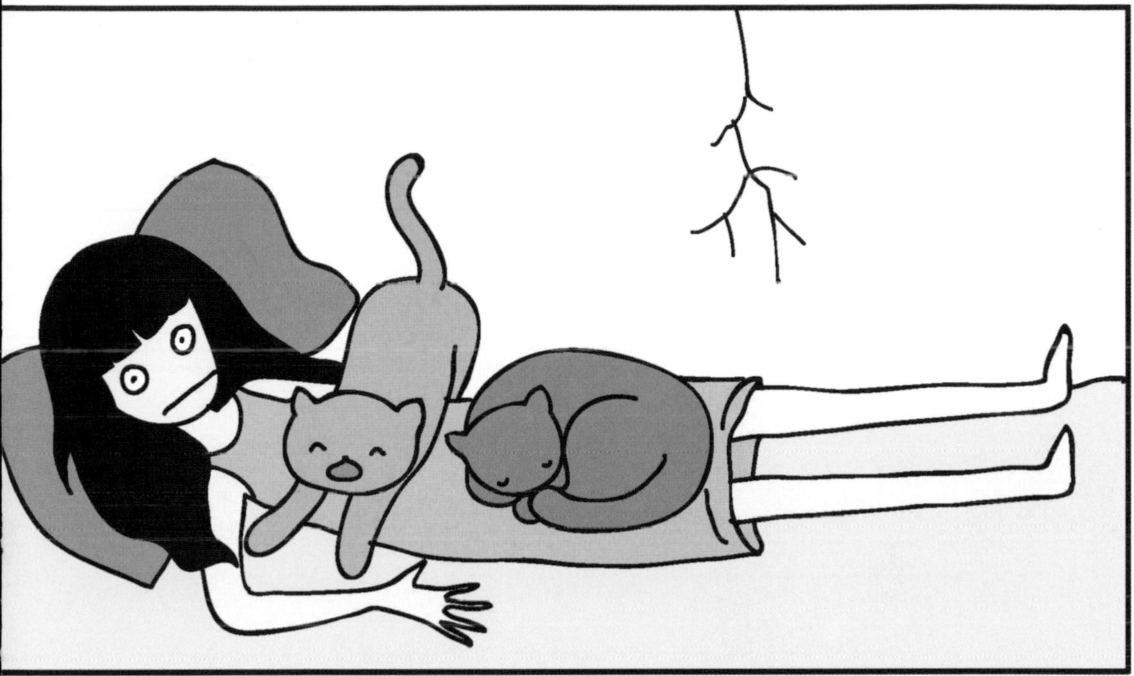

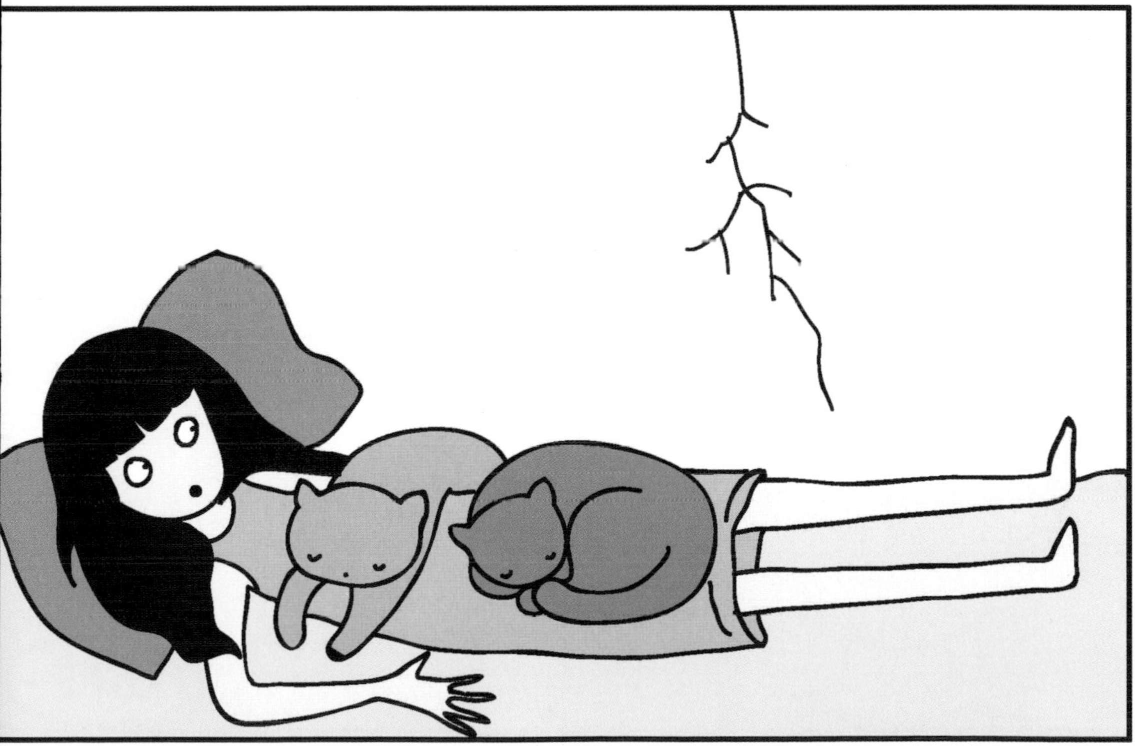

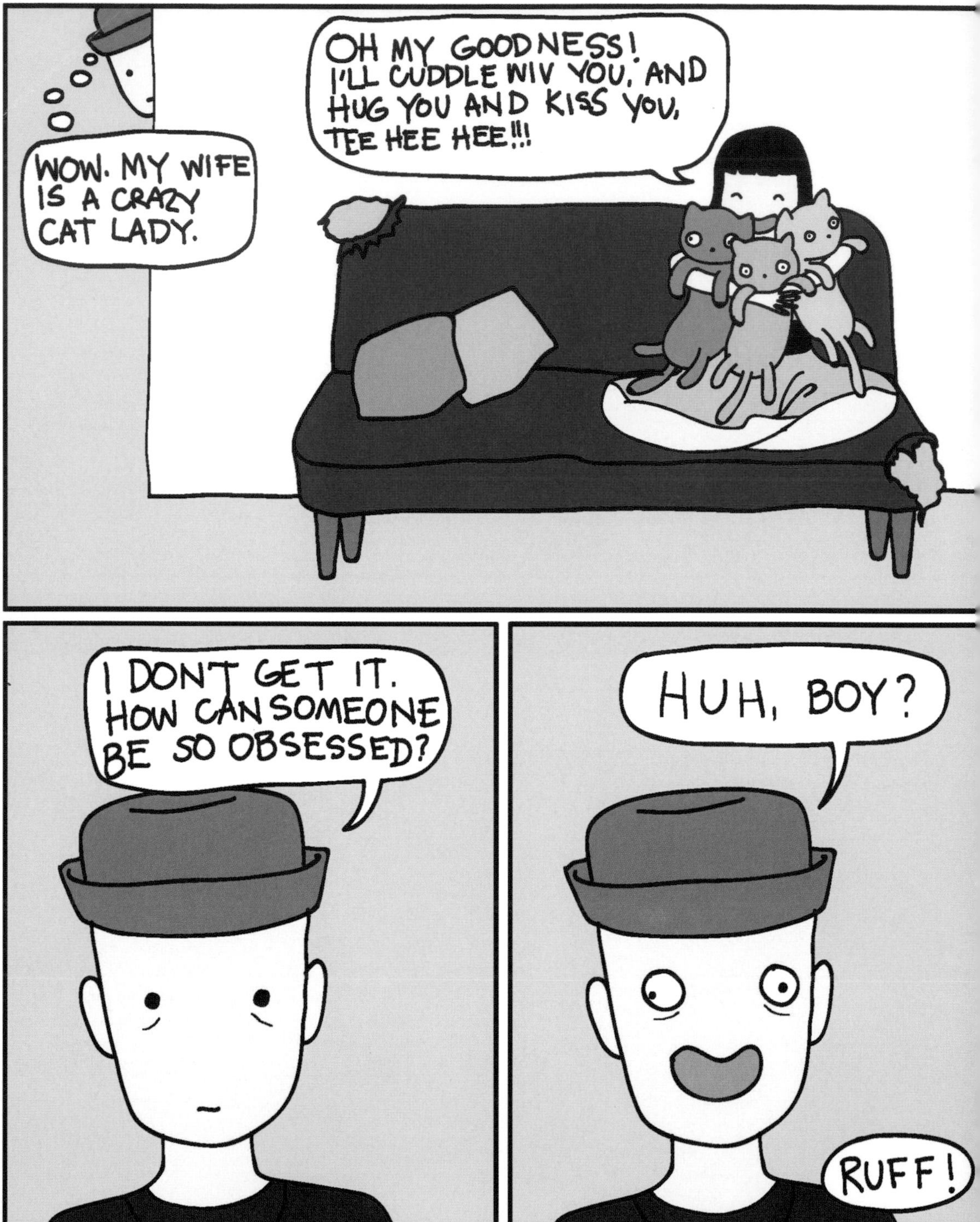
WOW. MY WIFE IS A CRAZY CAT LADY.
OH MY GOODNESS! I'LL CUDDLE WIV YOU, AND HUG YOU AND KISS YOU, TEE HEE HEE!!!
I DON'T GET IT. HOW CAN SOMEONE BE SO OBSESSED?
HUH, BOY?
RUFF!

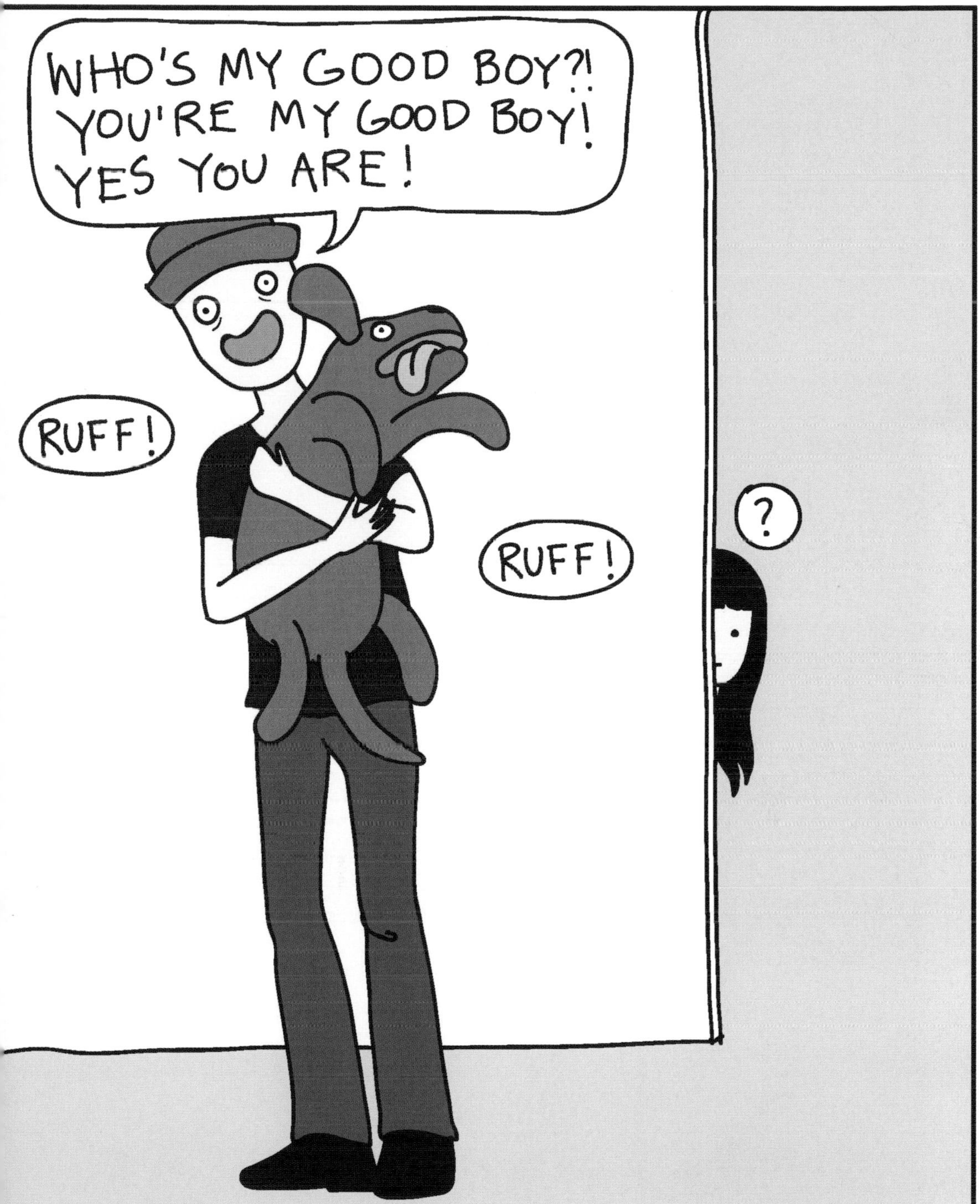
WHO'S MY GOOD BOY?! YOU'RE MY GOOD BOY! YES YOU ARE!
RUFF!
RUFF!
?

FIERCE LITTLE HUNTER

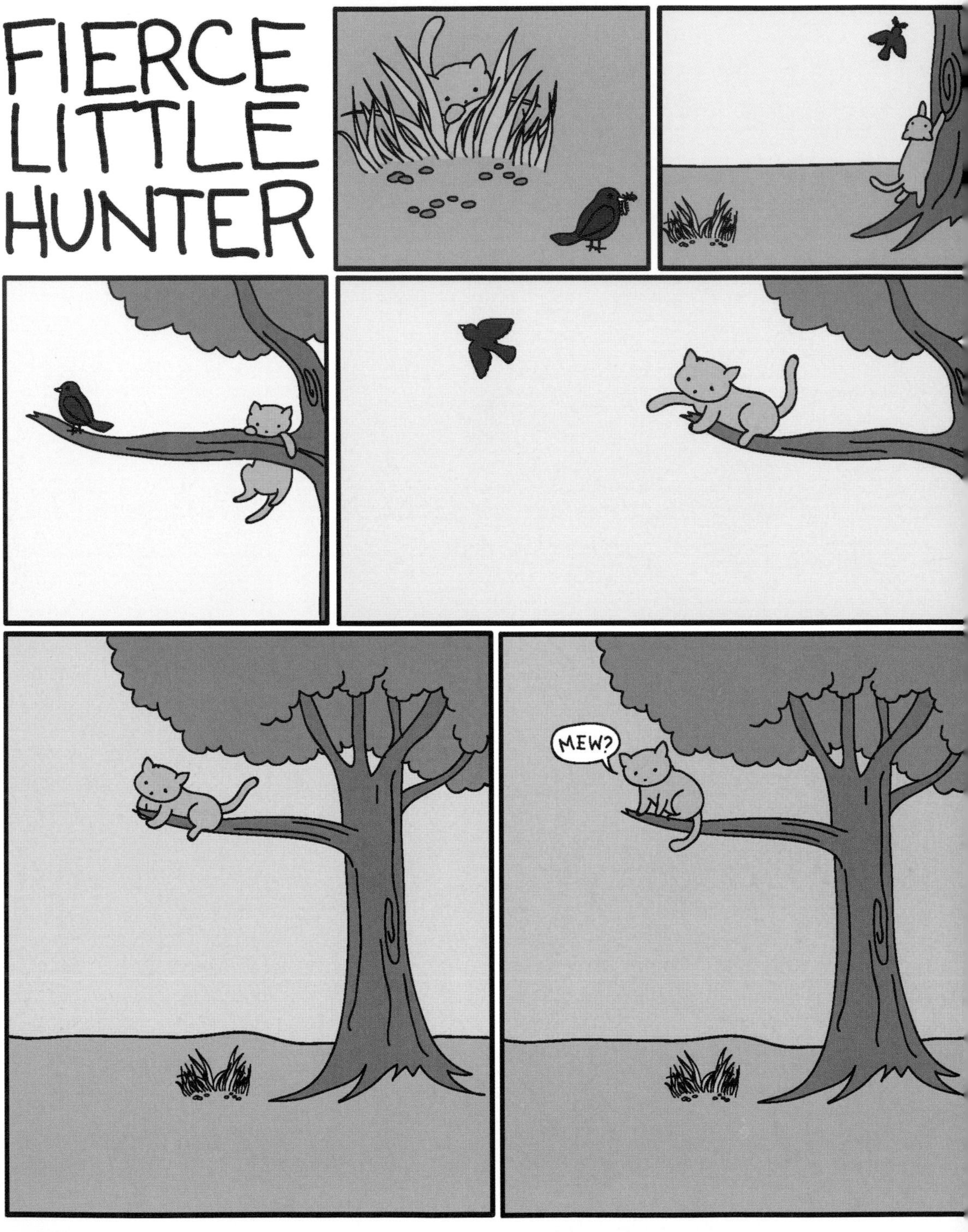

MEW?

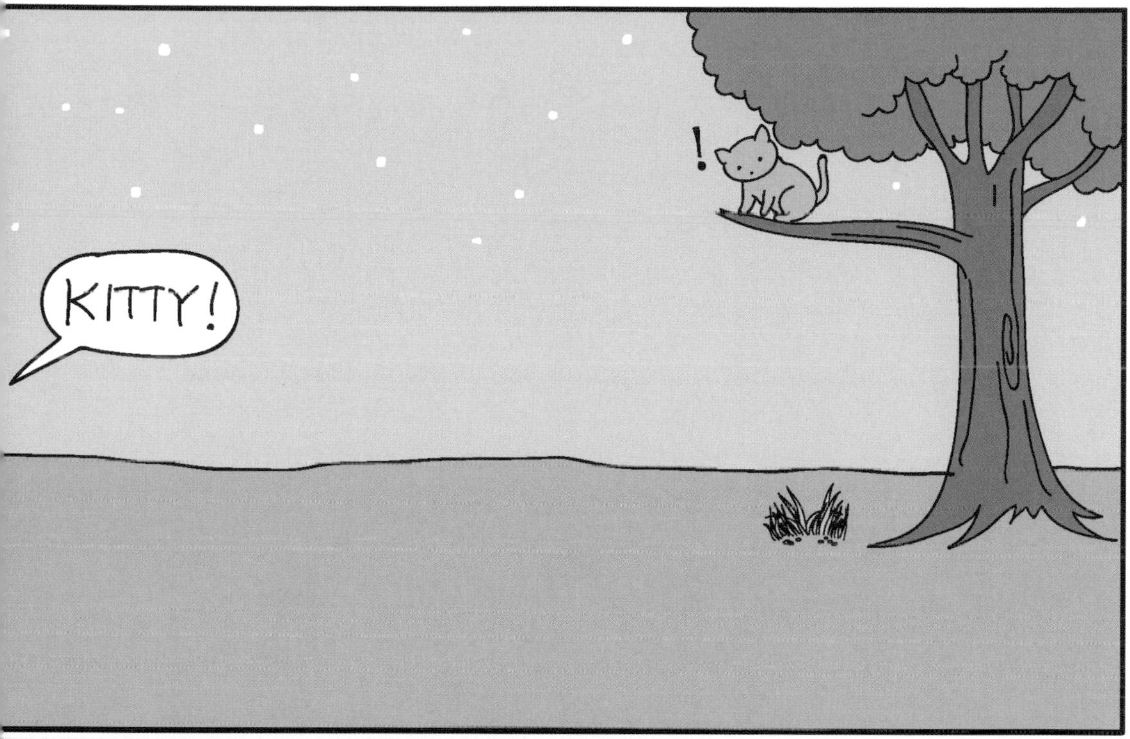
!
KITTY!

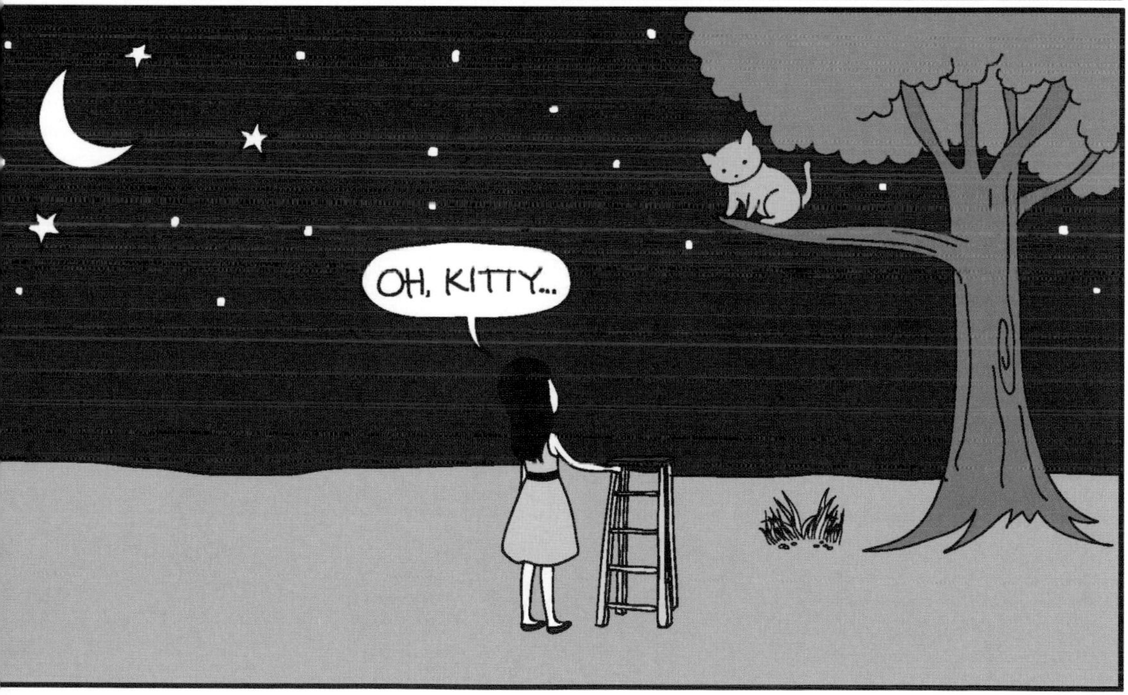
OH, KITTY...

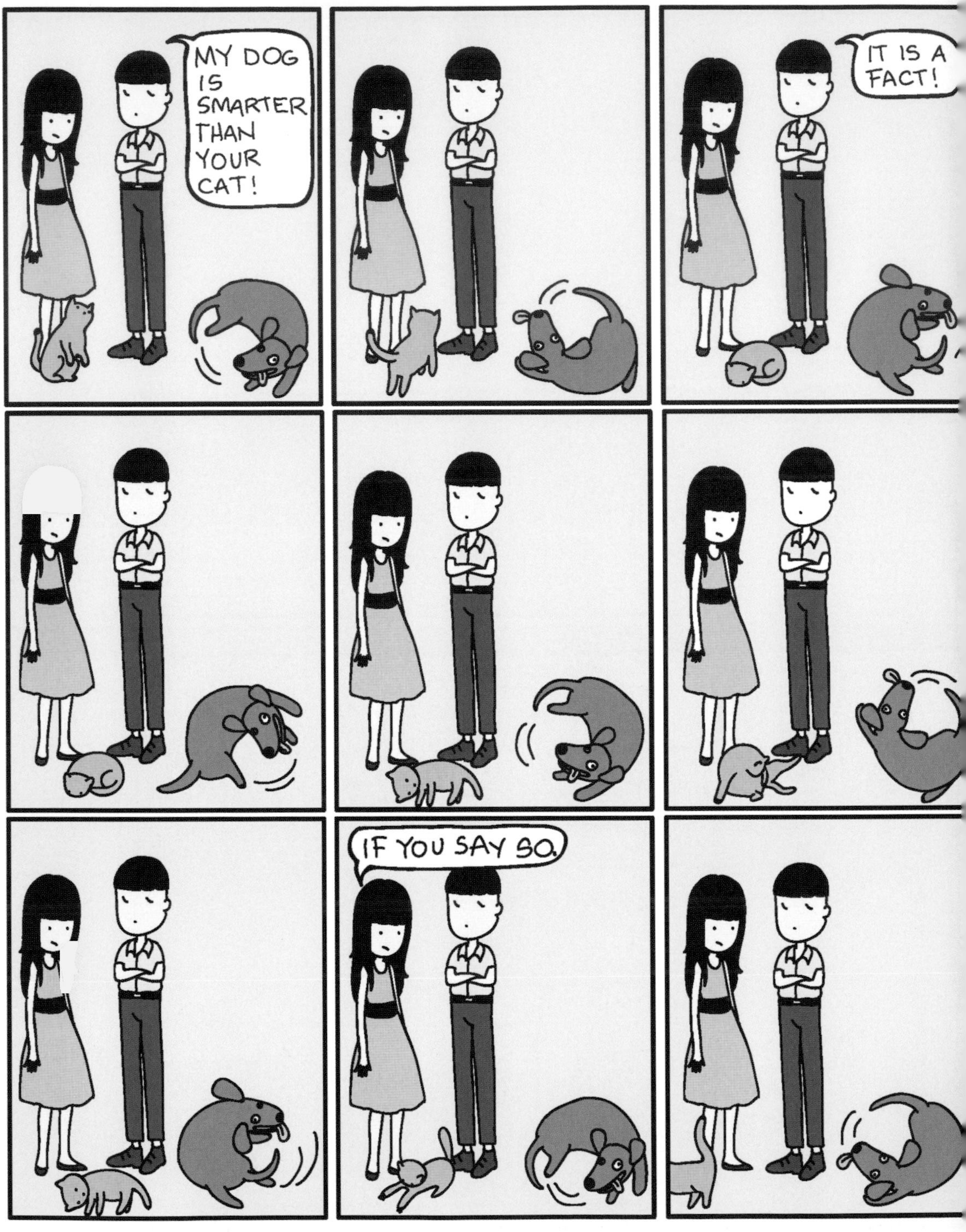
MY DOG IS SMARTER THAN YOUR CAT!
IT IS A FACT!
IF YOU SAY SO.

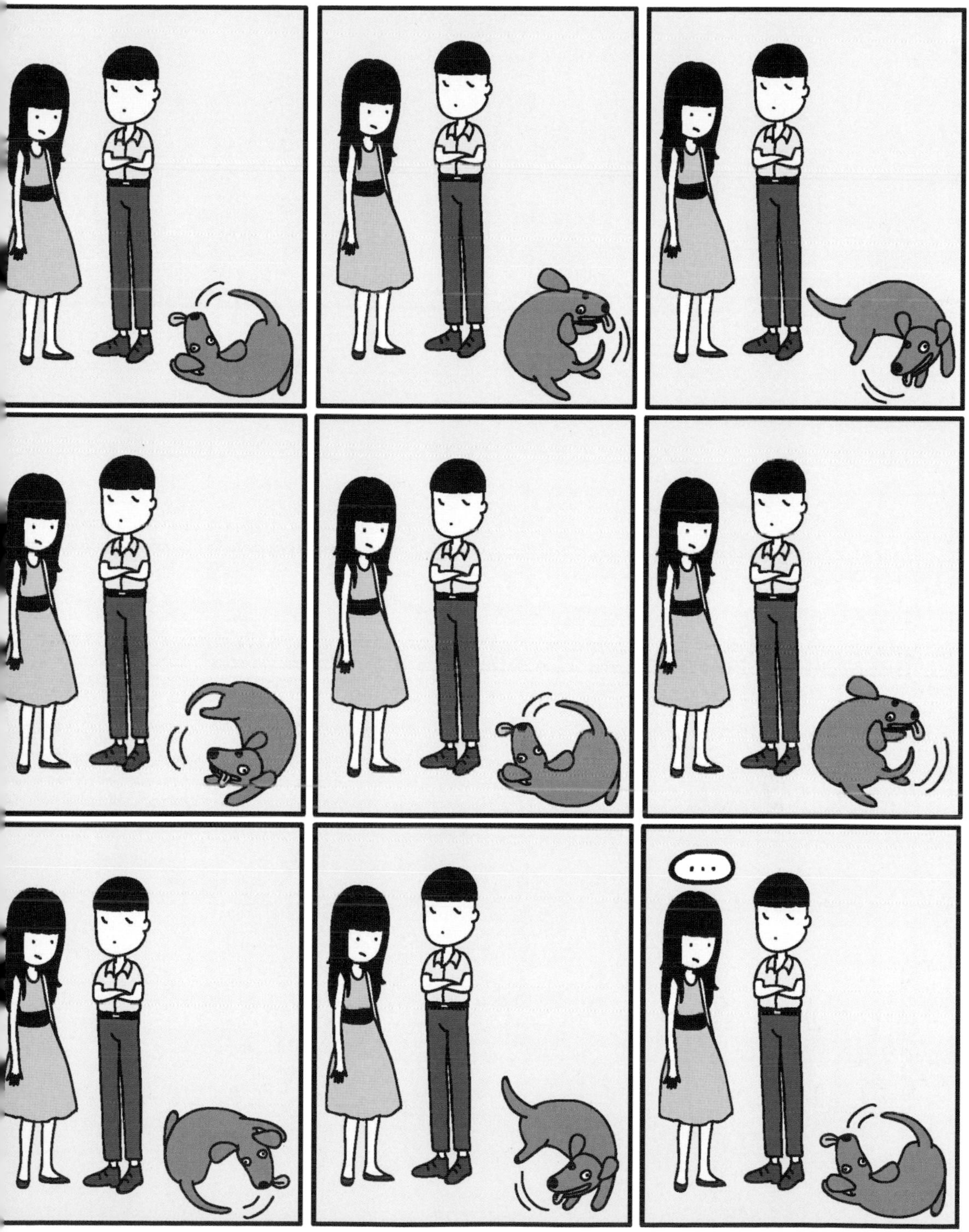
...

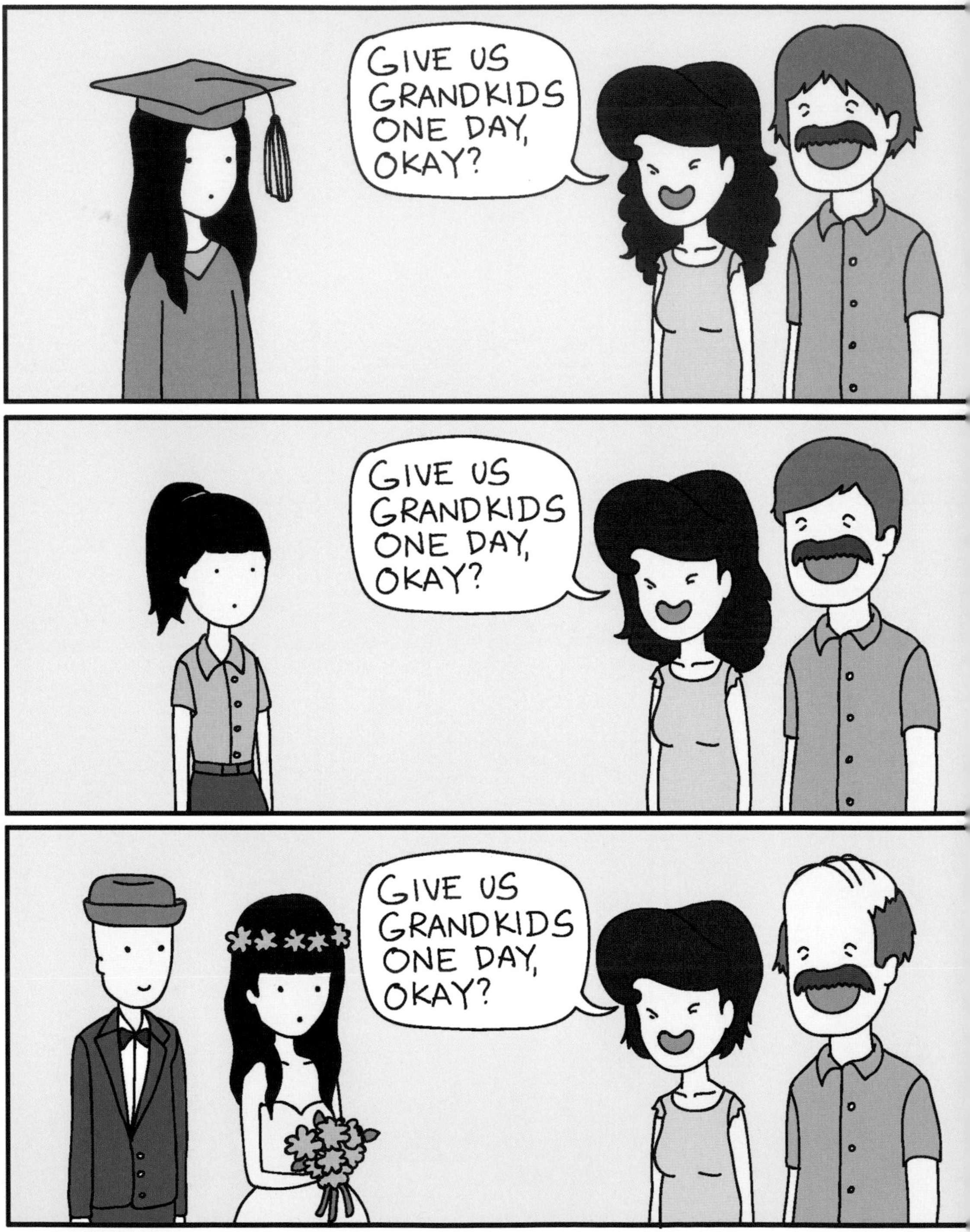
GIVE US GRANDKIDS ONE DAY, OKAY?
GIVE US GRANDKIDS ONE DAY, OKAY?
GIVE US GRANDKIDS ONE DAY, OKAY?

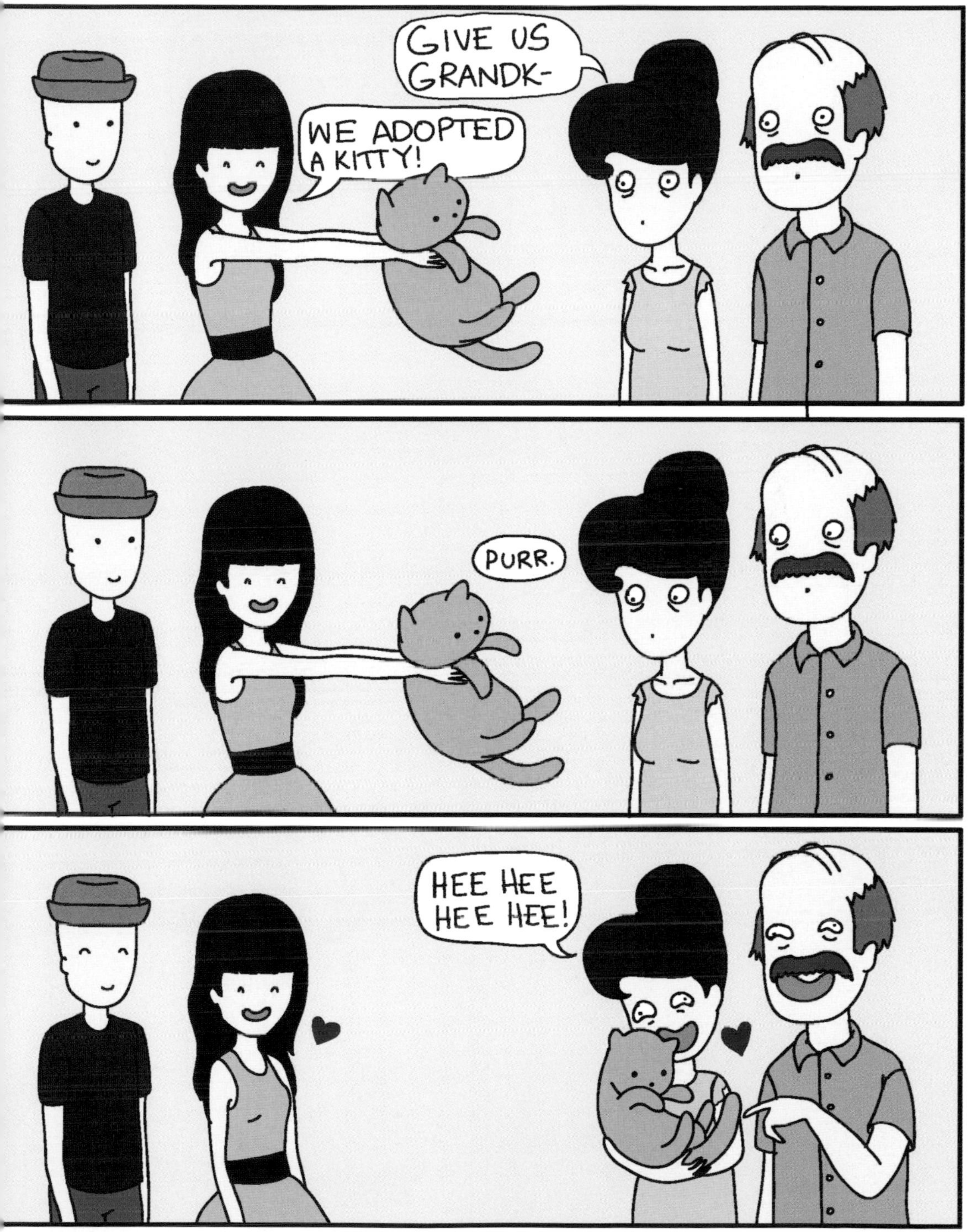
GIVE US GRANDK-
WE ADOPTED A KITTY!
PURR.
HEE HEE HEE HEE!

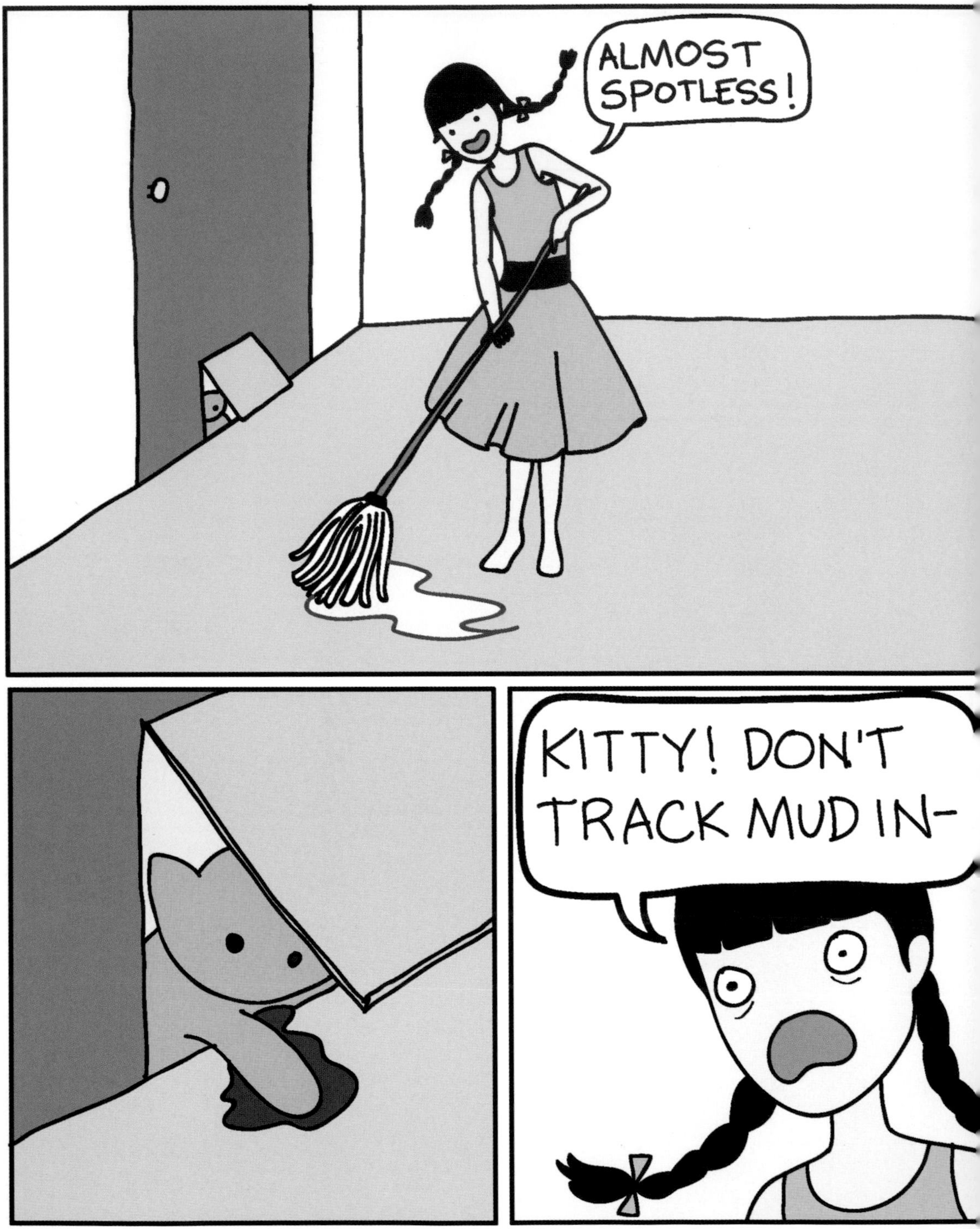
ALMOST SPOTLESS!
KITTY! DON'T TRACK MUD IN-

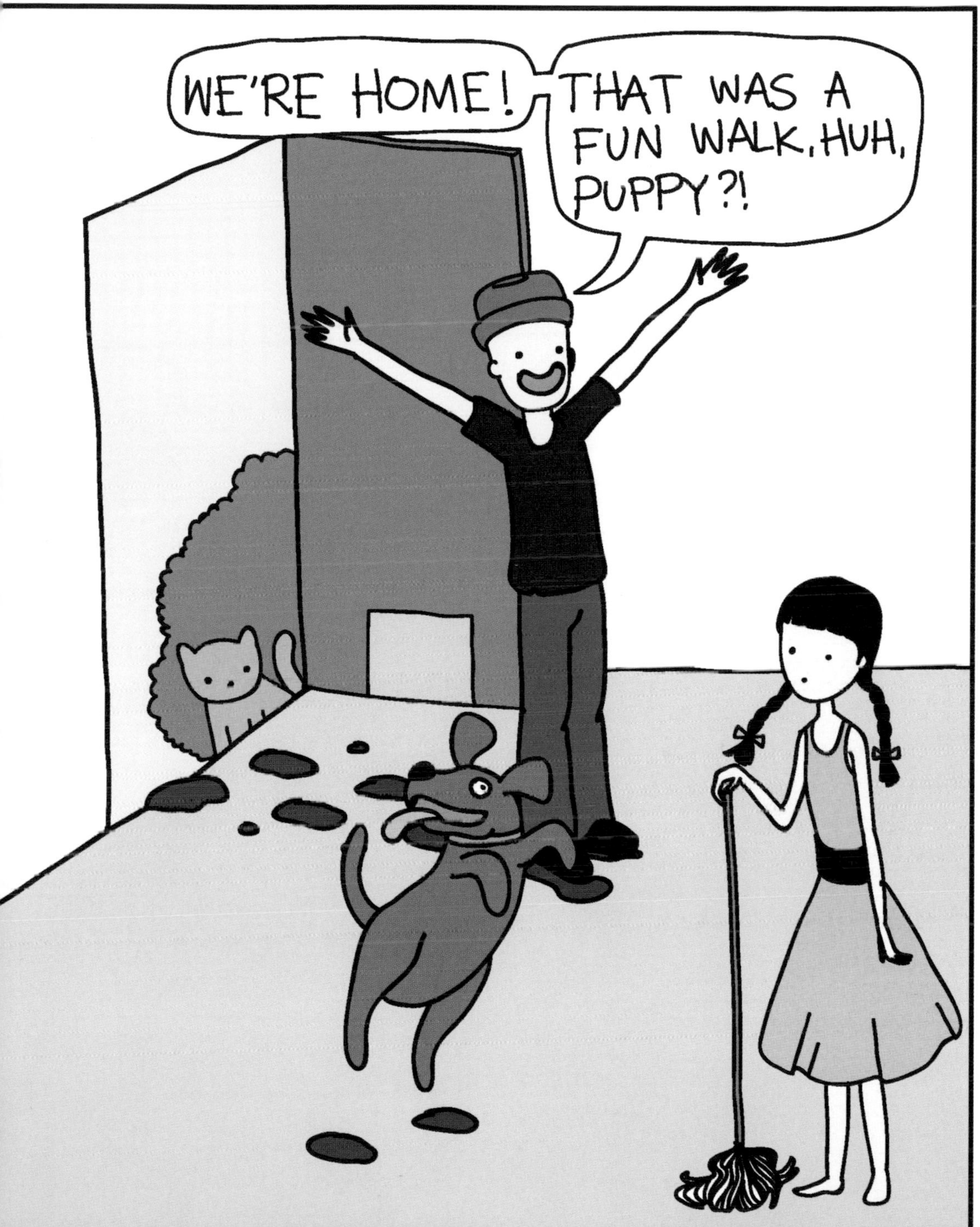
WE'RE HOME!
THAT WAS A FUN WALK, HUH, PUPPY?!

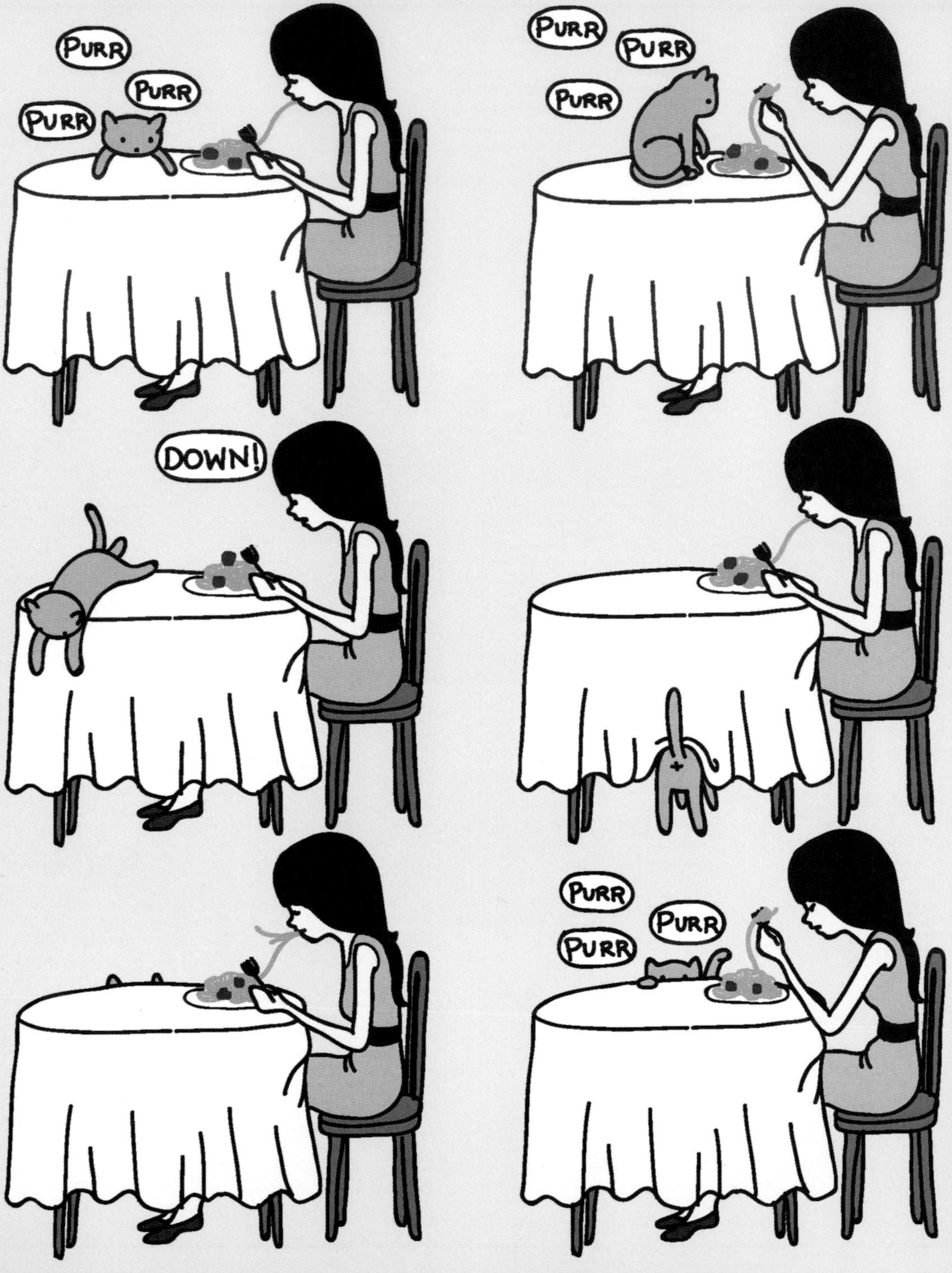
PURR
PURR
PURR
PURR
PURR
PURR
DOWN!
PURR
PURR
PURR

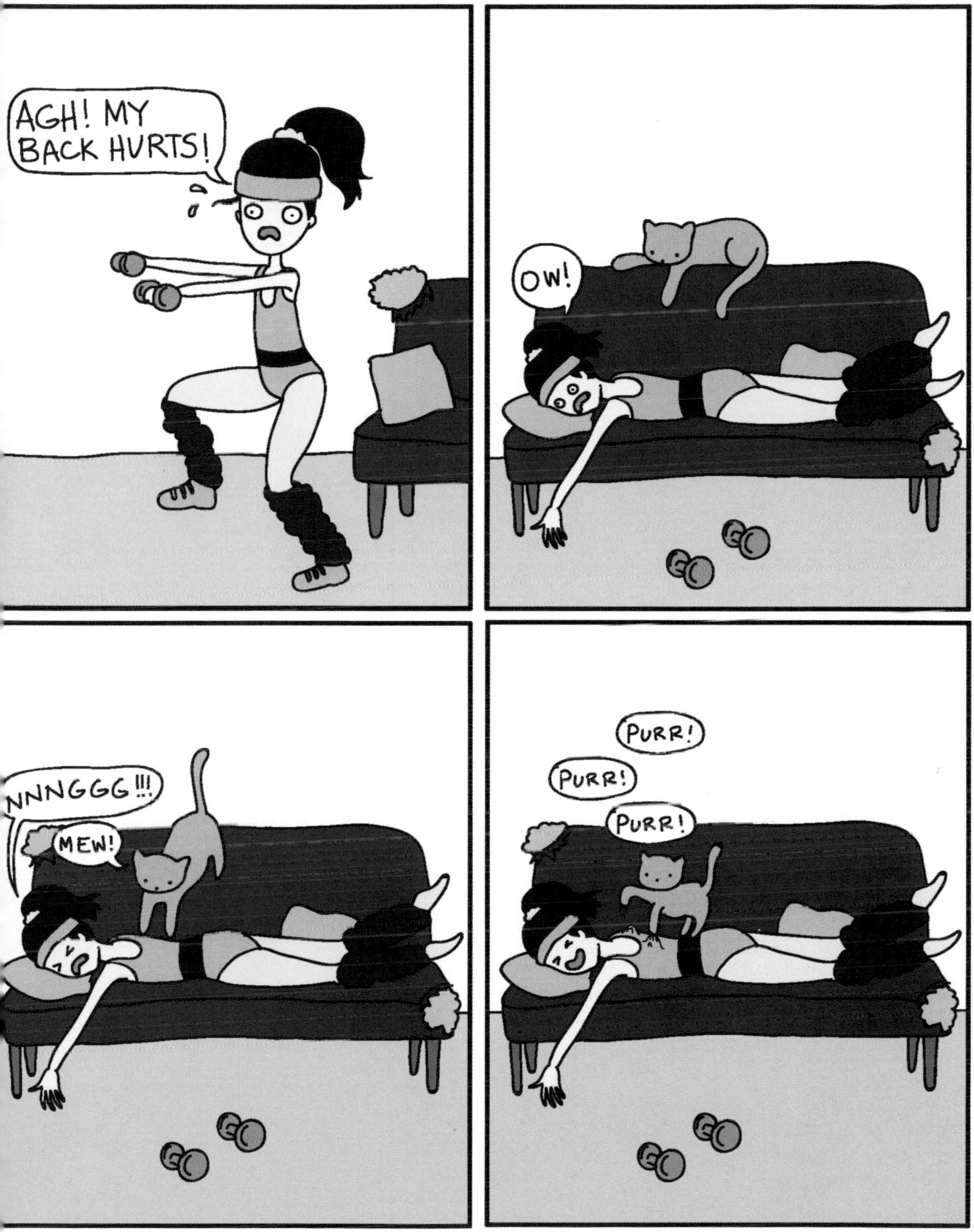
AGH! MY BACK HURTS!
OW!
NNNGGG!!!
MEW!
PURR!
PURR!
PURR!

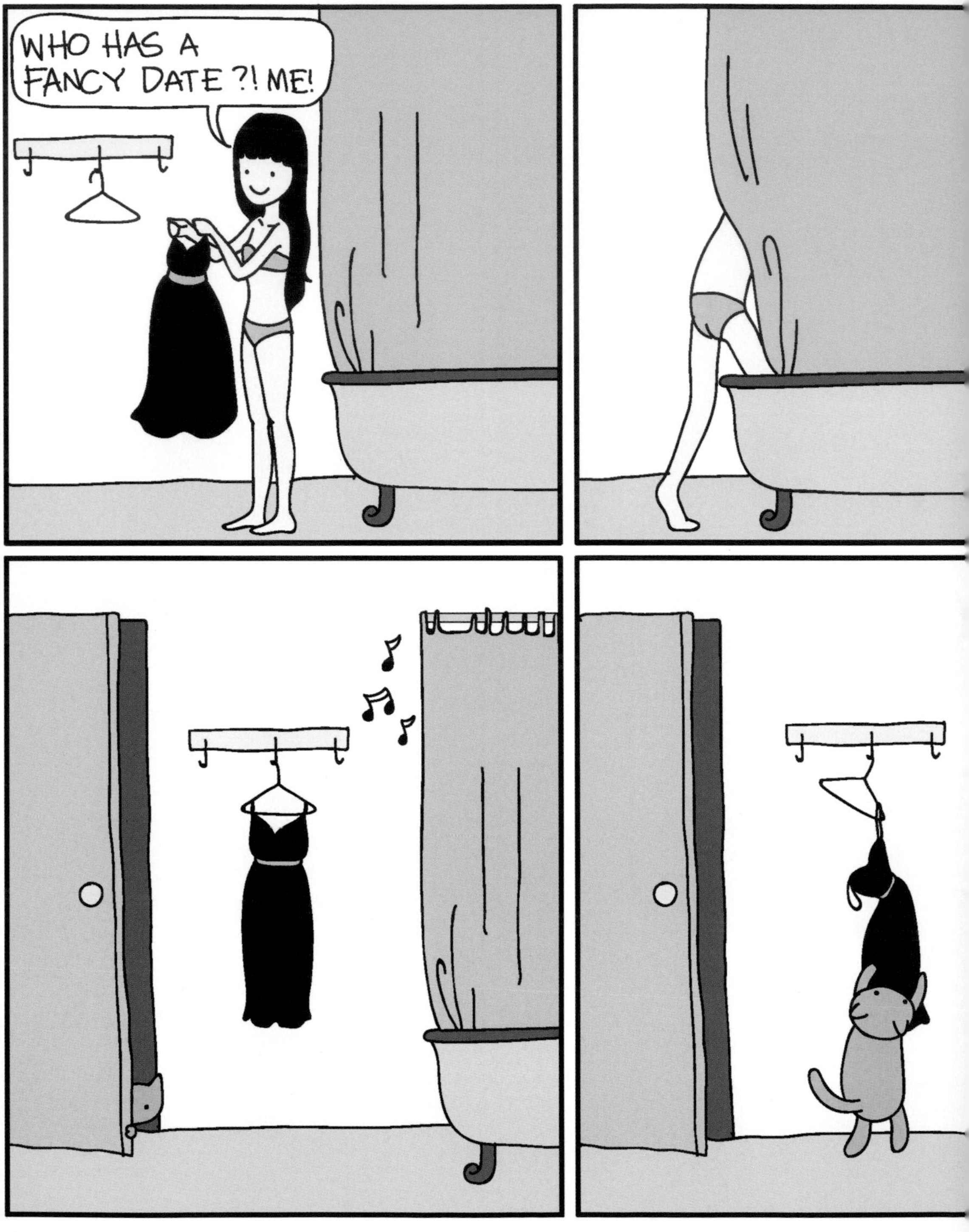
WHO HAS A FANCY DATE ?! ME!

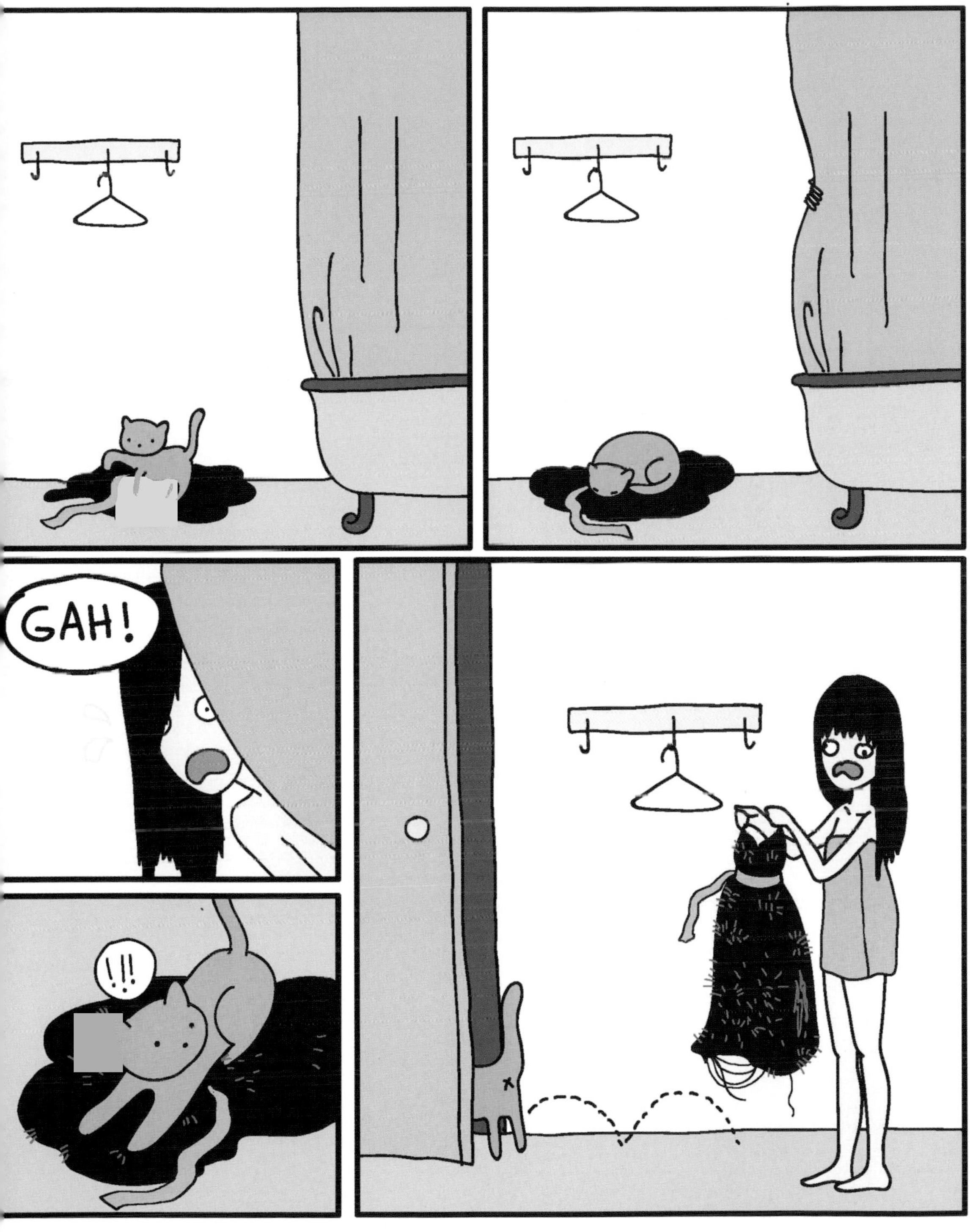
GAH!
!!!

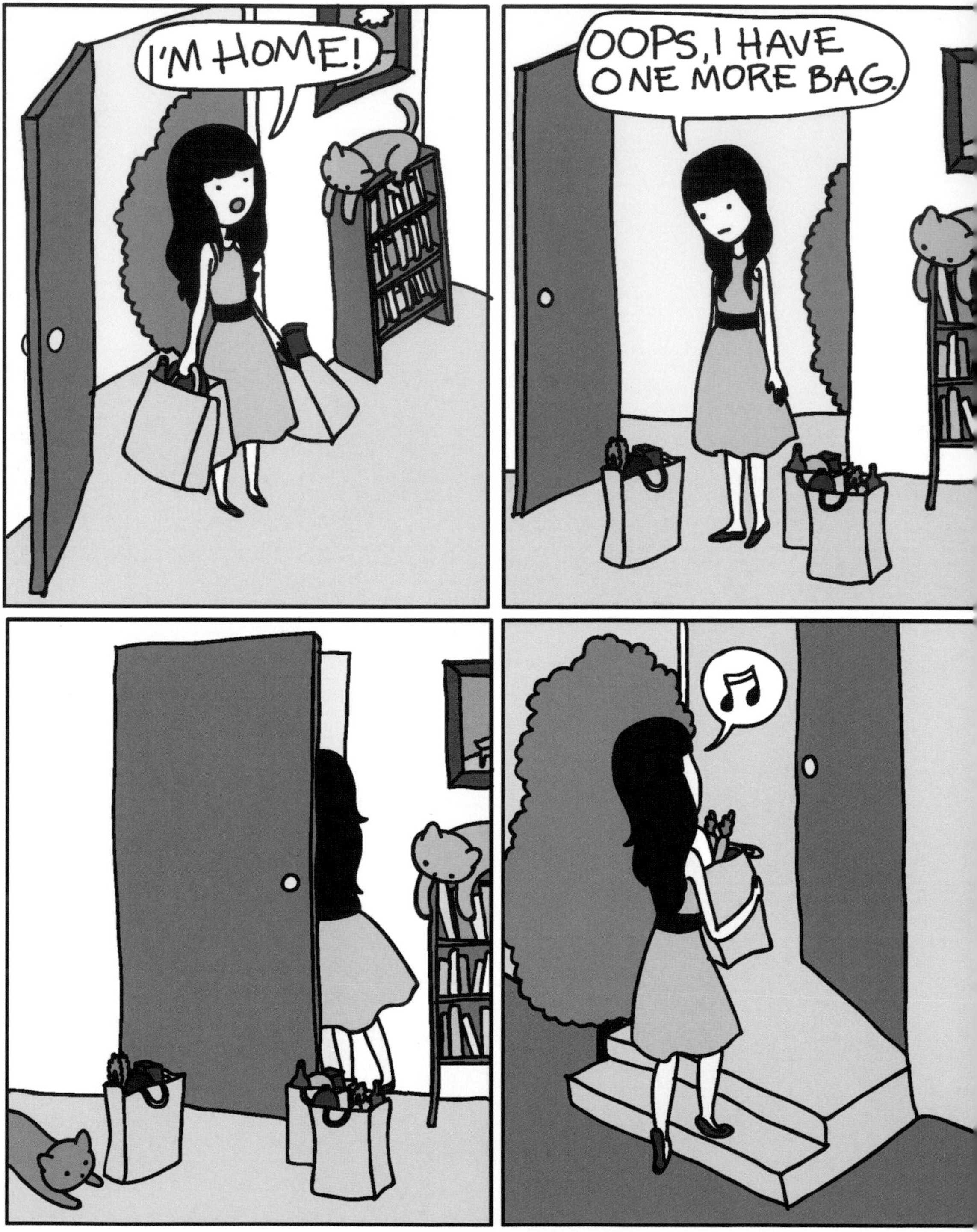
I'M HOME!
OOPS, I HAVE ONE MORE BAG.

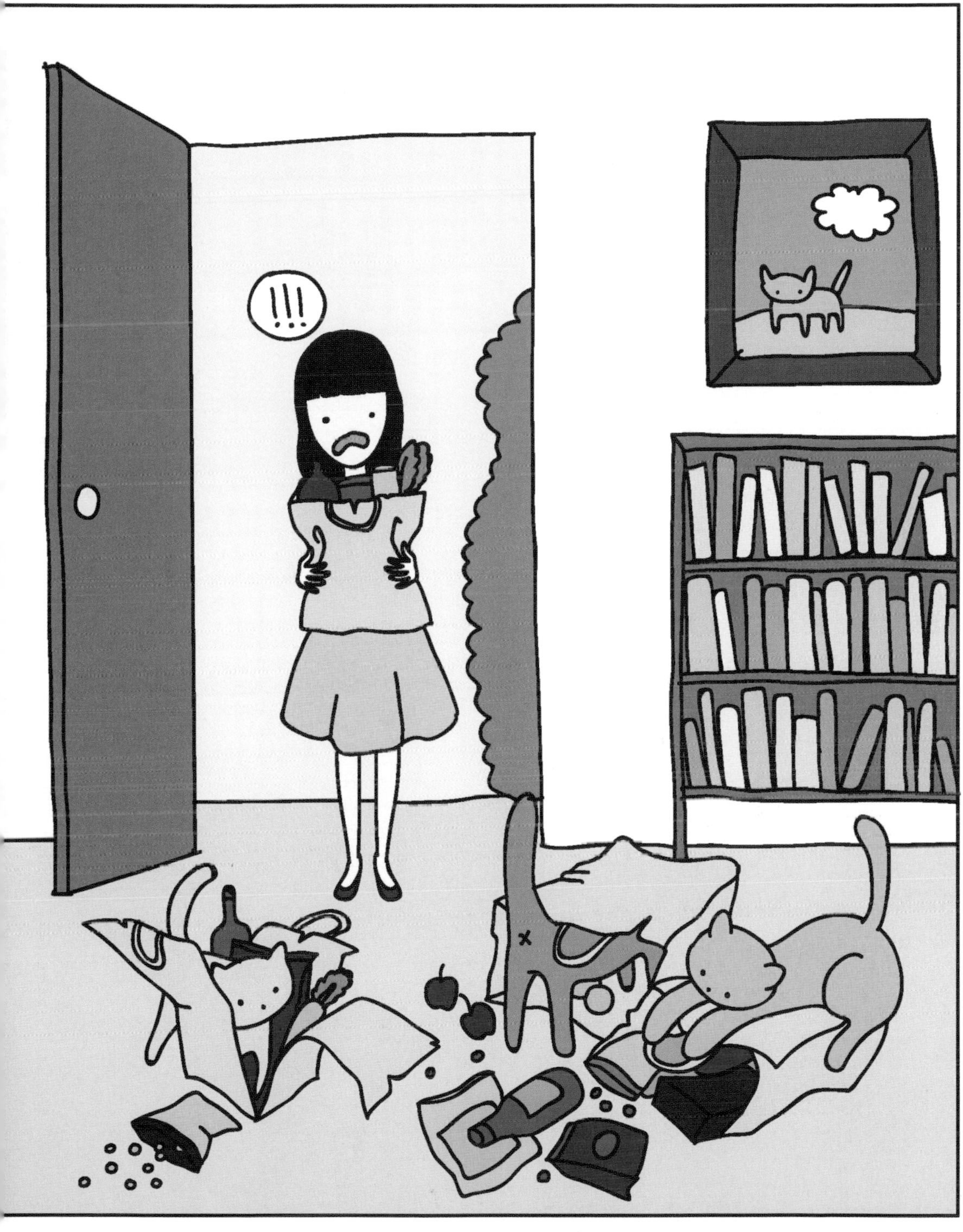
!!!

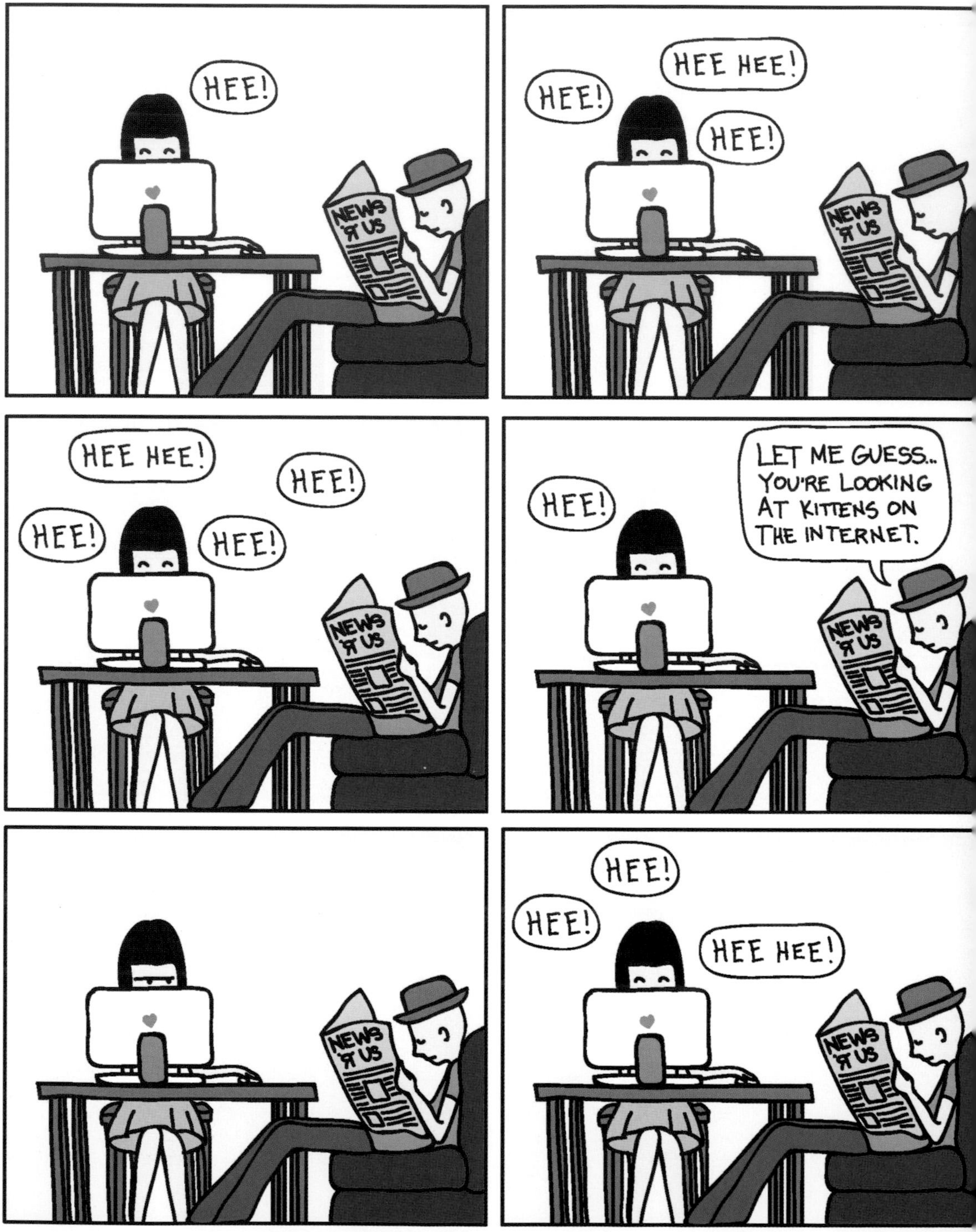
HEE!
HEE!
HEE HEE!
HEE!
HEE HEE!
HEE!
HEE!
HEE!
HEE!
LET ME GUESS.. YOU'RE LOOKING AT KITTENS ON THE INTERNET.
NEWS 'R' US
HEE!
HEE!
HEE HEE!

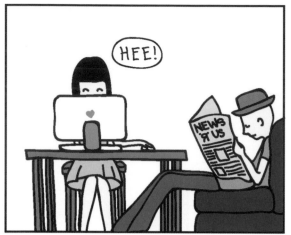

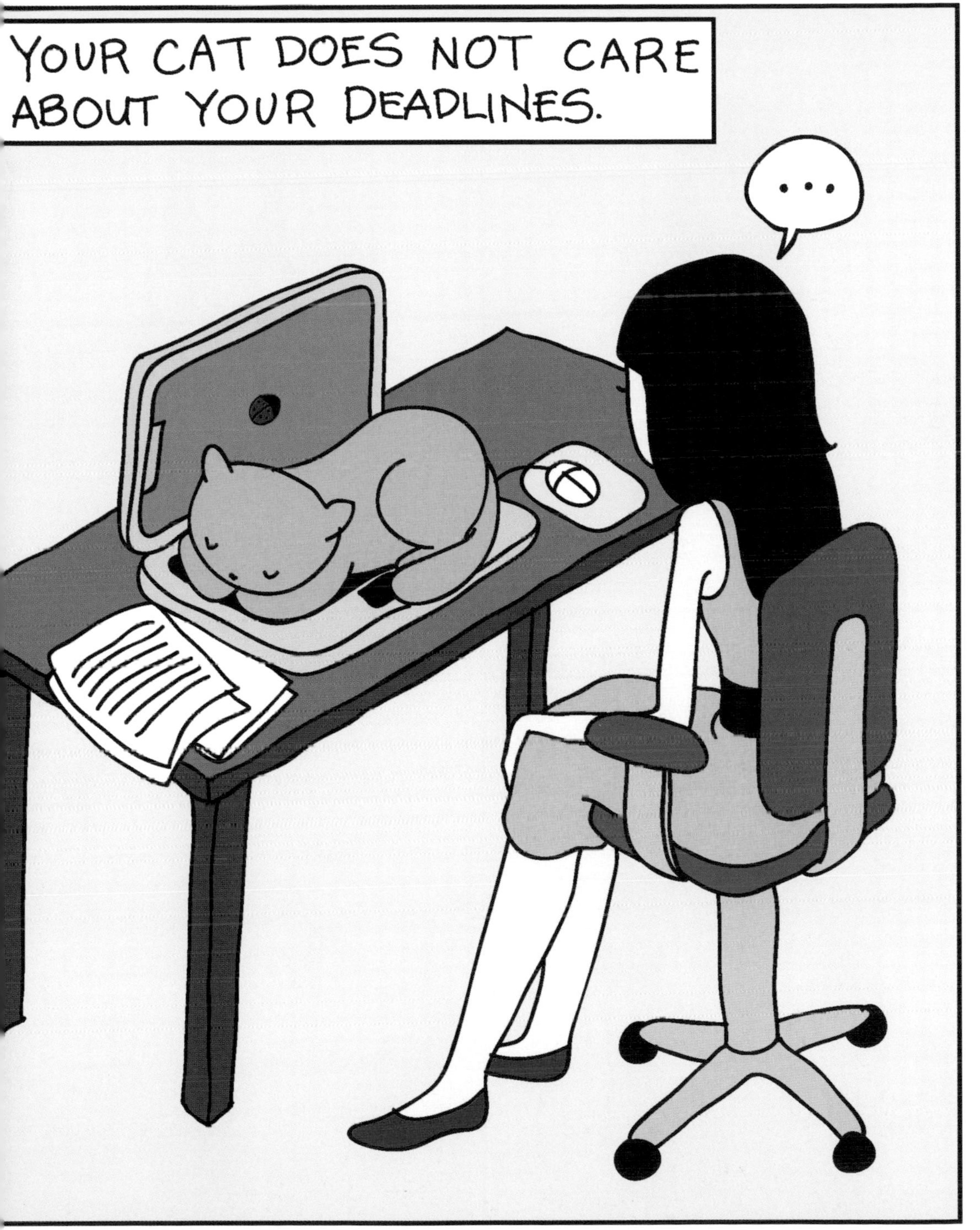
YOUR CAT DOES NOT CARE ABOUT YOUR DEADLINES.
...

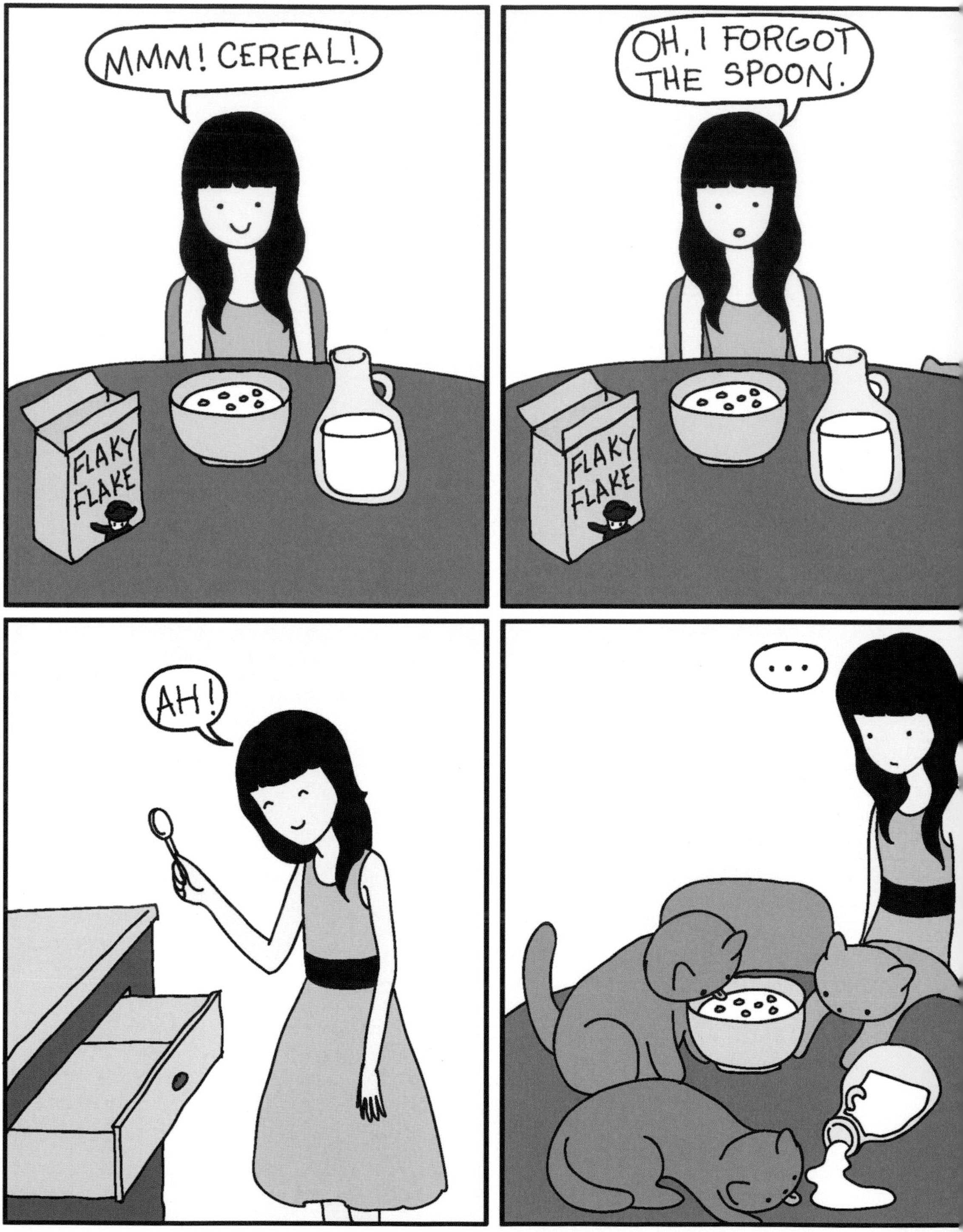
MMM! CEREAL!
FLAKY FLAKE
OH, I FORGOT THE SPOON.
FLAKY FLAKE
AH!
...

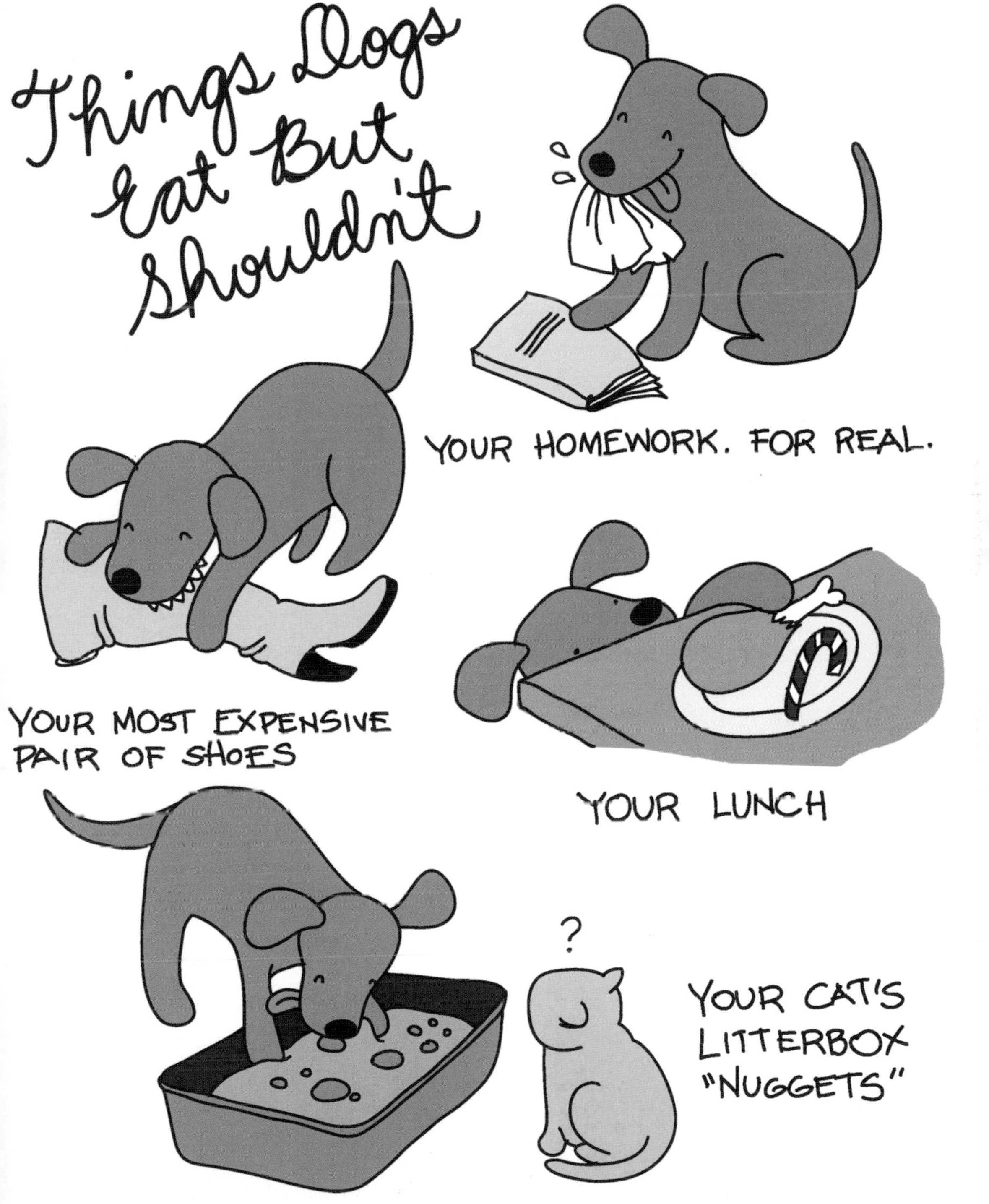
Things Dogs Eat But Shouldn't
YOUR HOMEWORK. FOR REAL.
YOUR MOST EXPENSIVE PAIR OF SHOES
YOUR LUNCH
?
YOUR CAT'S LITTERBOX "NUGGETS"

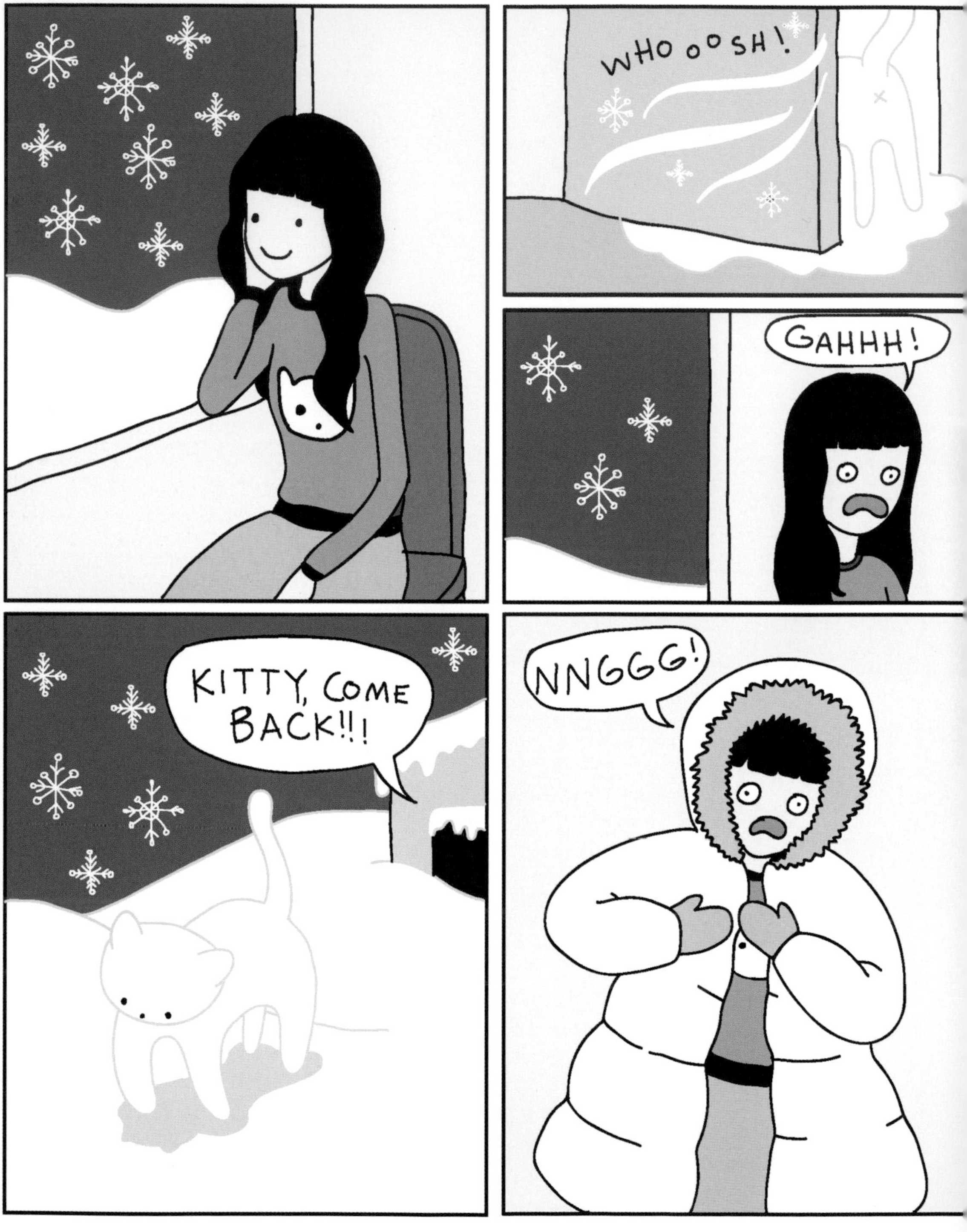
WHOOOSH!
GAHHH!
KITTY, COME BACK!!!
NNGGG!

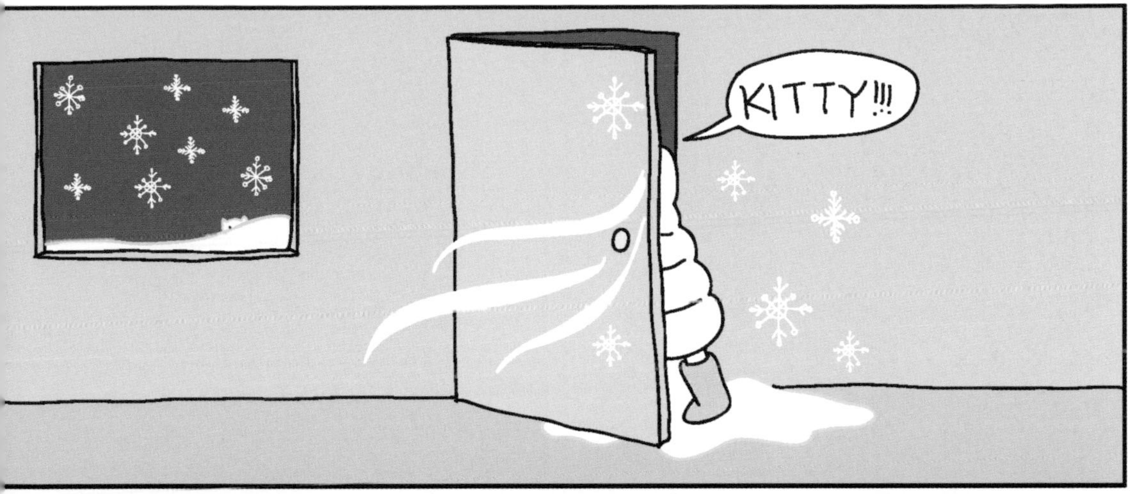
KITTY!!!
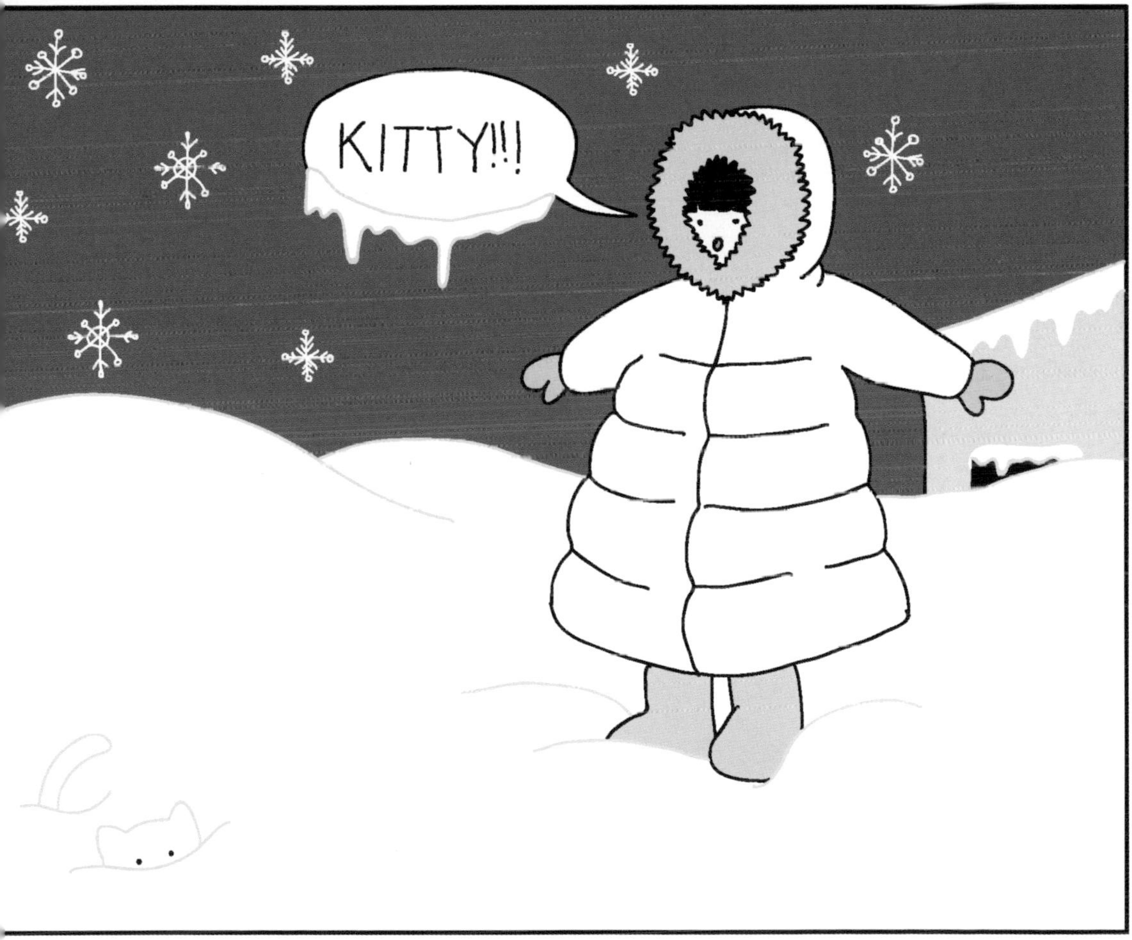
KITTY!!!

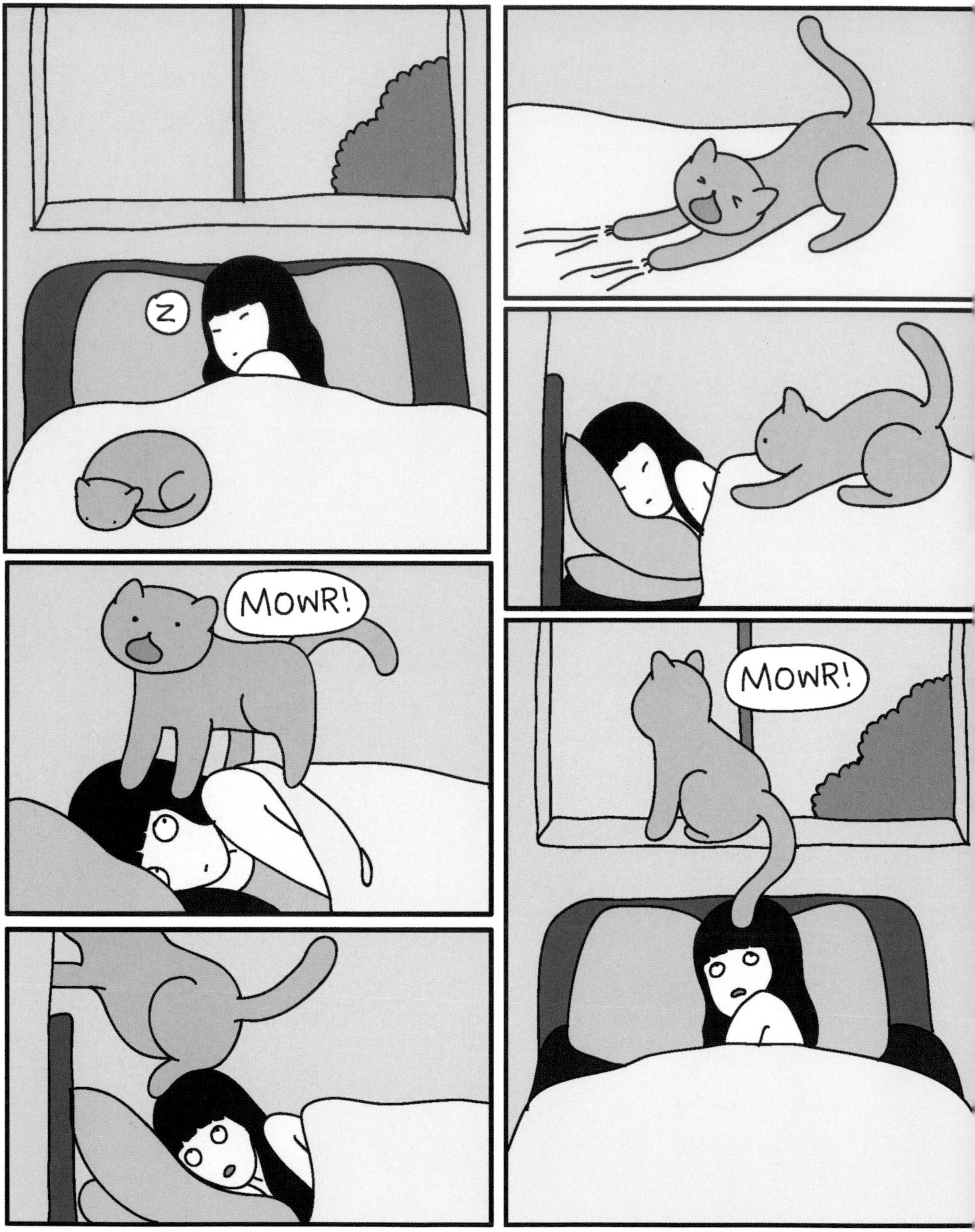
Z
MOWR!
MOWR!

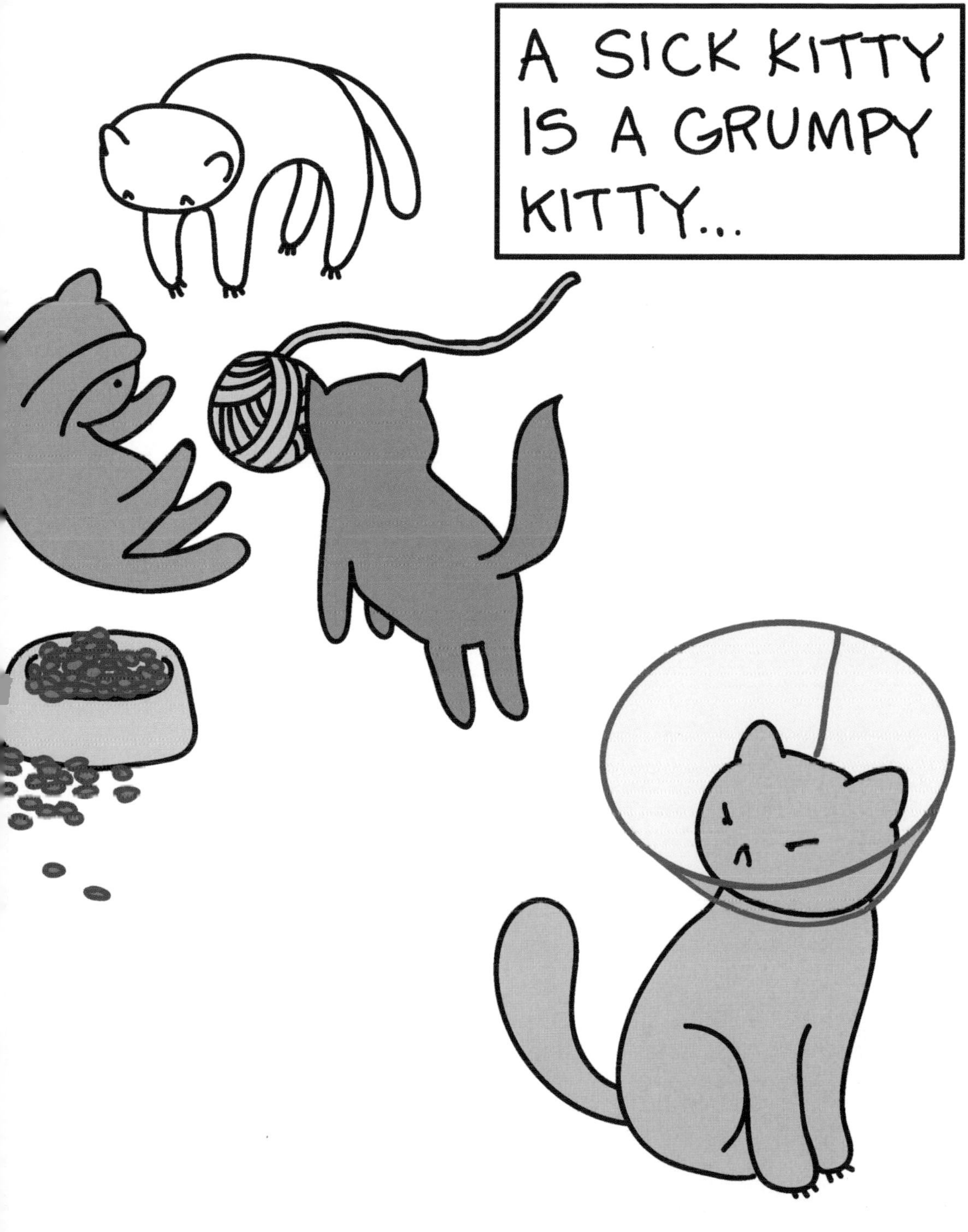
A SICK KITTY IS A GRUMPY KITTY...

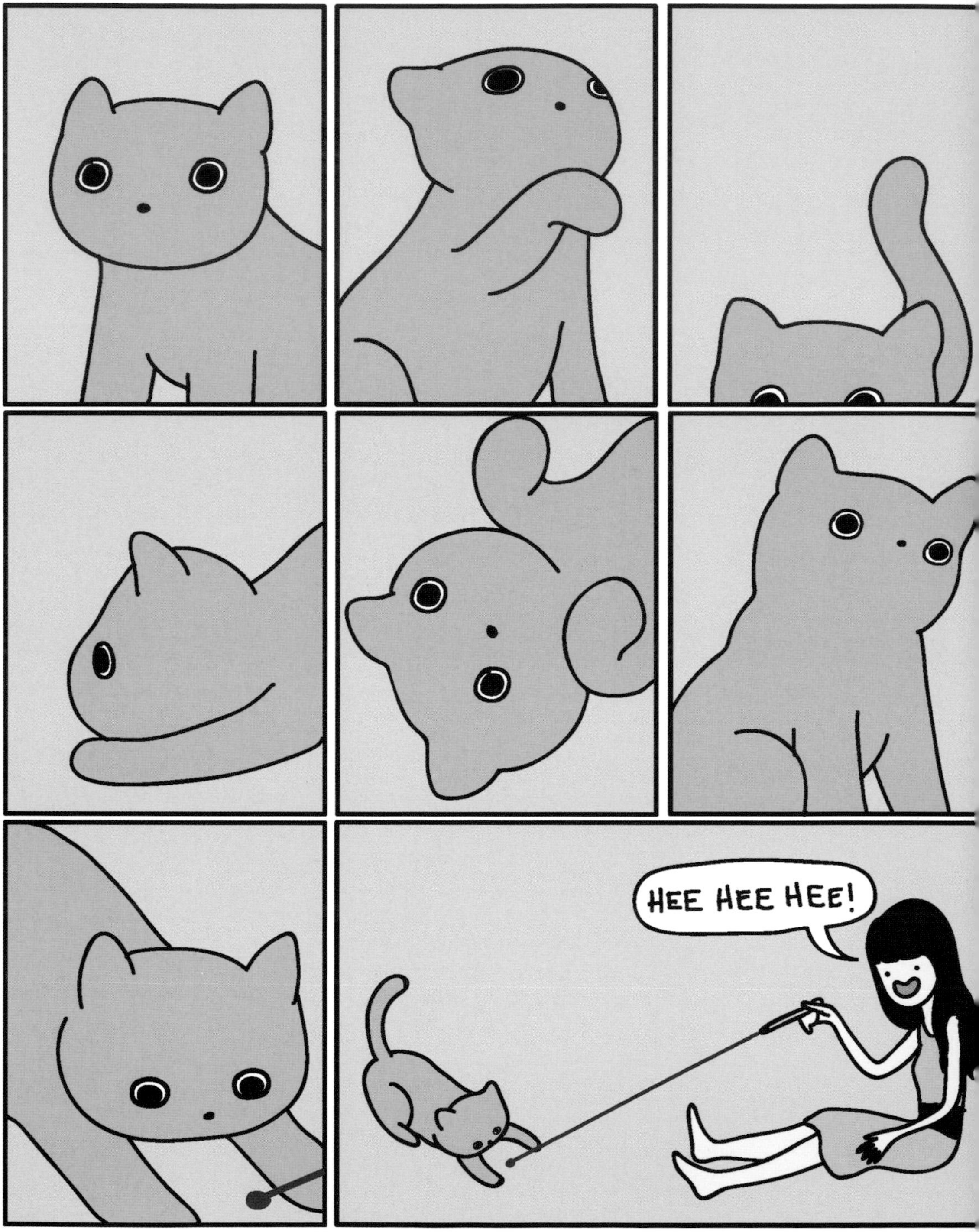
HEE HEE HEE!

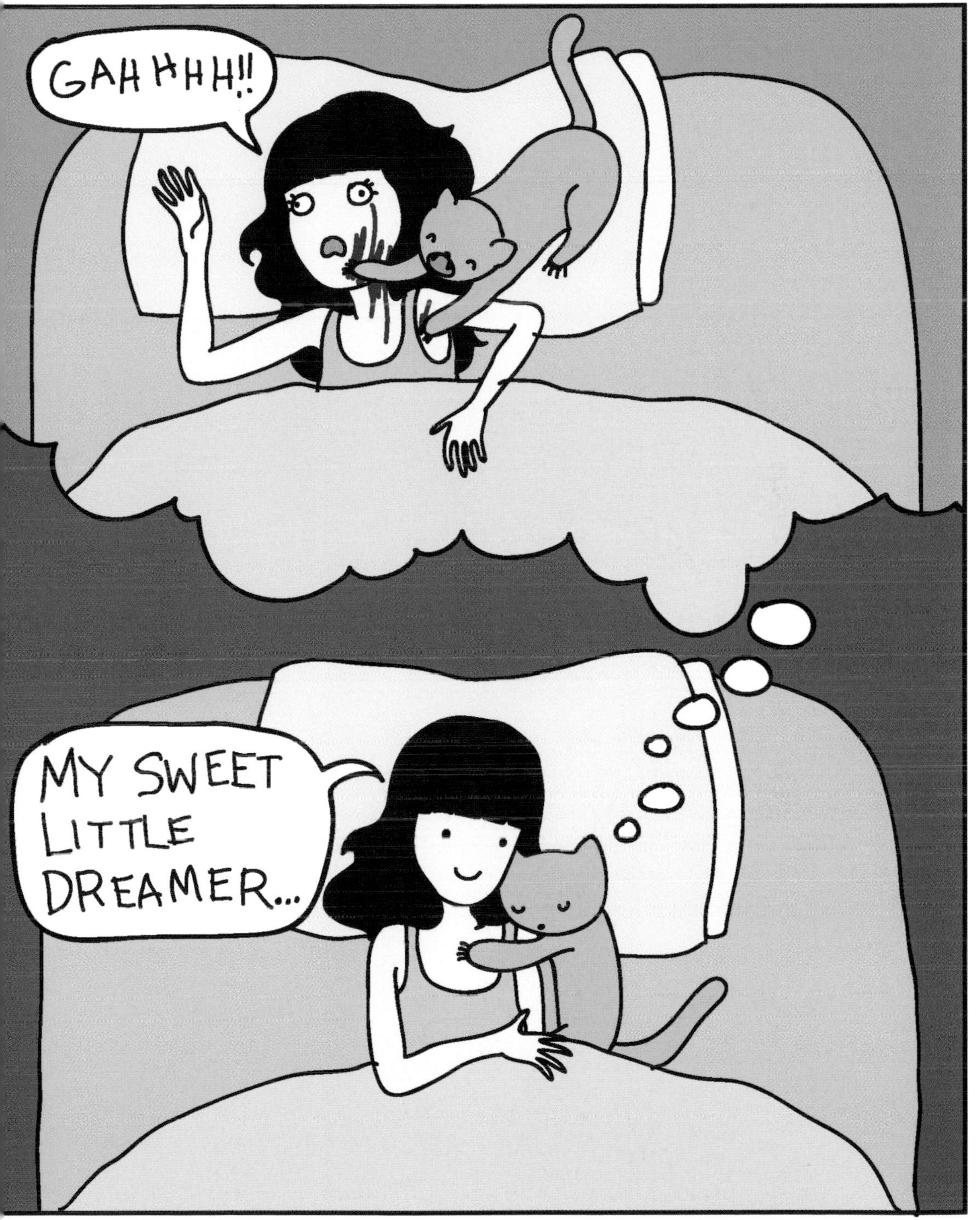
GAHHHH!!
MY SWEET LITTLE DREAMER...

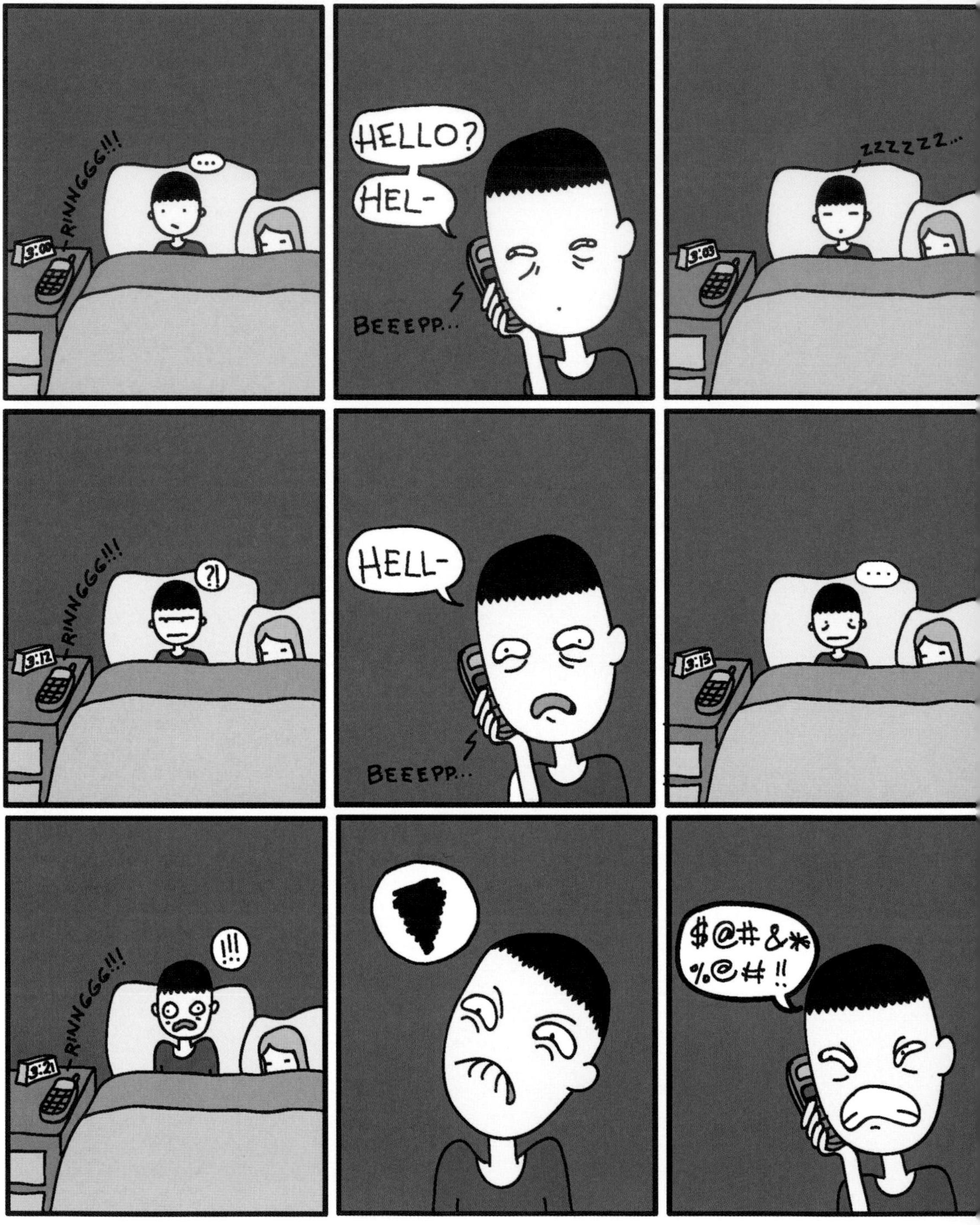

RINNGGG!!!
...
HELLO?
HEL-
BEEEPP...
ZZZZZZ...
RINNGGG!!!
?!
HELL-
BEEEPP...
...
RINNGGG!!!
!!!
$@#&*
%@#!!

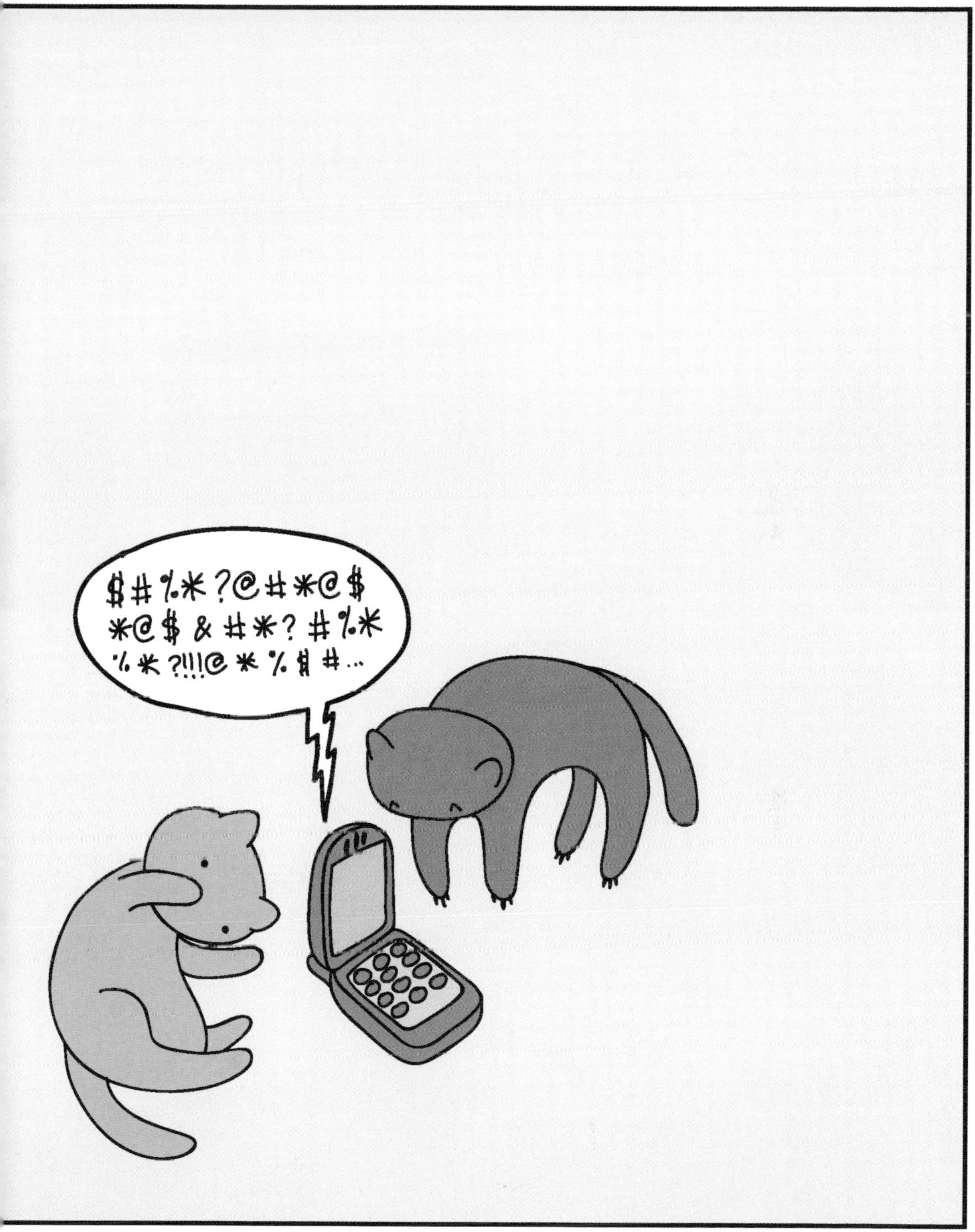
$#%*?@#*@$
@$ & #? #%*
%*?!!!@*%$#...

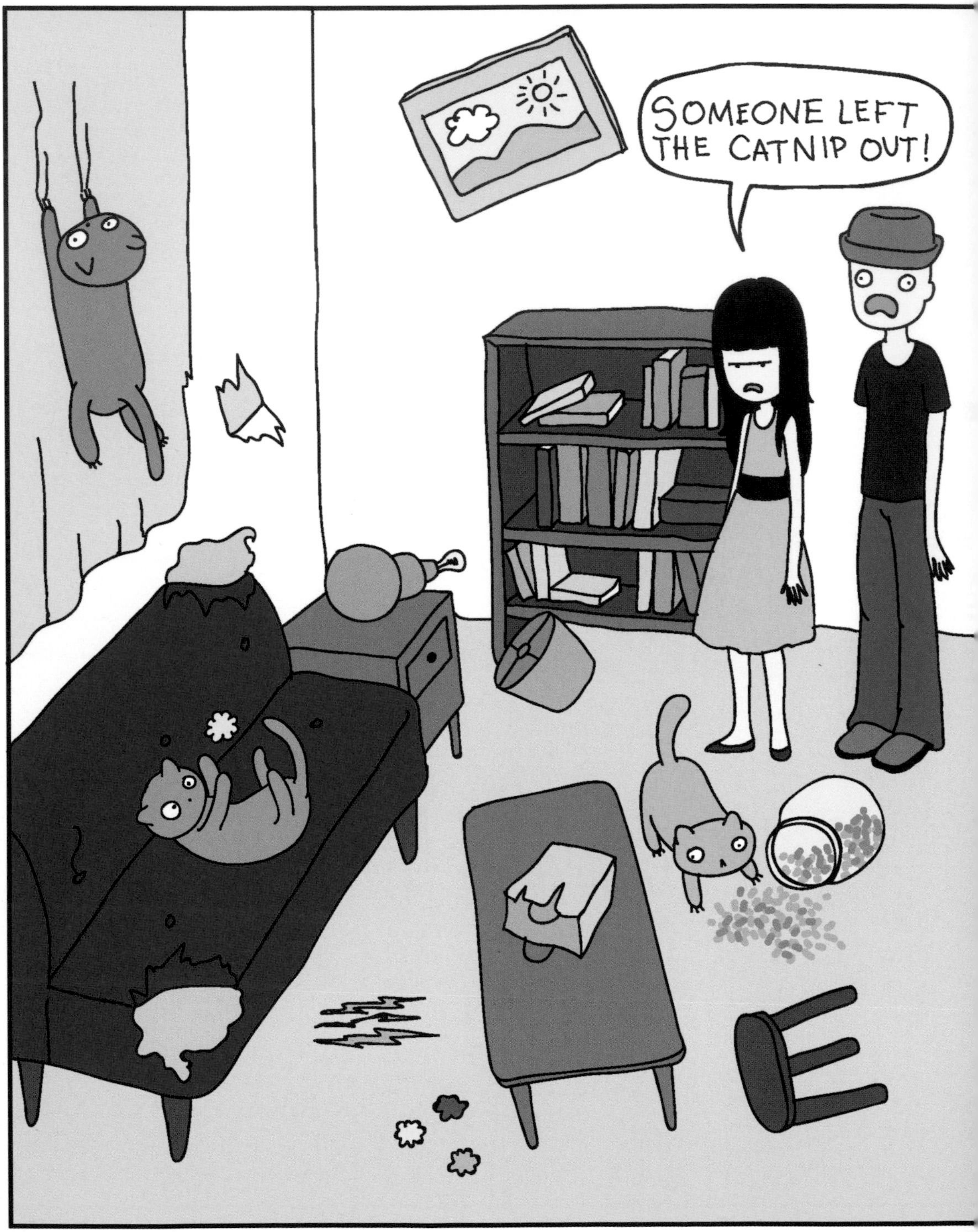
SOMEONE LEFT THE CATNIP OUT!

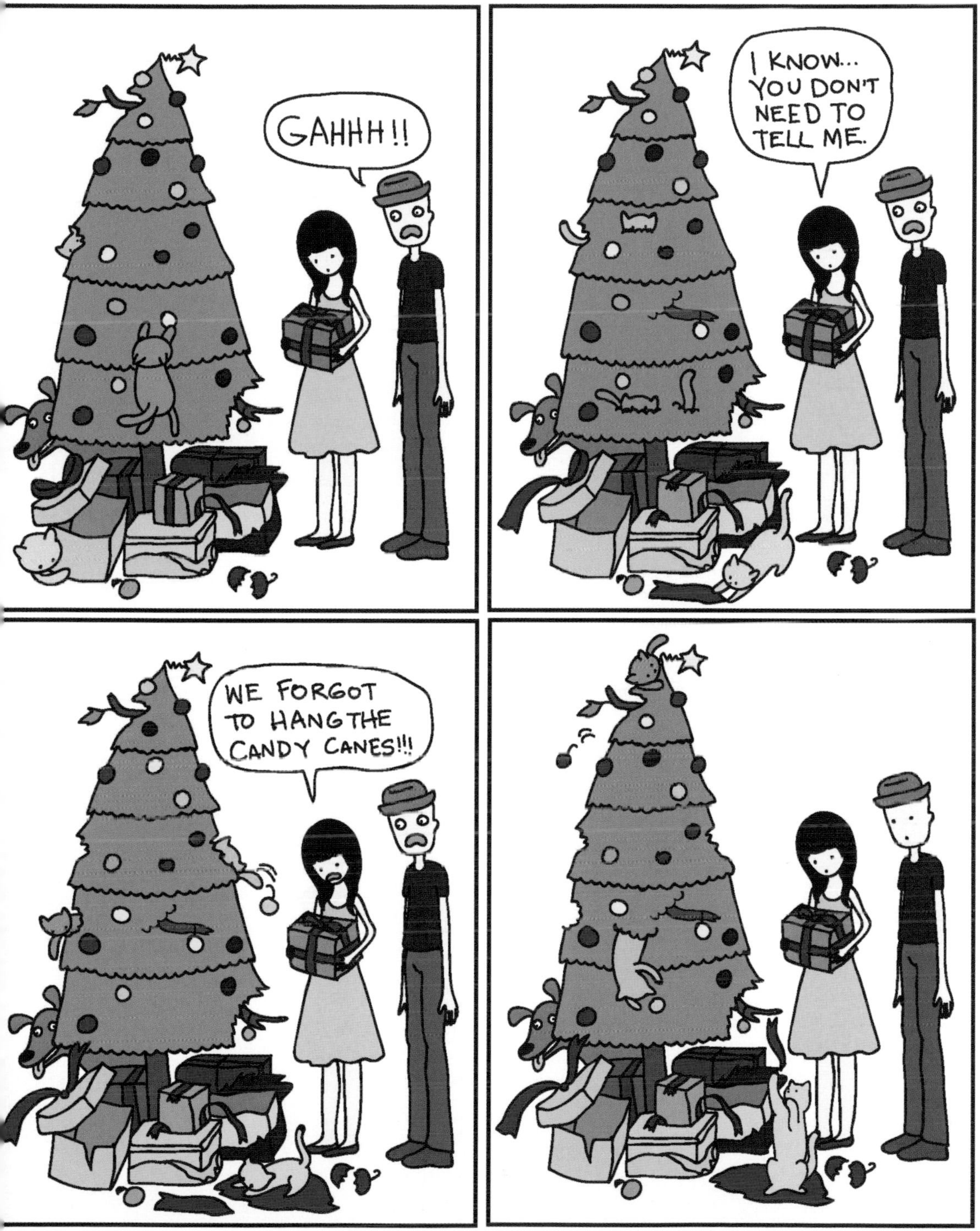
GAHHH!!
I KNOW... YOU DON'T NEED TO TELL ME.
WE FORGOT TO HANG THE CANDY CANES!!!

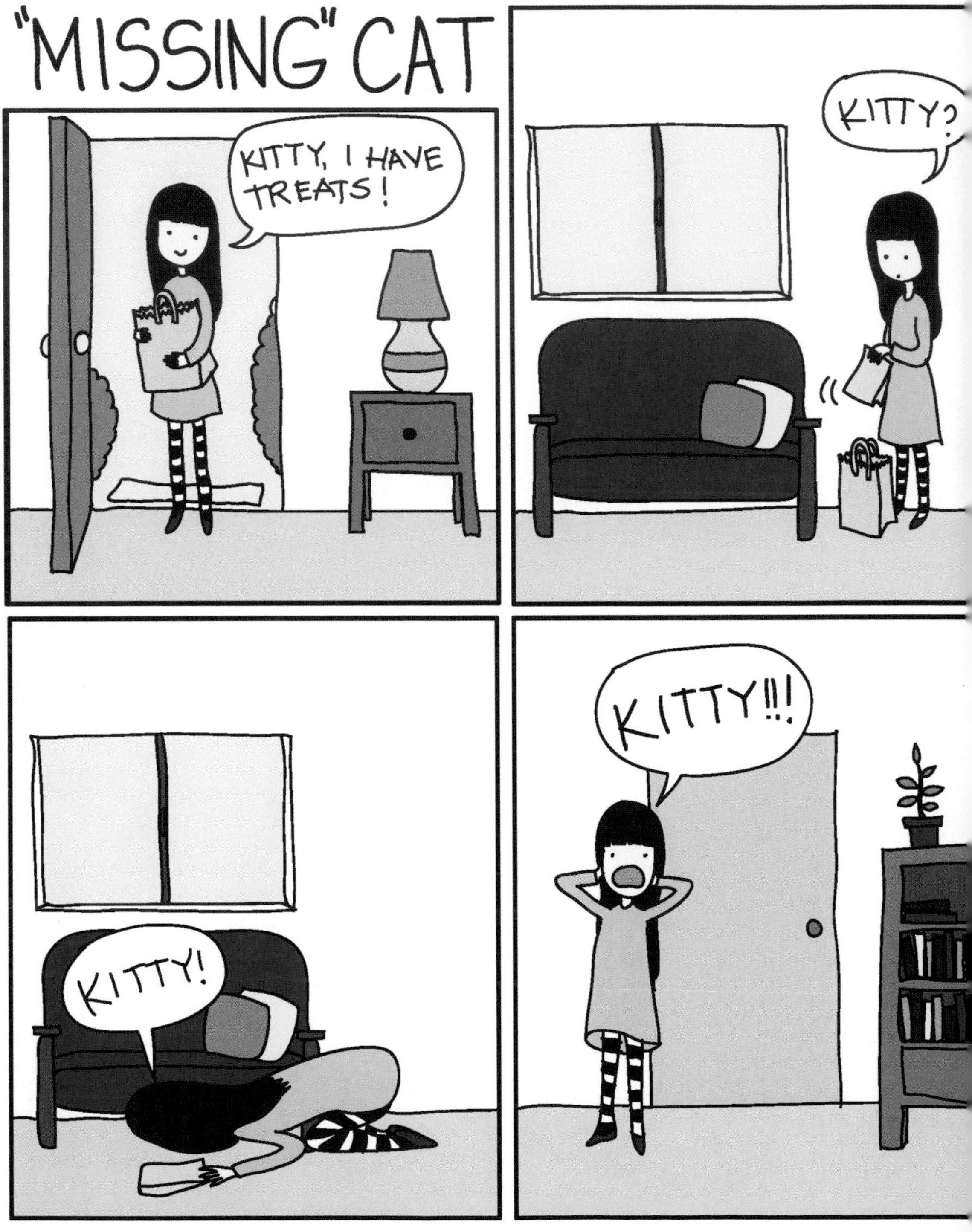
"MISSING" CAT
KITTY, I HAVE TREATS!
KITTY?
KITTY!
KITTY!!!

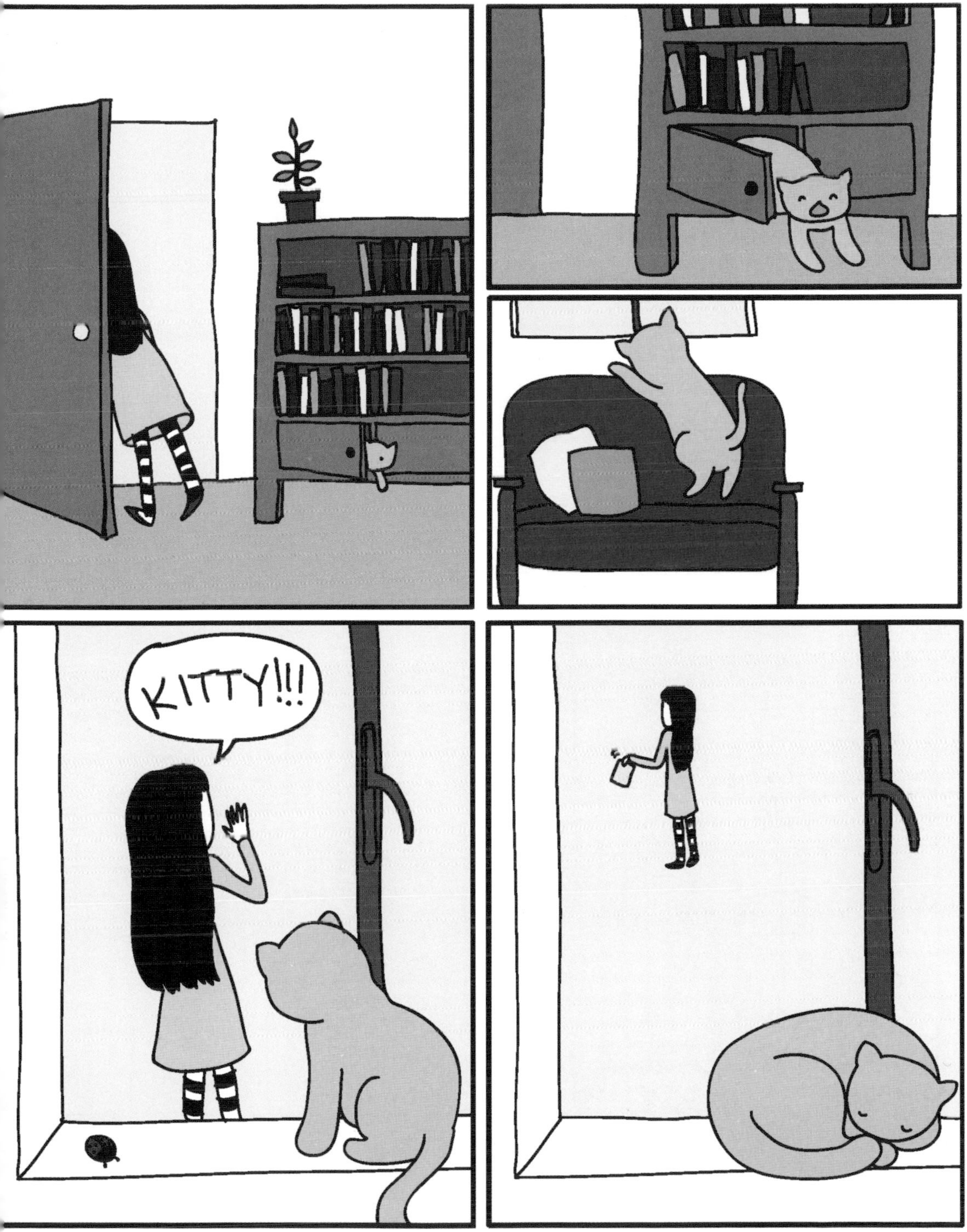
KITTY!!!

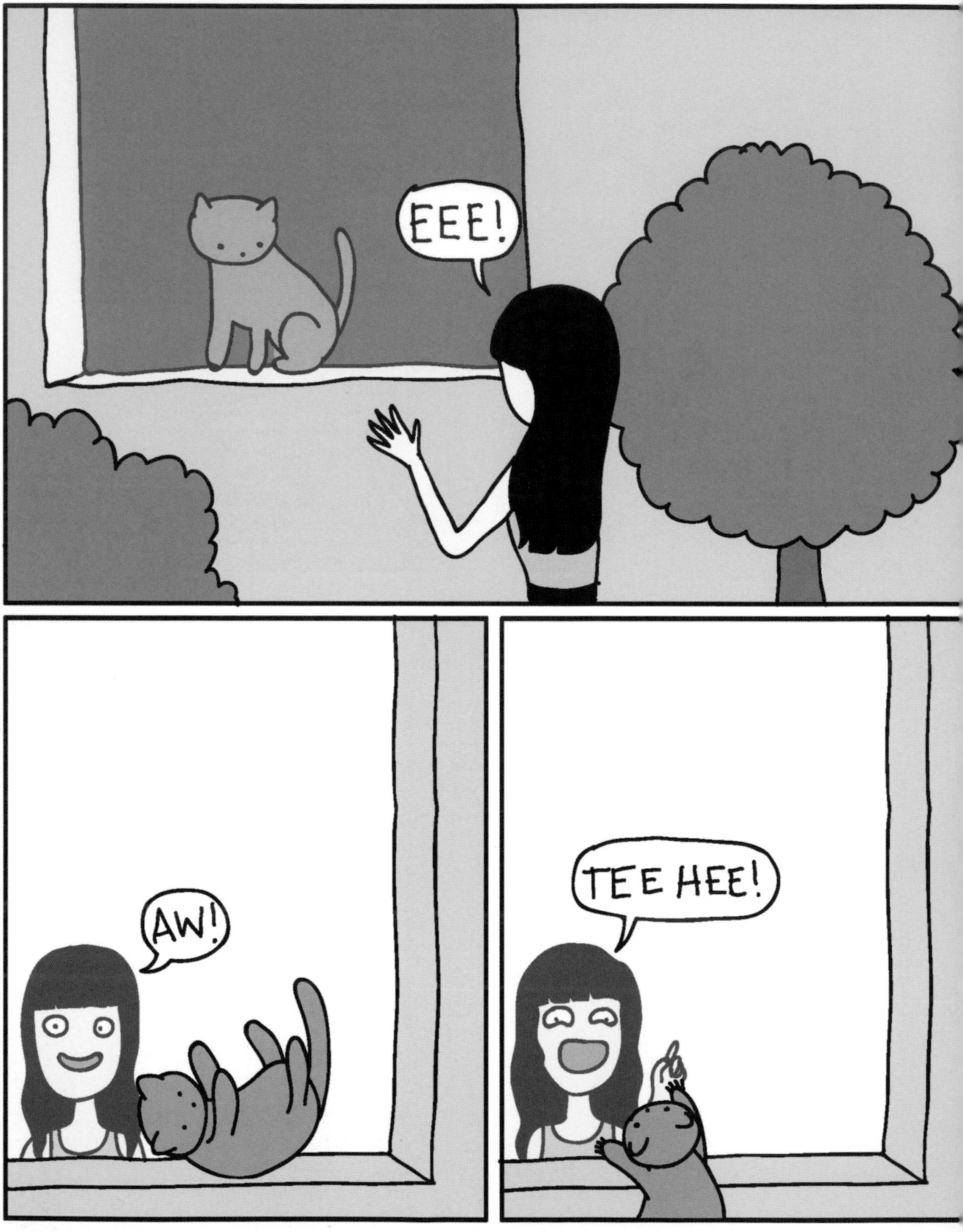
EEE!
AW!
TEE HEE!

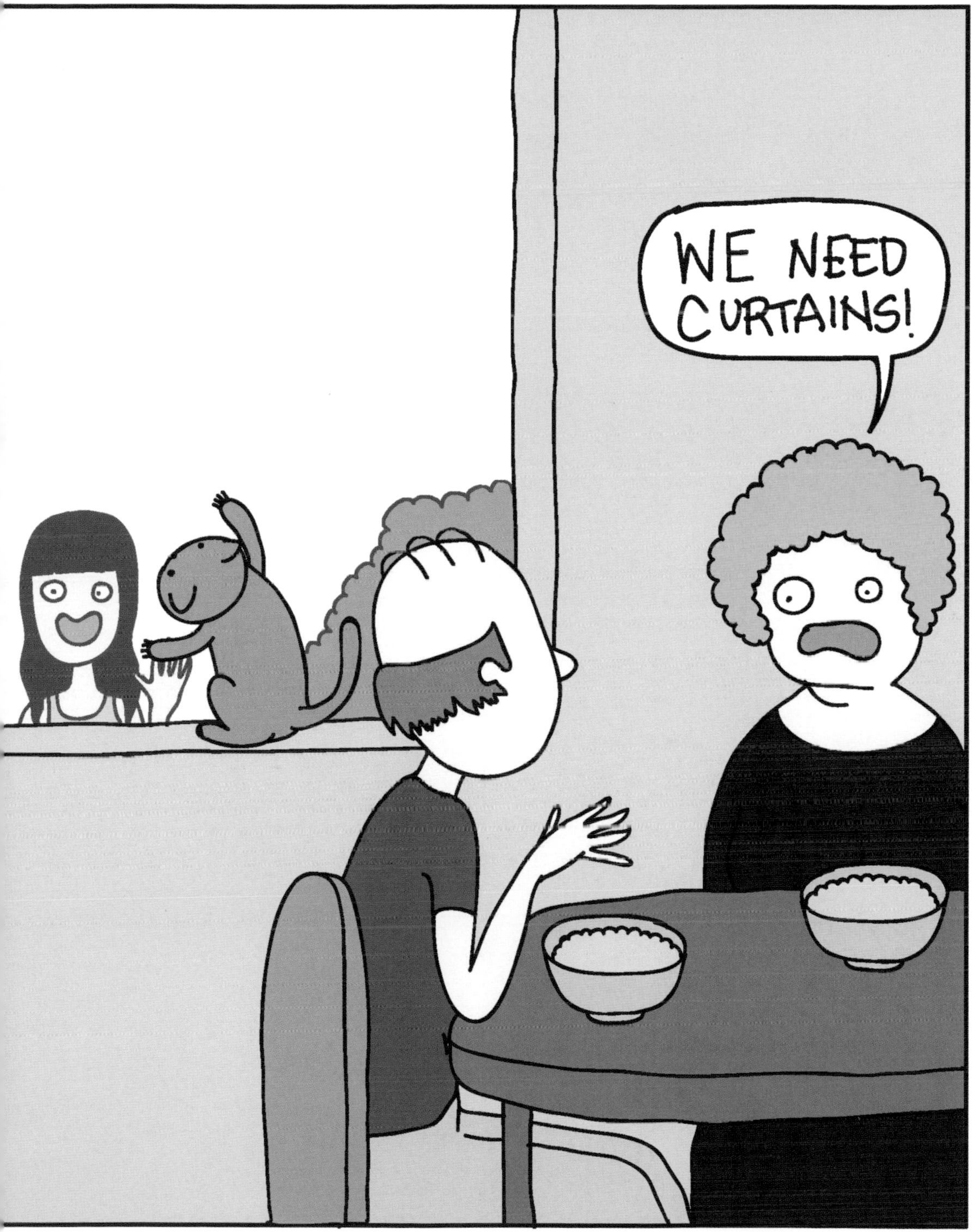
WE NEED CURTAINS!

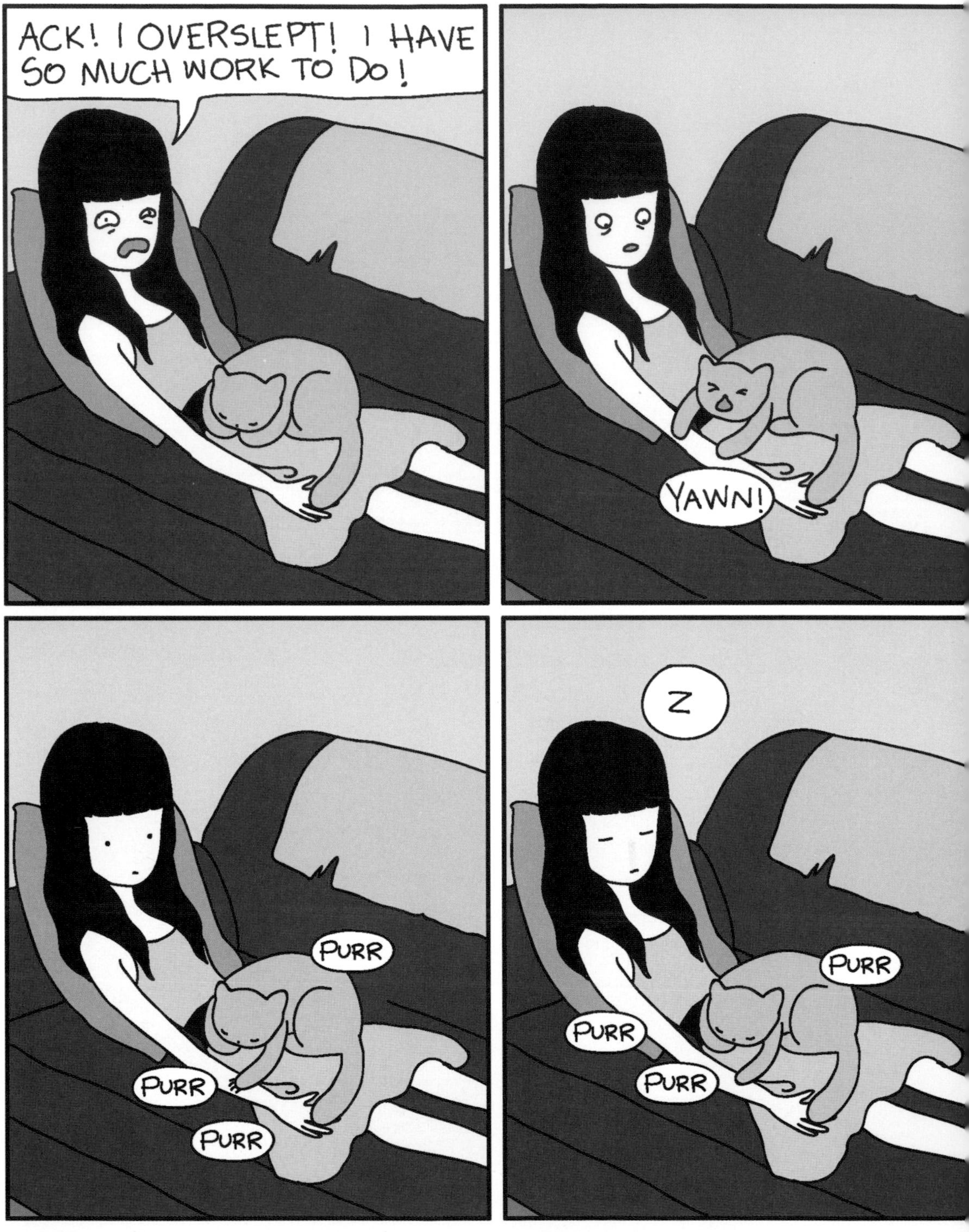
ACK! I OVERSLEPT! I HAVE SO MUCH WORK TO DO!
YAWN!
PURR
PURR
PURR
Z
PURR
PURR
PURR

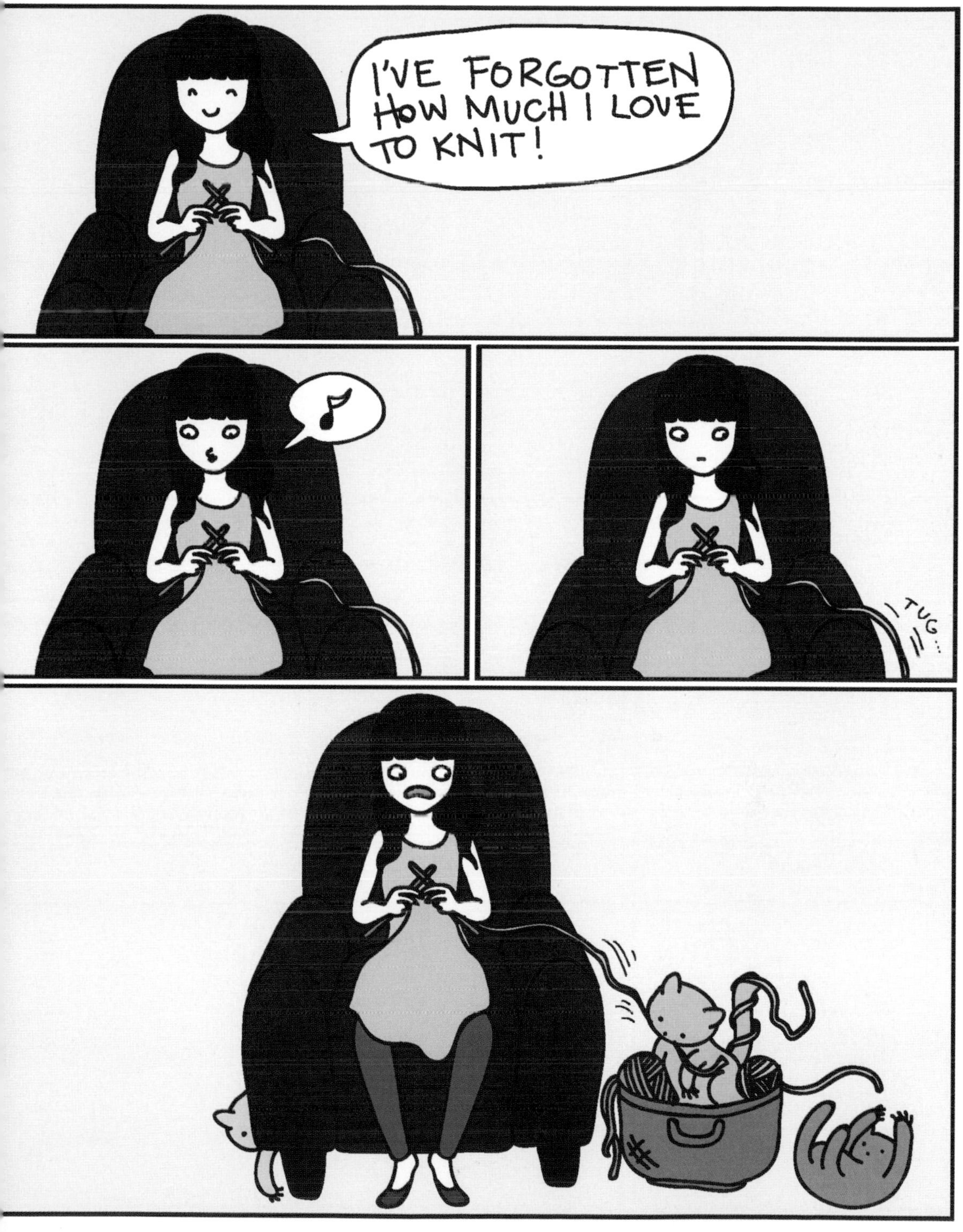
I'VE FORGOTTEN HOW MUCH I LOVE TO KNIT!
TUG...

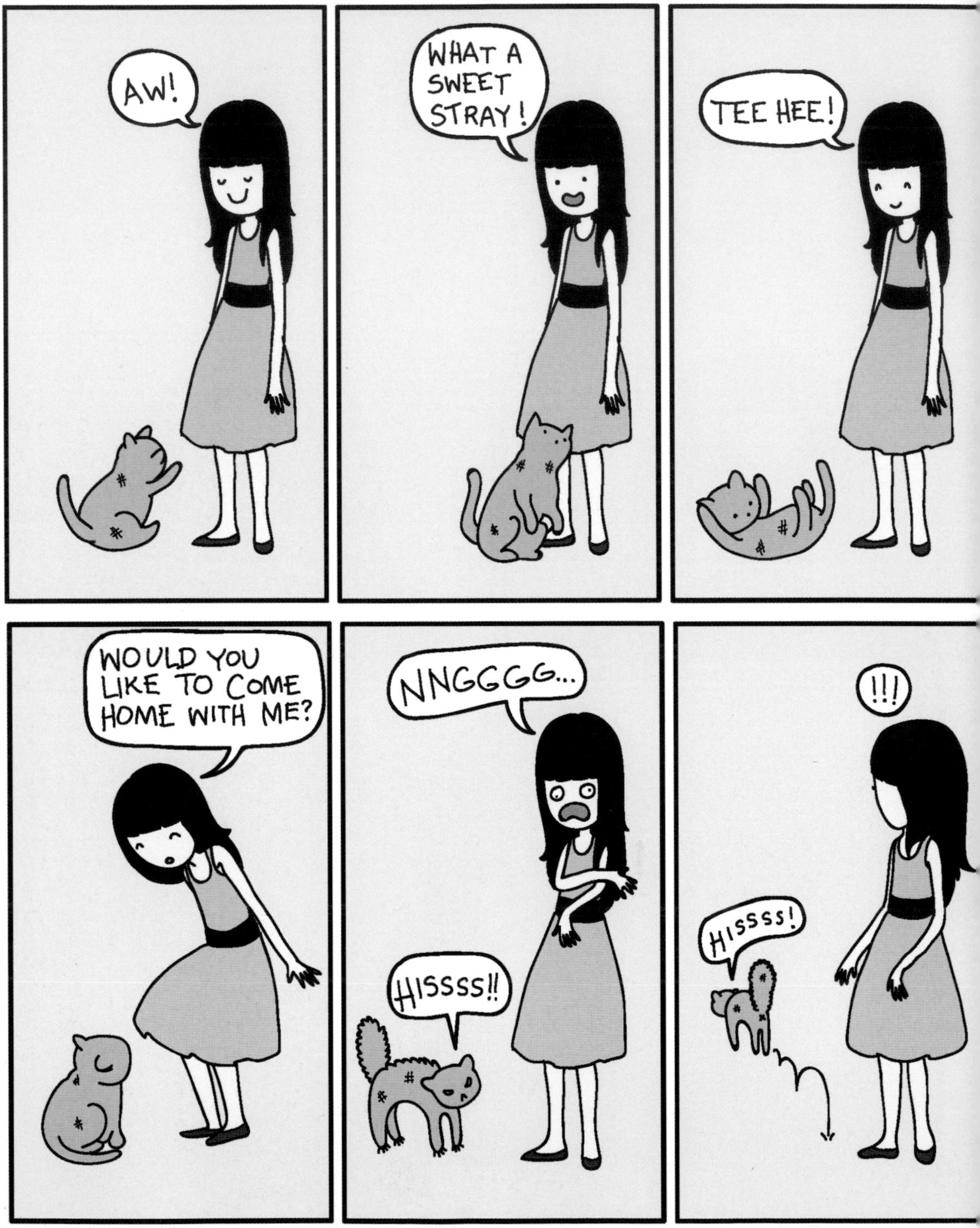
AW!
WHAT A SWEET STRAY!
TEE HEE!
WOULD YOU LIKE TO COME HOME WITH ME?
NNGGGG...
HISSSS!!
!!!
HISSSS!

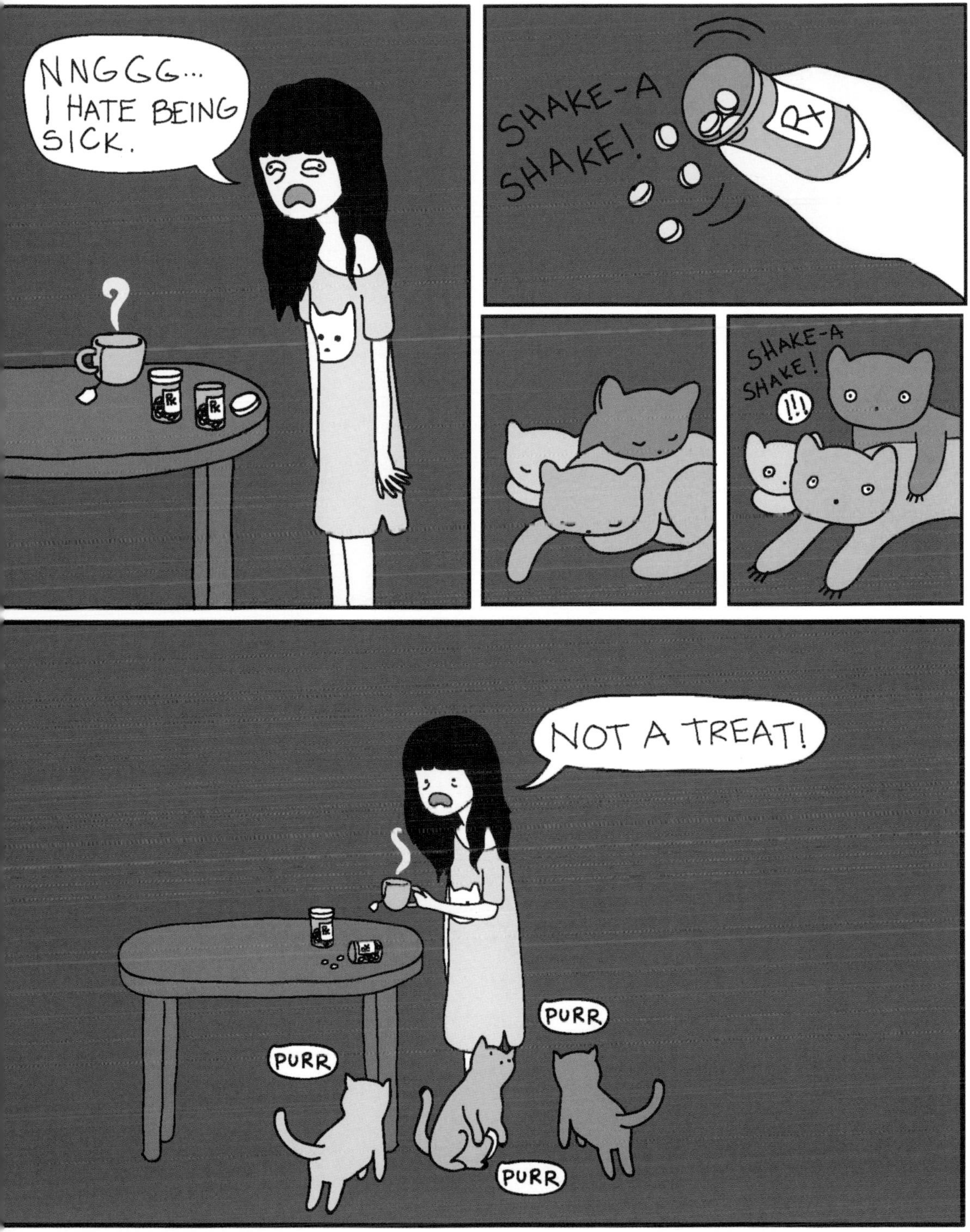
NNGGG...
I HATE BEING
SICK.
SHAKE-A
SHAKE!
SHAKE-A
SHAKE!
!!!
NOT A TREAT!
PURR
PURR
PURR

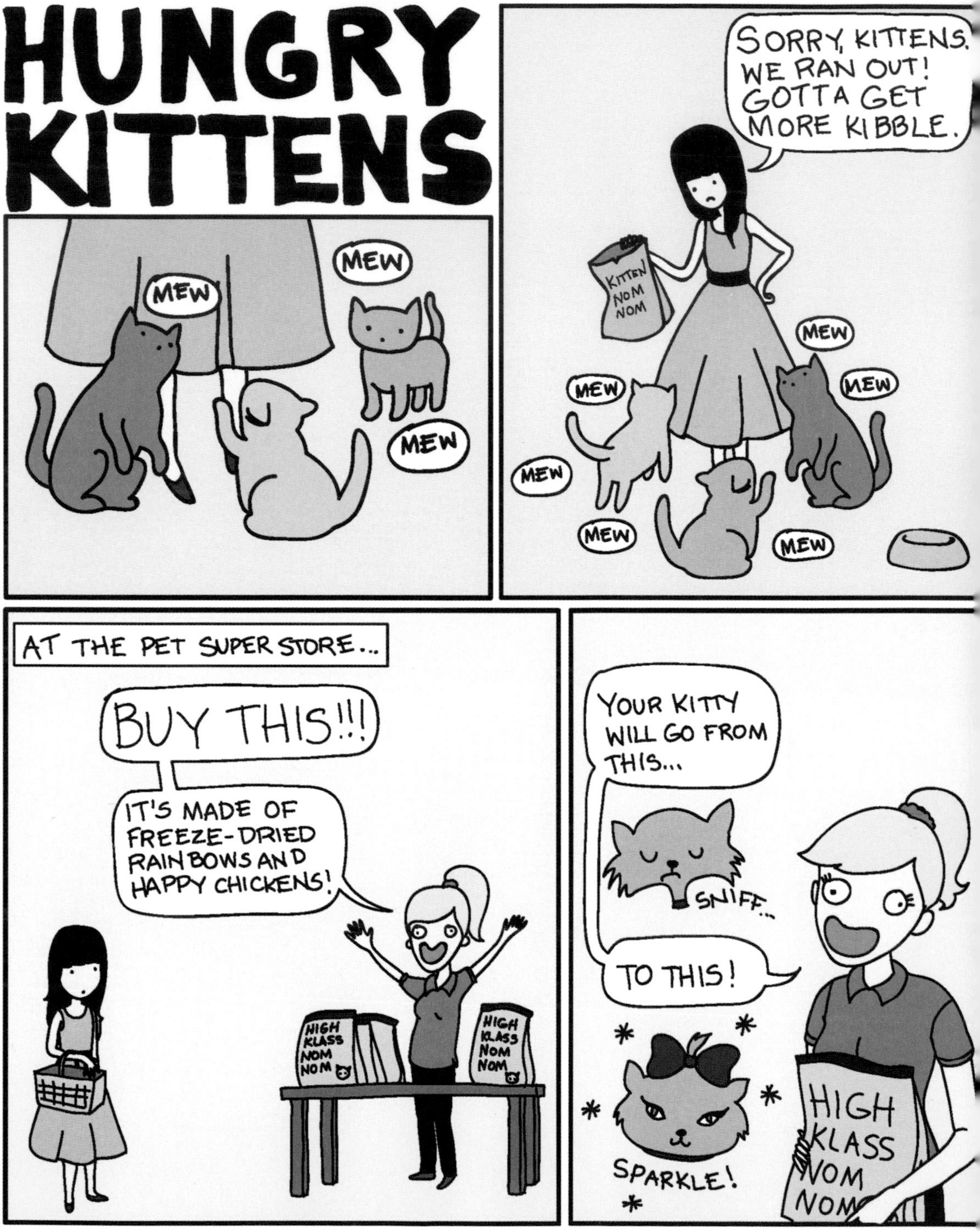
HUNGRY KITTENS
MEW
MEW
MEW
SORRY, KITTENS. WE RAN OUT! GOTTA GET MORE KIBBLE.
KITTEN NOM NOM
MEW
MEW
MEW
MEW
MEW
MEW
AT THE PET SUPER STORE...
BUY THIS!!!
IT'S MADE OF FREEZE-DRIED RAINBOWS AND HAPPY CHICKENS!
HIGH KLASS NOM NOM
HIGH KLASS NOM NOM
YOUR KITTY WILL GO FROM THIS...
SNIFF...
TO THIS!
SPARKLE!
HIGH KLASS NOM NOM

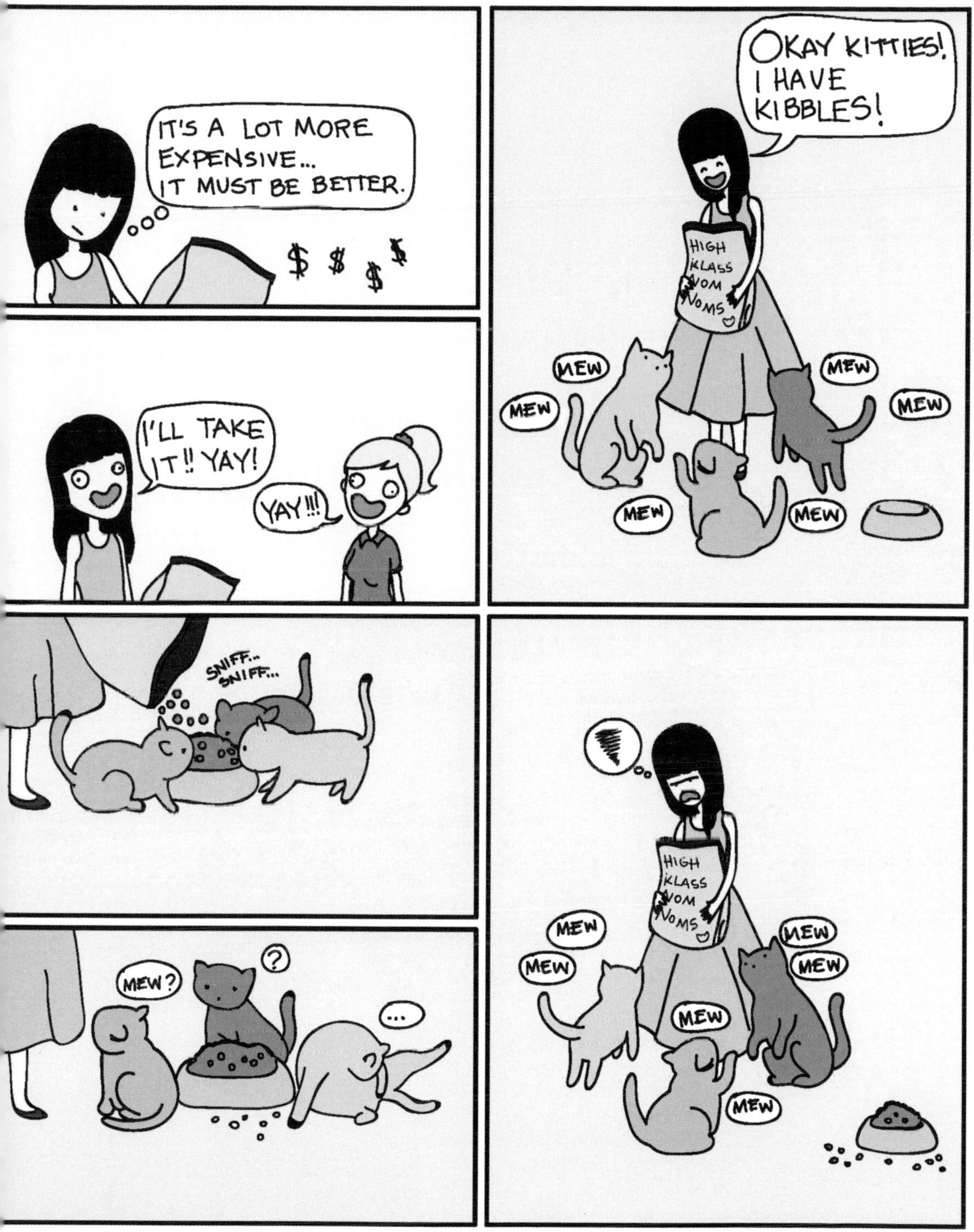
IT'S A LOT MORE EXPENSIVE... IT MUST BE BETTER.
$ $ $ $
I'LL TAKE IT!! YAY!
YAY!!!
SNIFF... SNIFF...
MEW?
?
...
OKAY KITTIES! I HAVE KIBBLES!
HIGH KLASS NOM NOMS
MEW
MEW
MEW
MEW
MEW
MEW
HIGH KLASS NOM NOMS
MEW
MEW
MEW
MEW
MEW
MEW

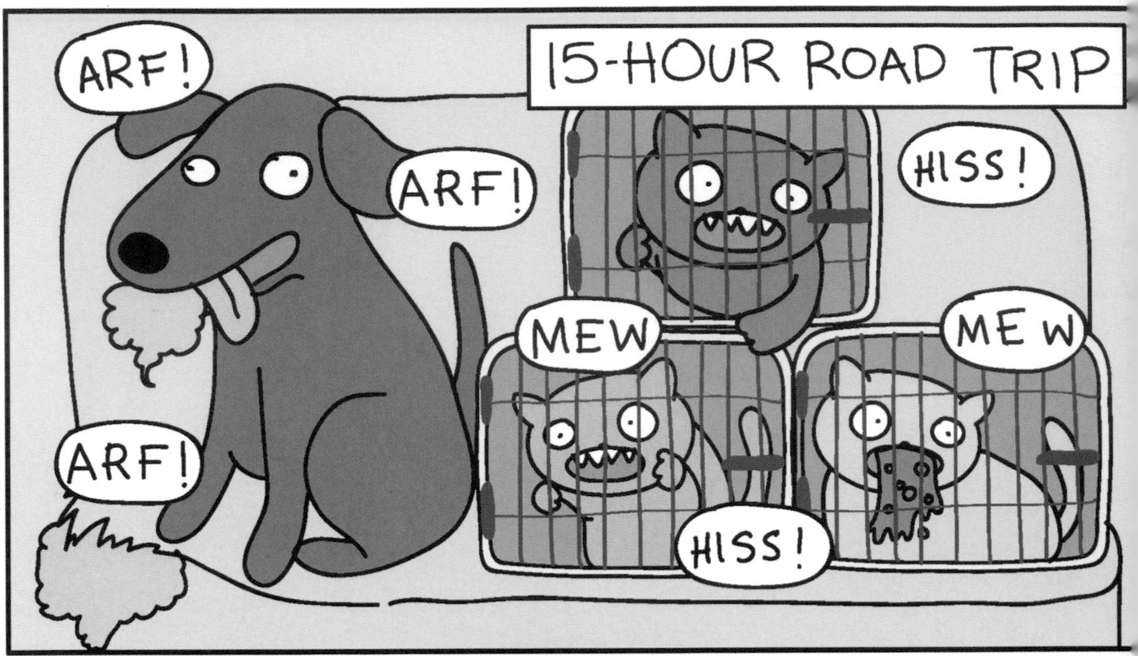
15-HOUR ROAD TRIP
ARF!
ARF!
ARF!
HISS!
MEW
MEW
HISS!

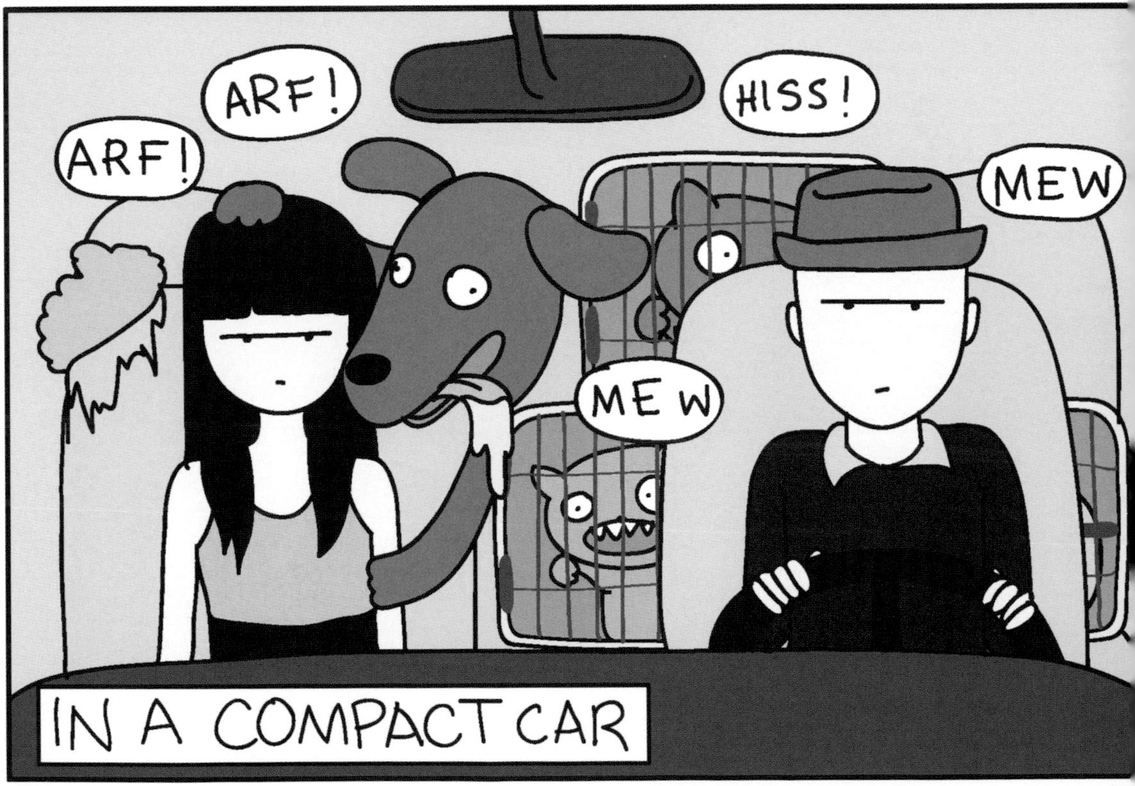
ARF!
ARF!
HISS!
MEW
MEW
IN A COMPACT CAR

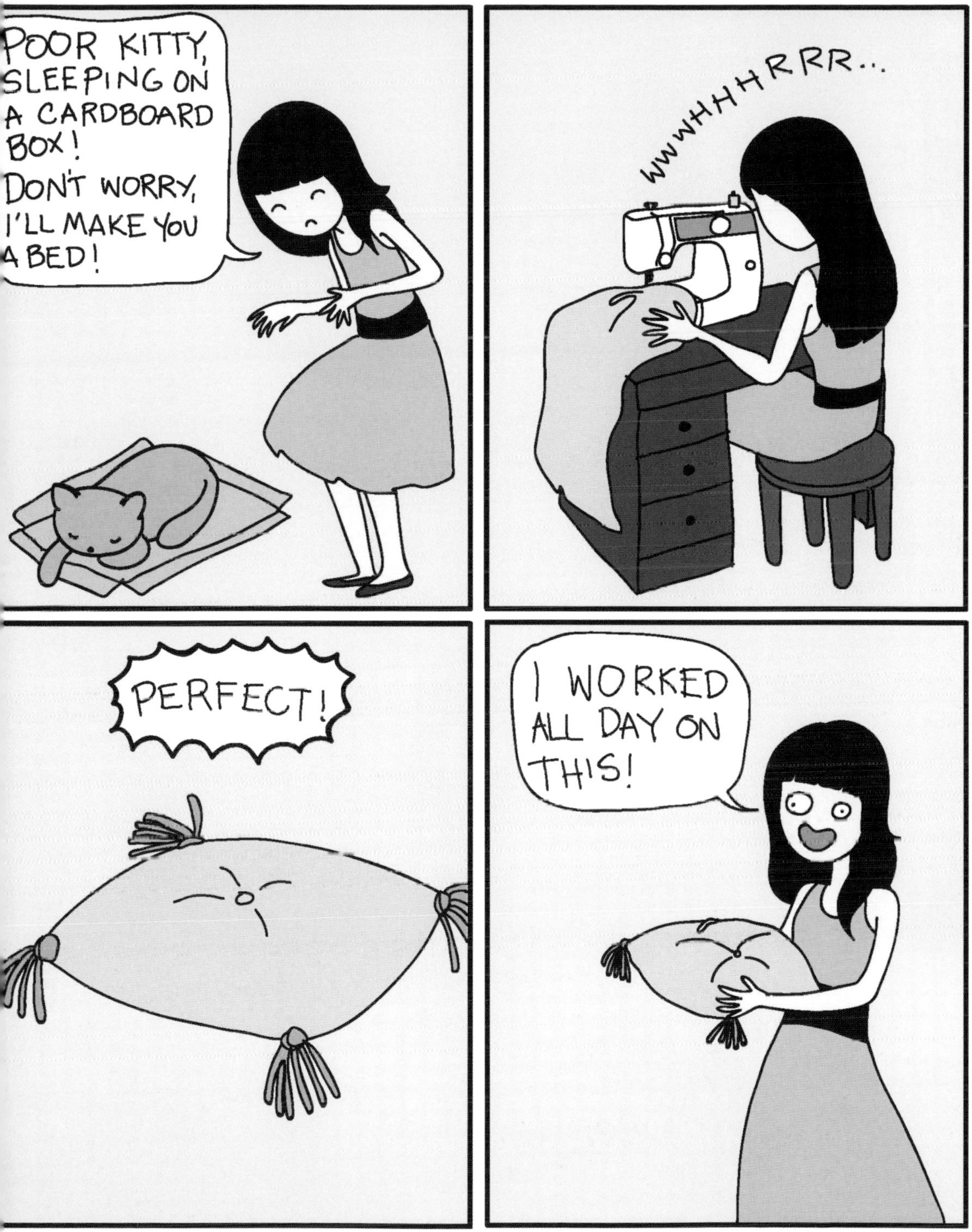
POOR KITTY, SLEEPING ON A CARDBOARD BOX! DON'T WORRY, I'LL MAKE YOU A BED!
WWWHHHHRRR...
PERFECT!
I WORKED ALL DAY ON THIS!

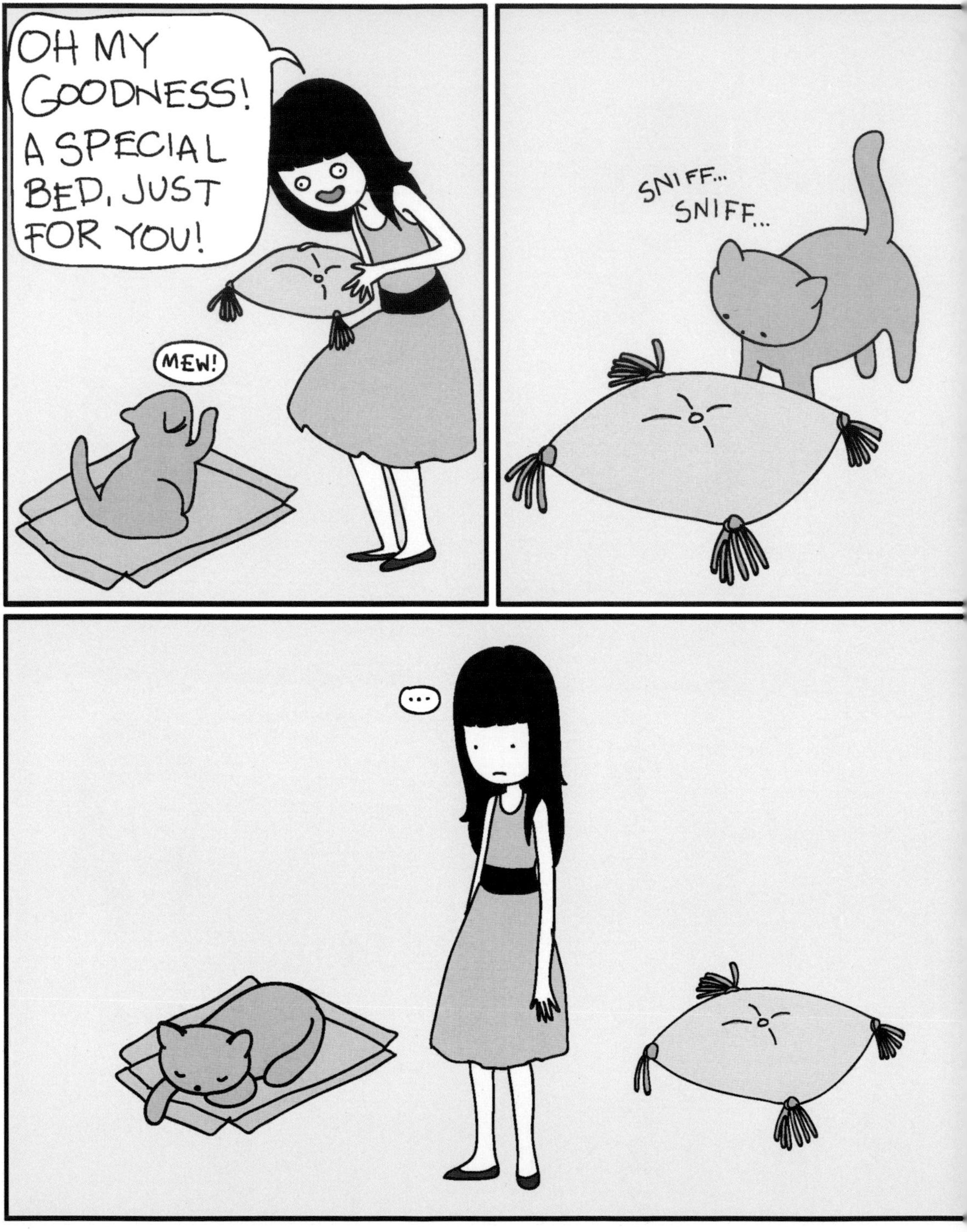
OH MY GOODNESS! A SPECIAL BED, JUST FOR YOU!
MEW!
SNIFF... SNIFF...
...

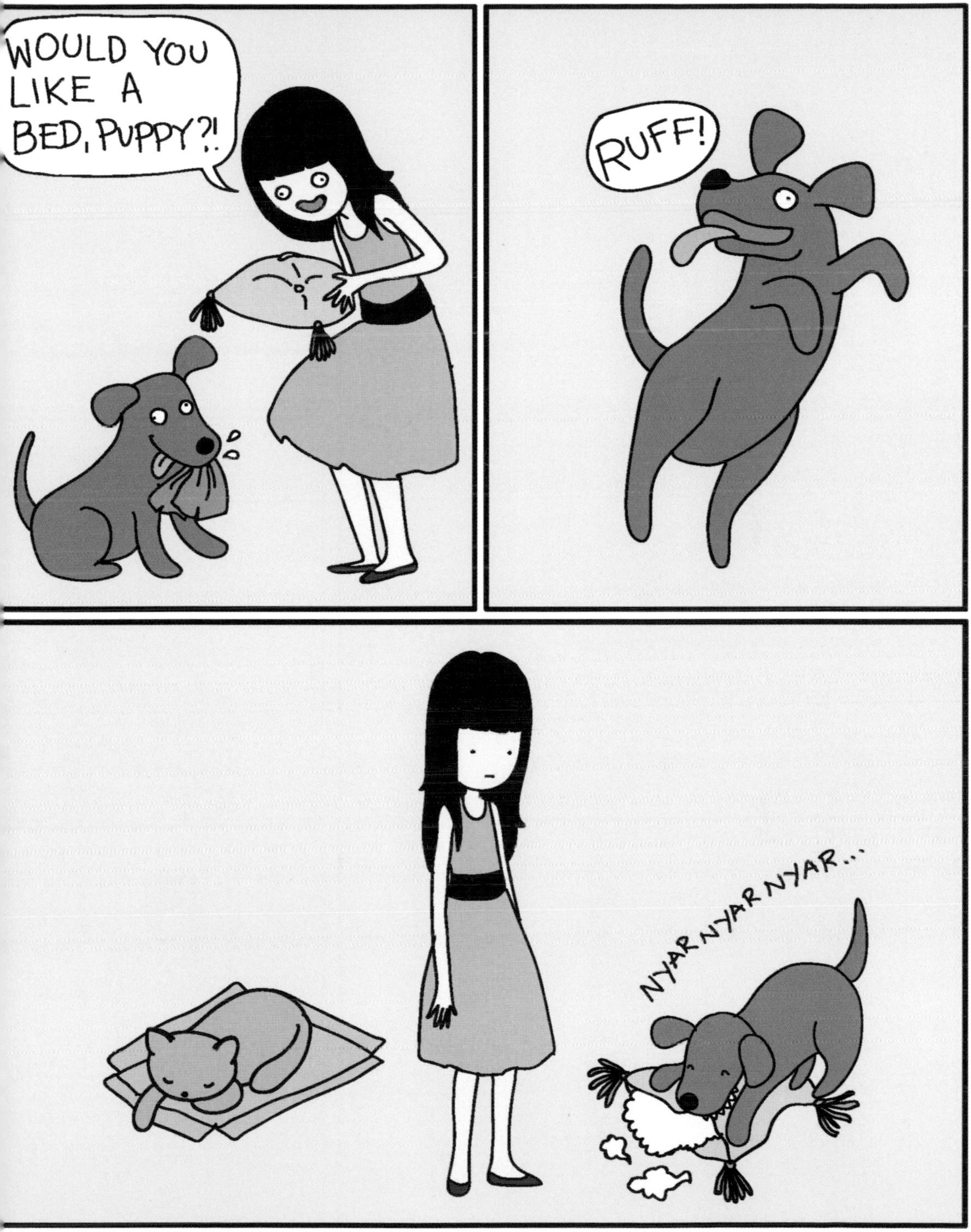
WOULD YOU LIKE A BED, PUPPY?!
RUFF!
NYAR NYAR NYAR...

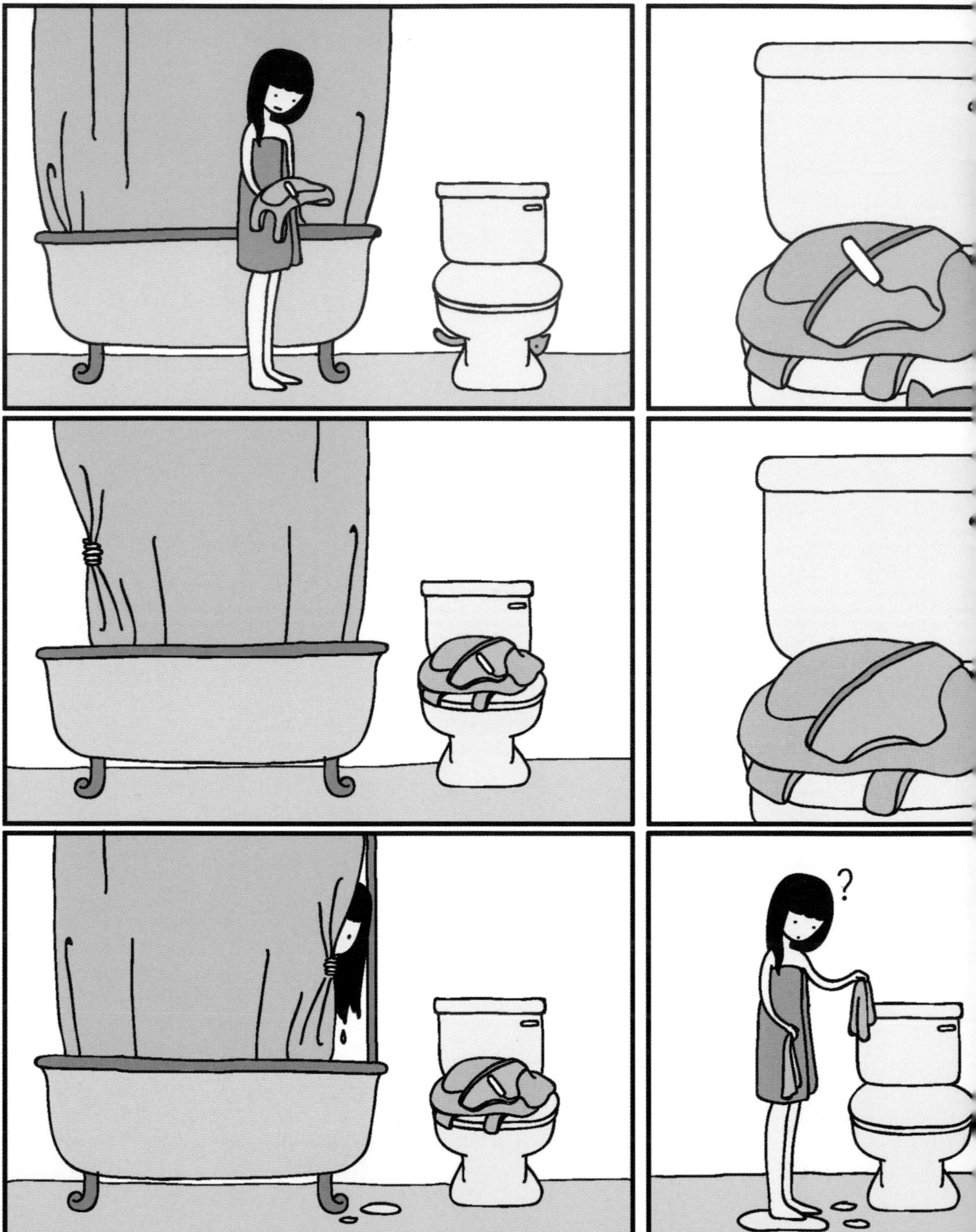
?

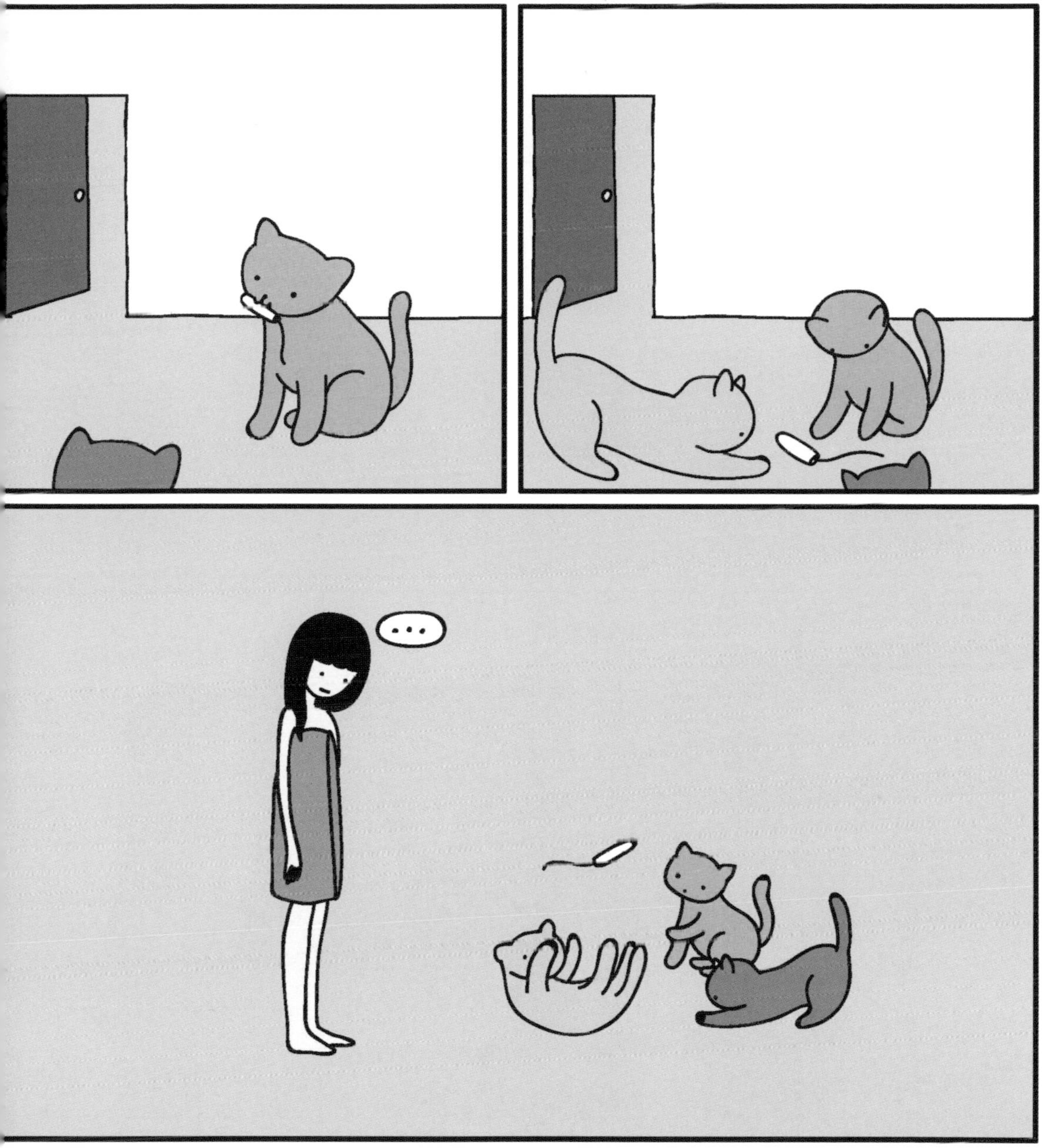
...

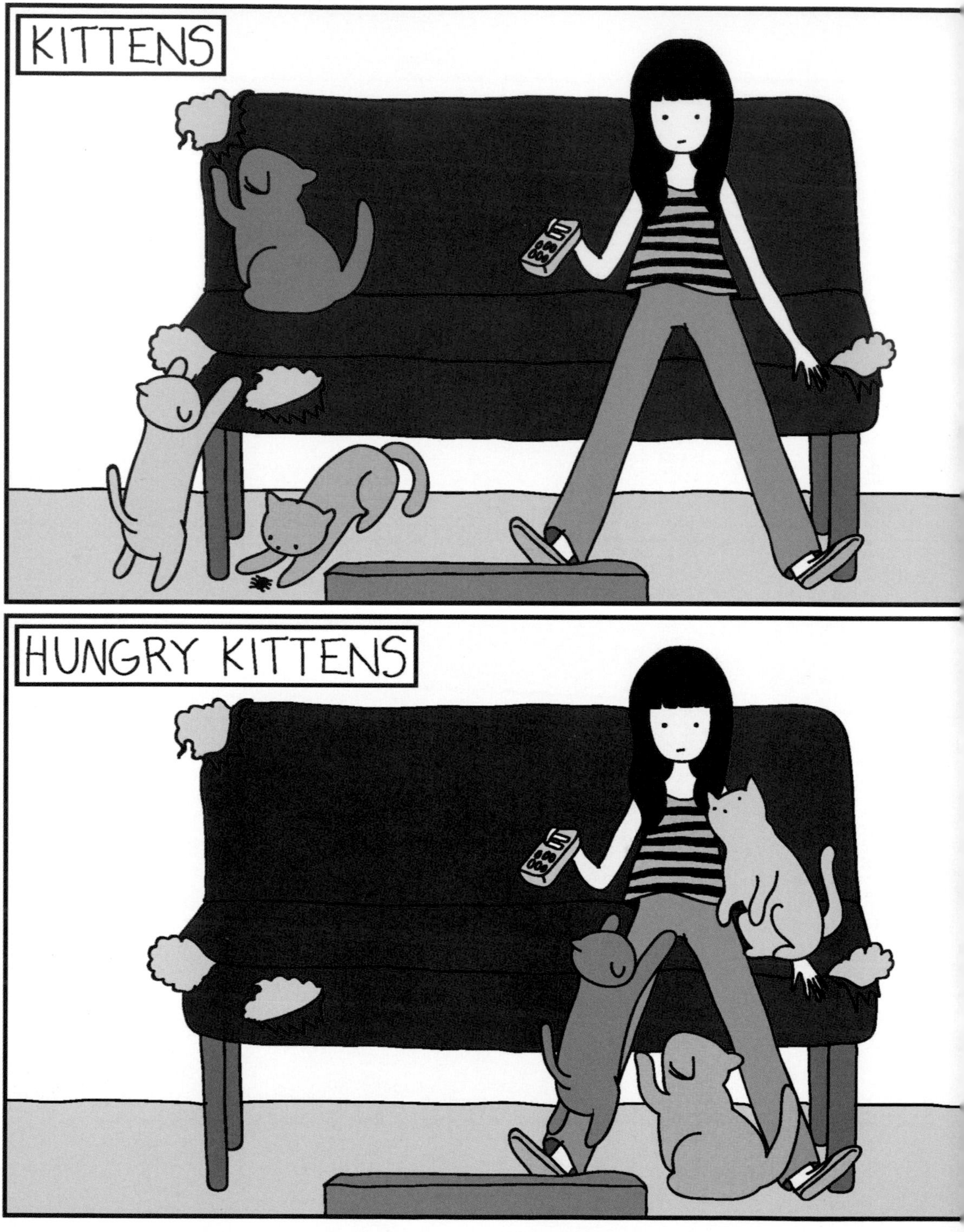
KITTENS
HUNGRY KITTENS

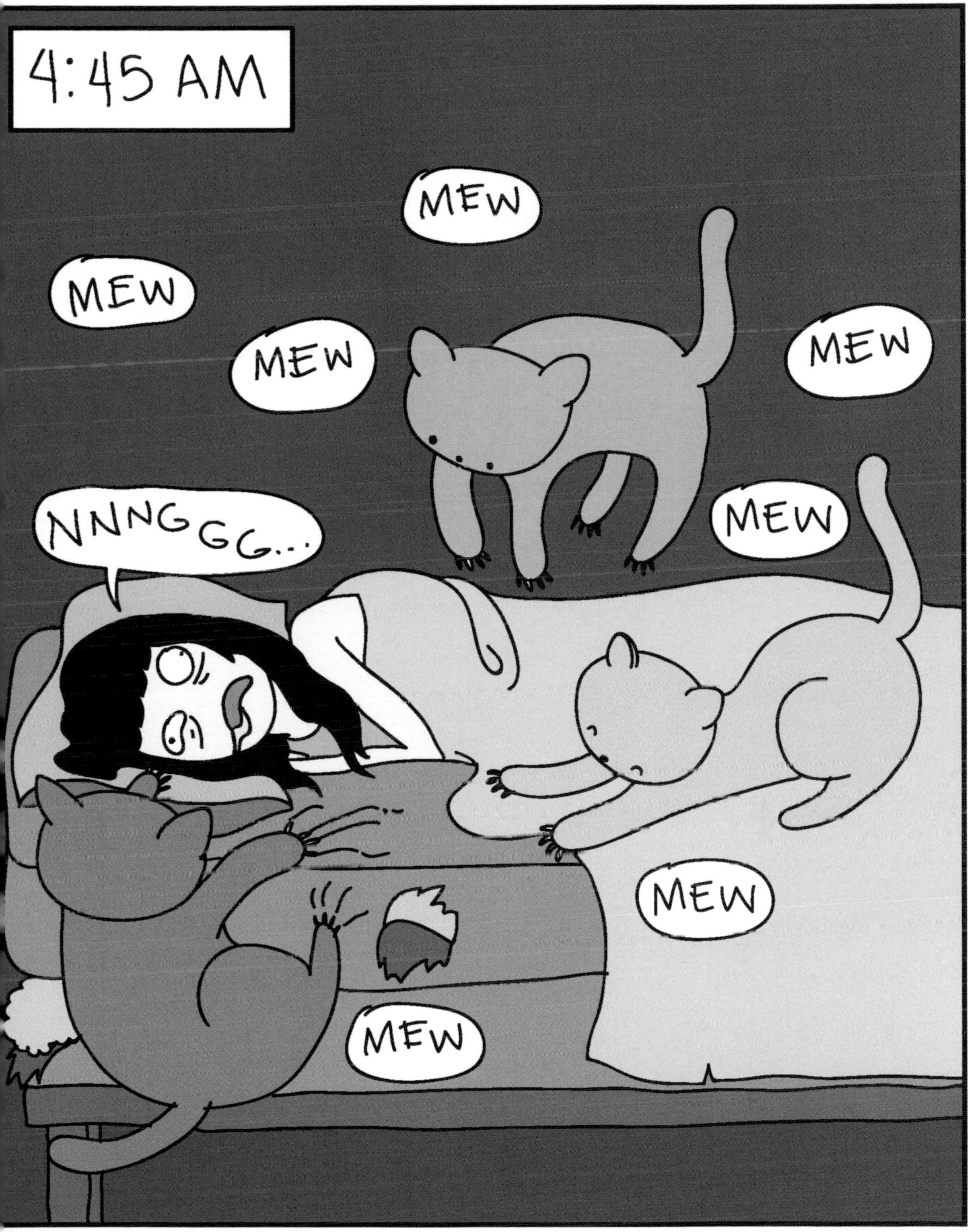
4:45 AM
MEW
MEW
MEW
MEW
NNNGGG...
MEW
MEW
MEW

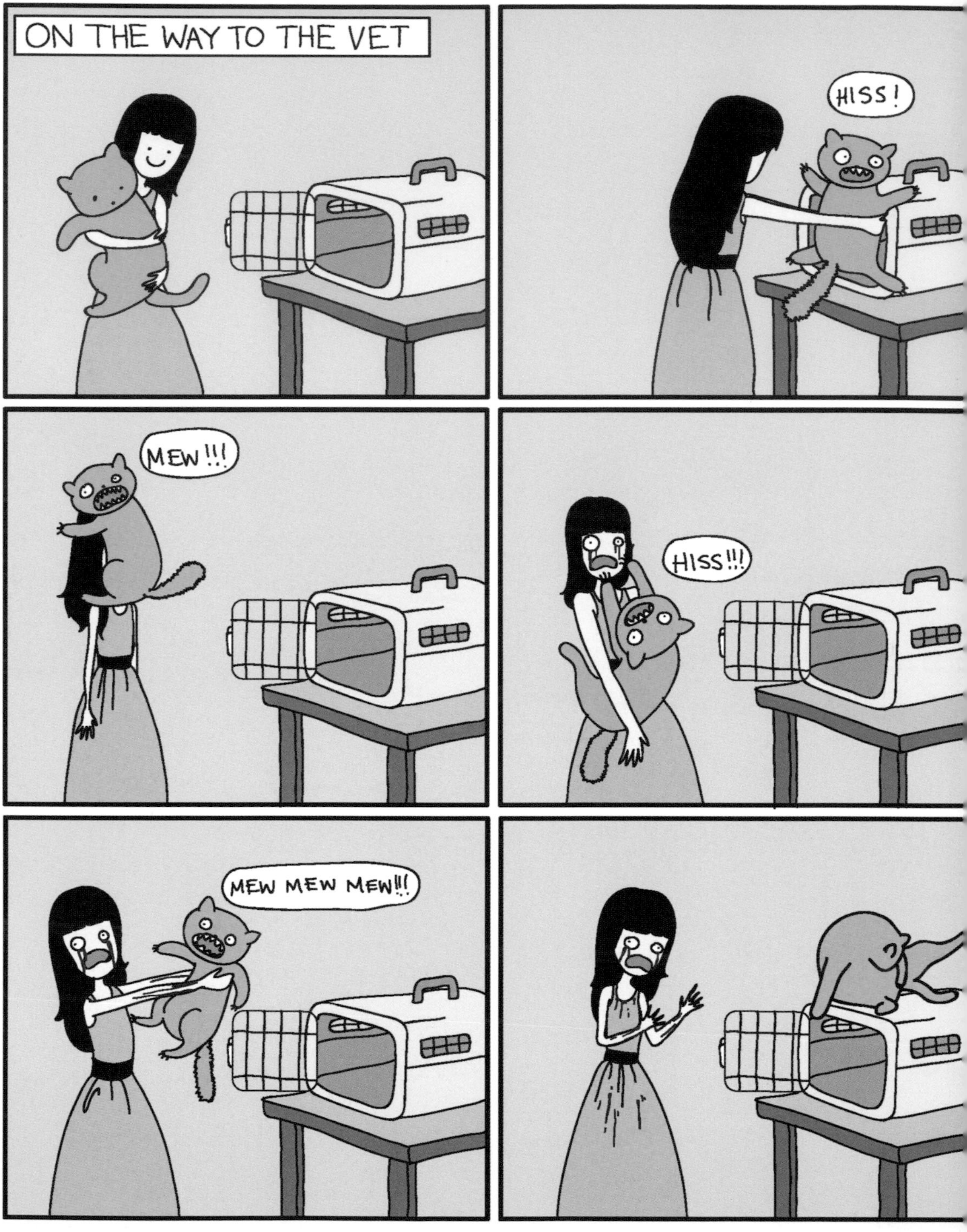
ON THE WAY TO THE VET
HISS!
MEW!!!
HISS!!!
MEW MEW MEW!!!

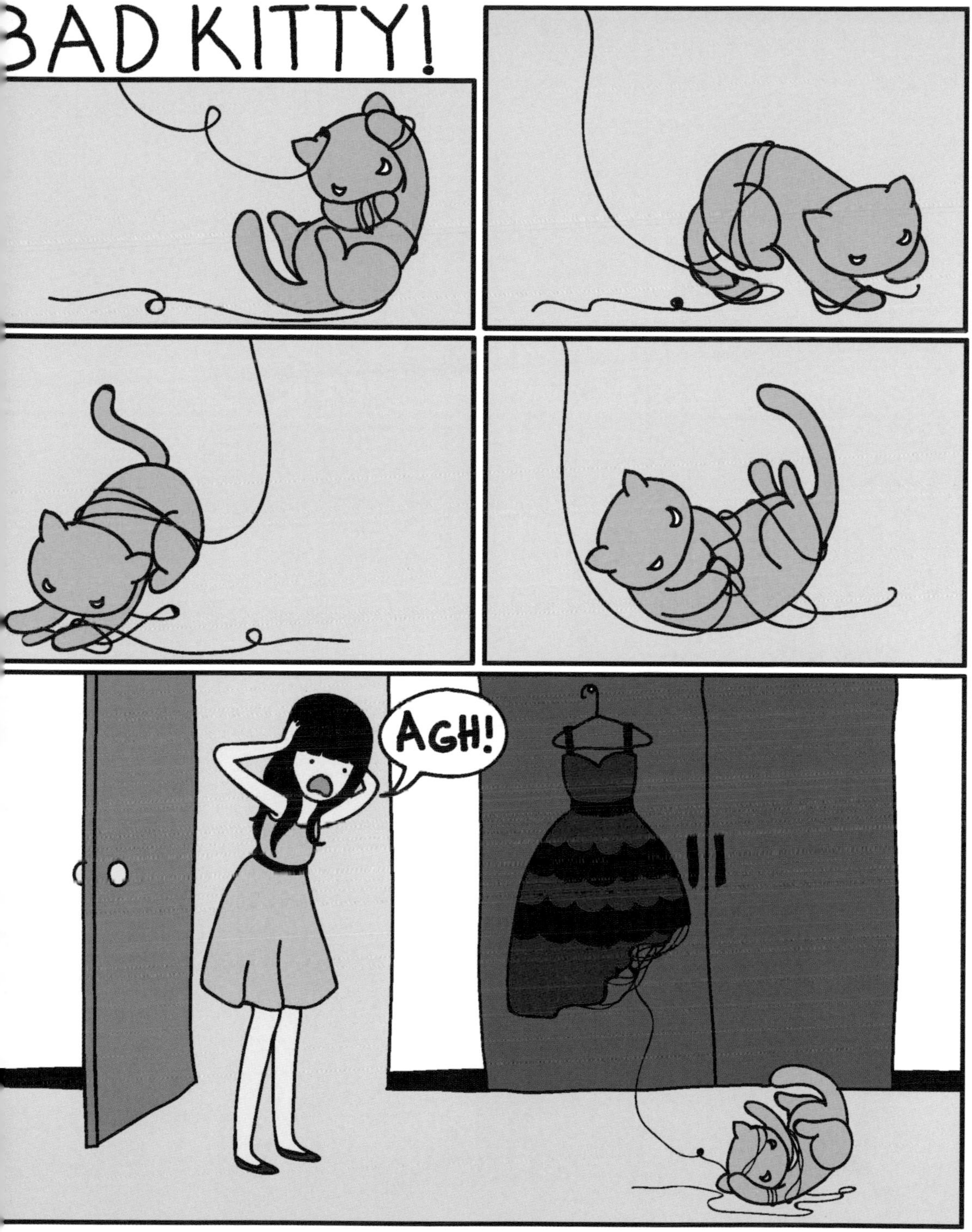
BAD KITTY!
AGH!

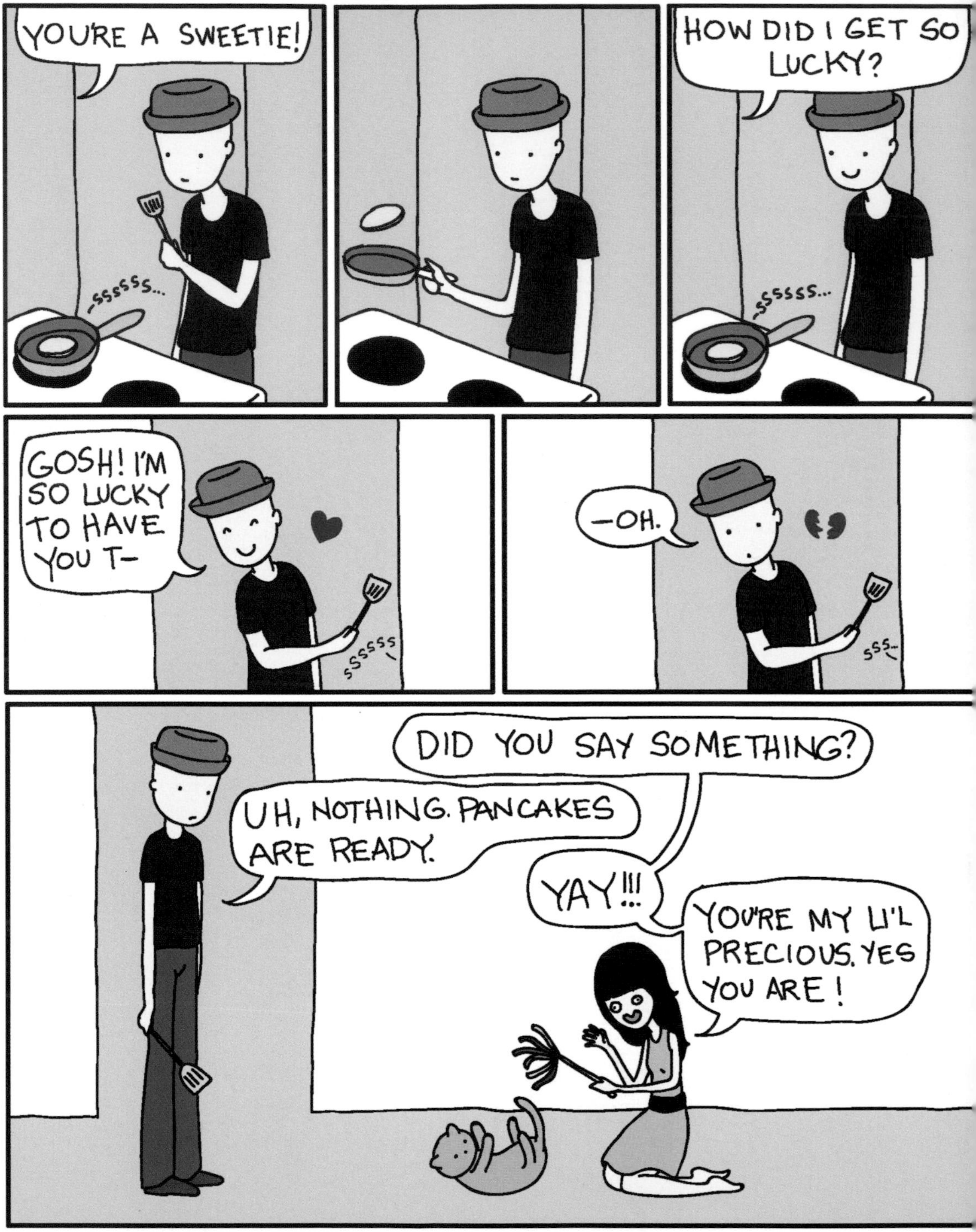
YOU'RE A SWEETIE!
SSSSSS...
HOW DID I GET SO LUCKY?
SSSSS...
GOSH! I'M SO LUCKY TO HAVE YOU T–
SSSSSS
–OH.
SSS..
DID YOU SAY SOMETHING?
UH, NOTHING. PANCAKES ARE READY.
YAY!!!
YOU'RE MY LI'L PRECIOUS. YES YOU ARE!

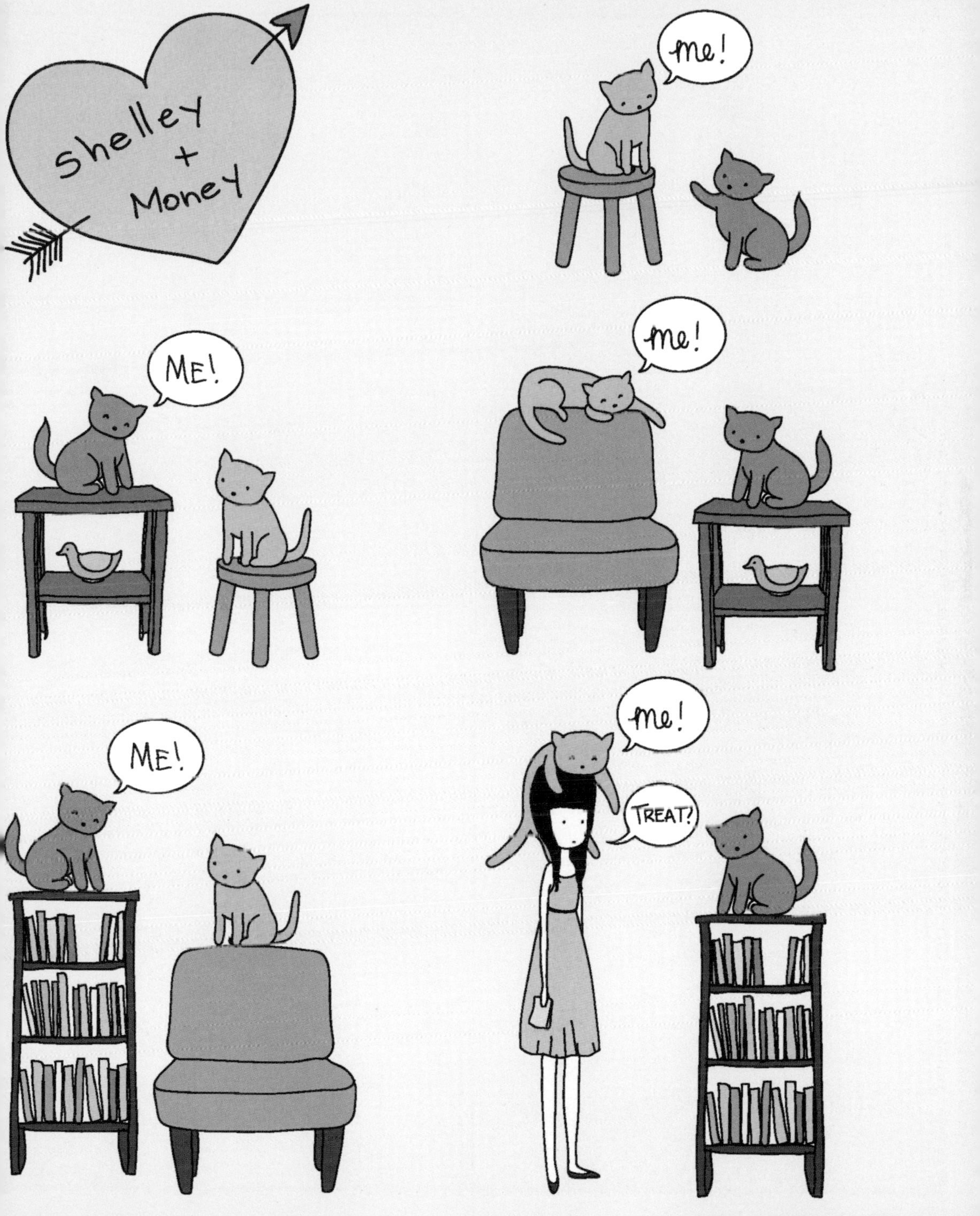
Shelley + Money
me!
ME!
me!
ME!
me!
TREAT?

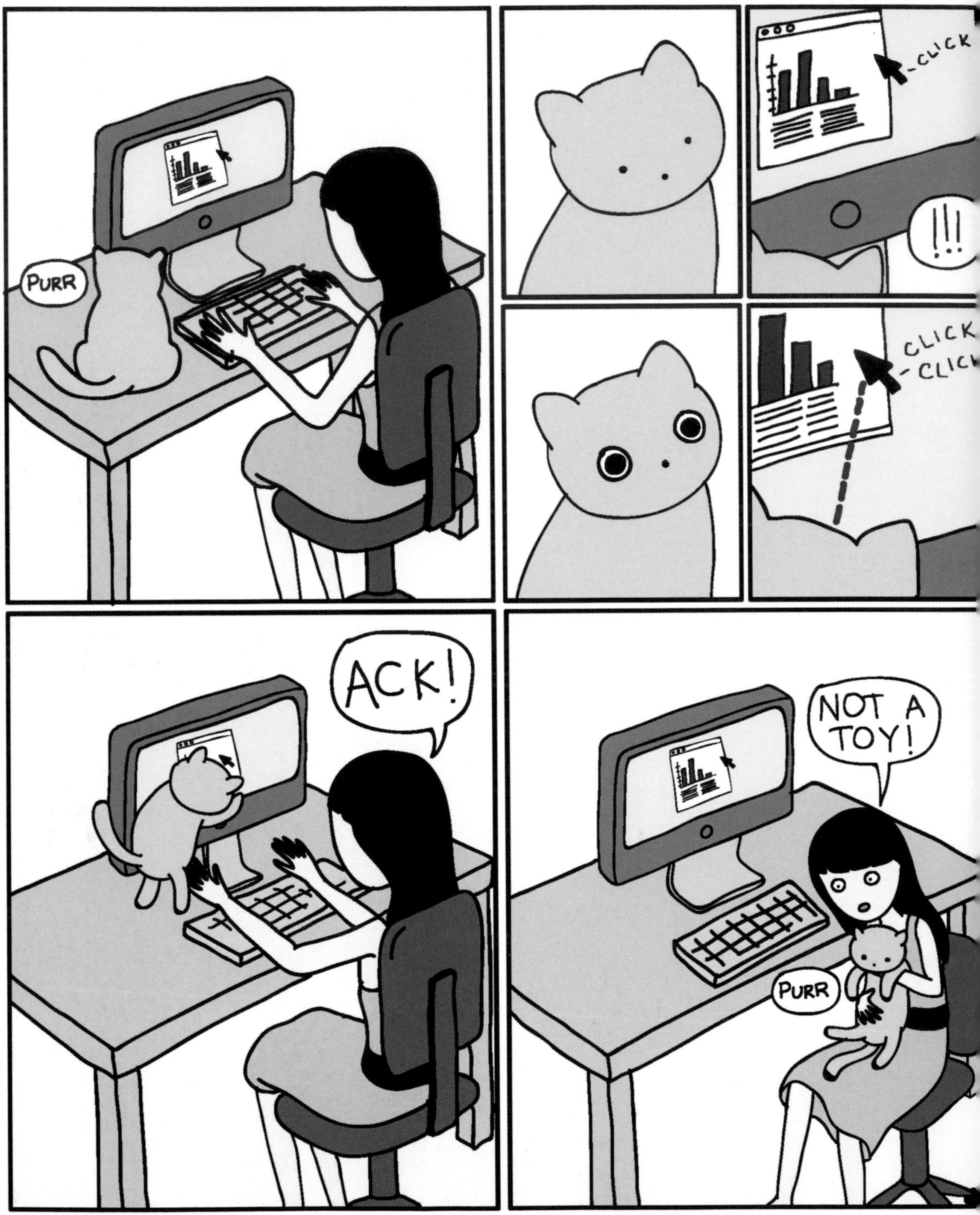
PURR
CLICK
!!!
CLICK
CLICK
ACK!
NOT A TOY!
PURR

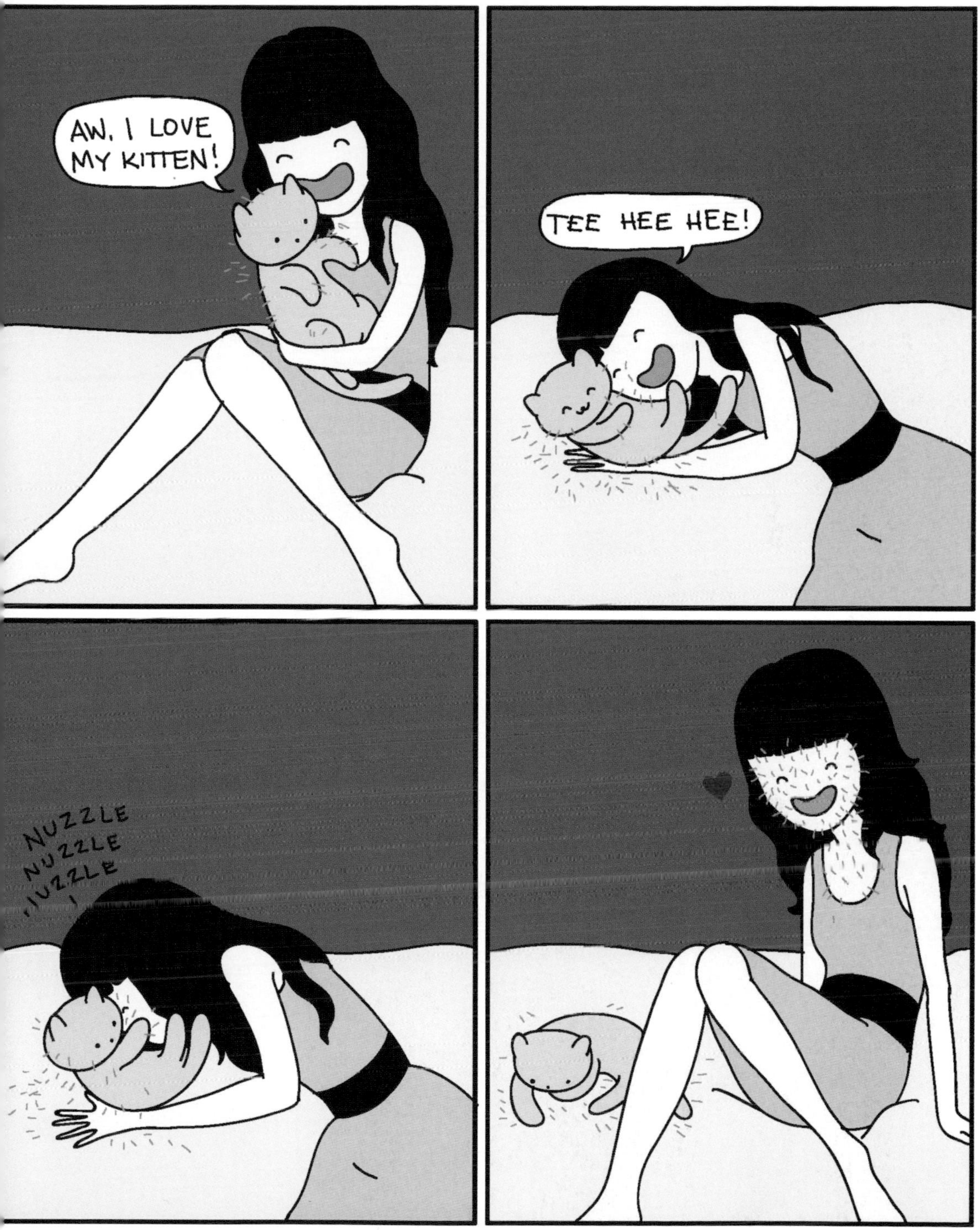

AW, I LOVE MY KITTEN!
TEE HEE HEE!
NUZZLE NUZZLE NUZZLE

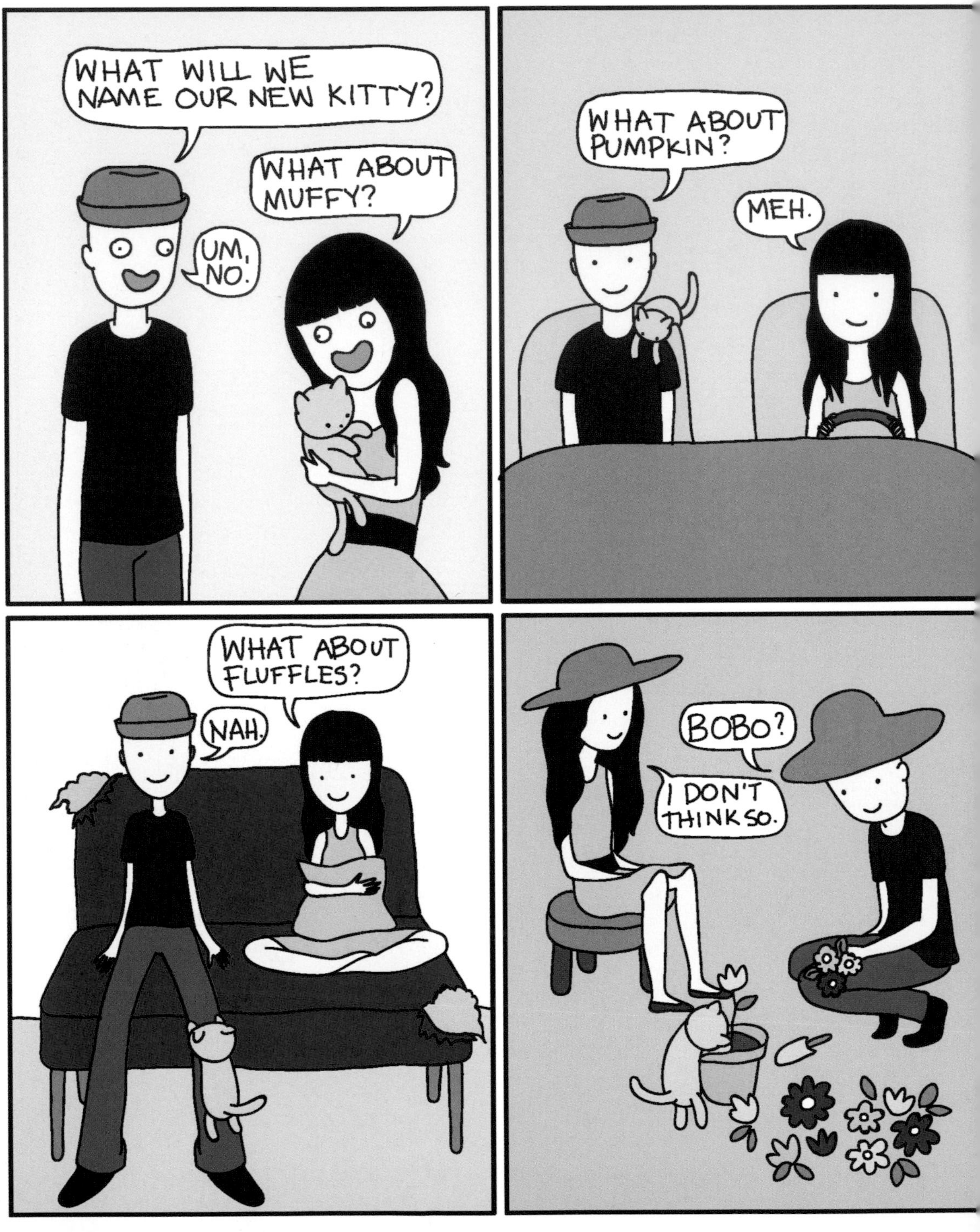
WHAT WILL WE NAME OUR NEW KITTY?
WHAT ABOUT MUFFY?
UM, NO.
WHAT ABOUT PUMPKIN?
MEH.
WHAT ABOUT FLUFFLES?
NAH.
BOBO?
I DON'T THINK SO.

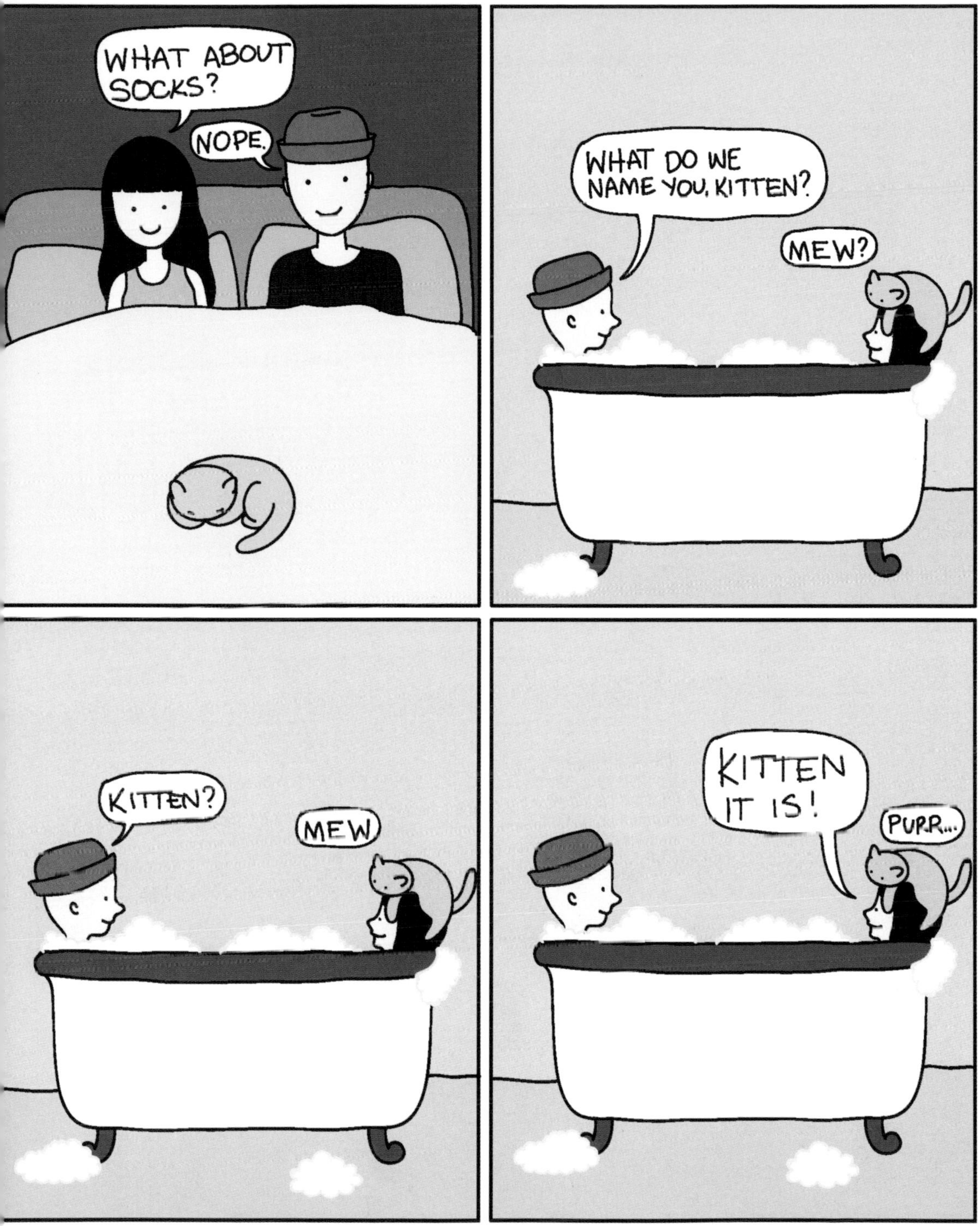
WHAT ABOUT SOCKS?
NOPE.
WHAT DO WE NAME YOU, KITTEN?
MEW?
KITTEN?
MEW
KITTEN IT IS!
PURR...

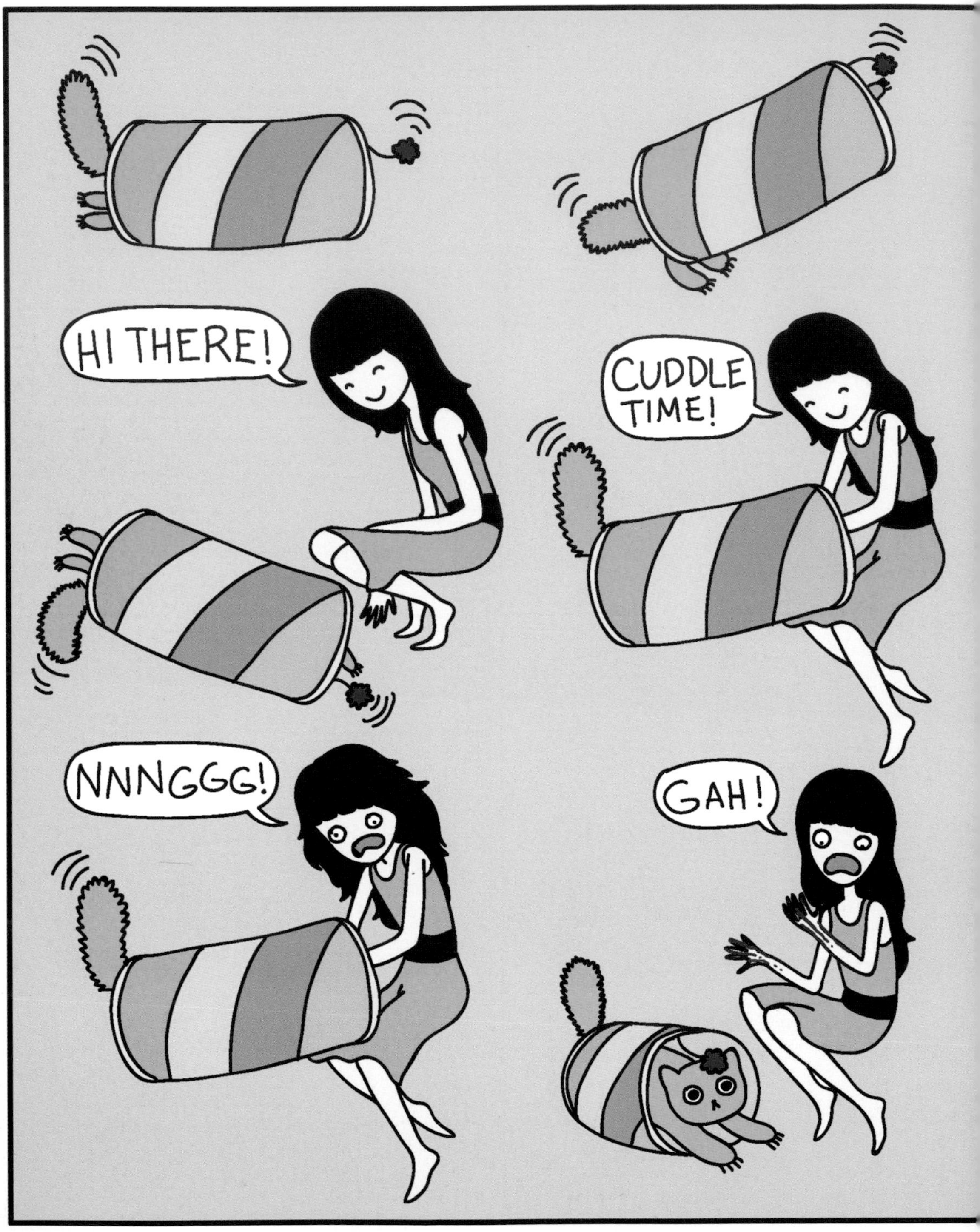
HI THERE!
CUDDLE TIME!
NNNGGG!
GAH!

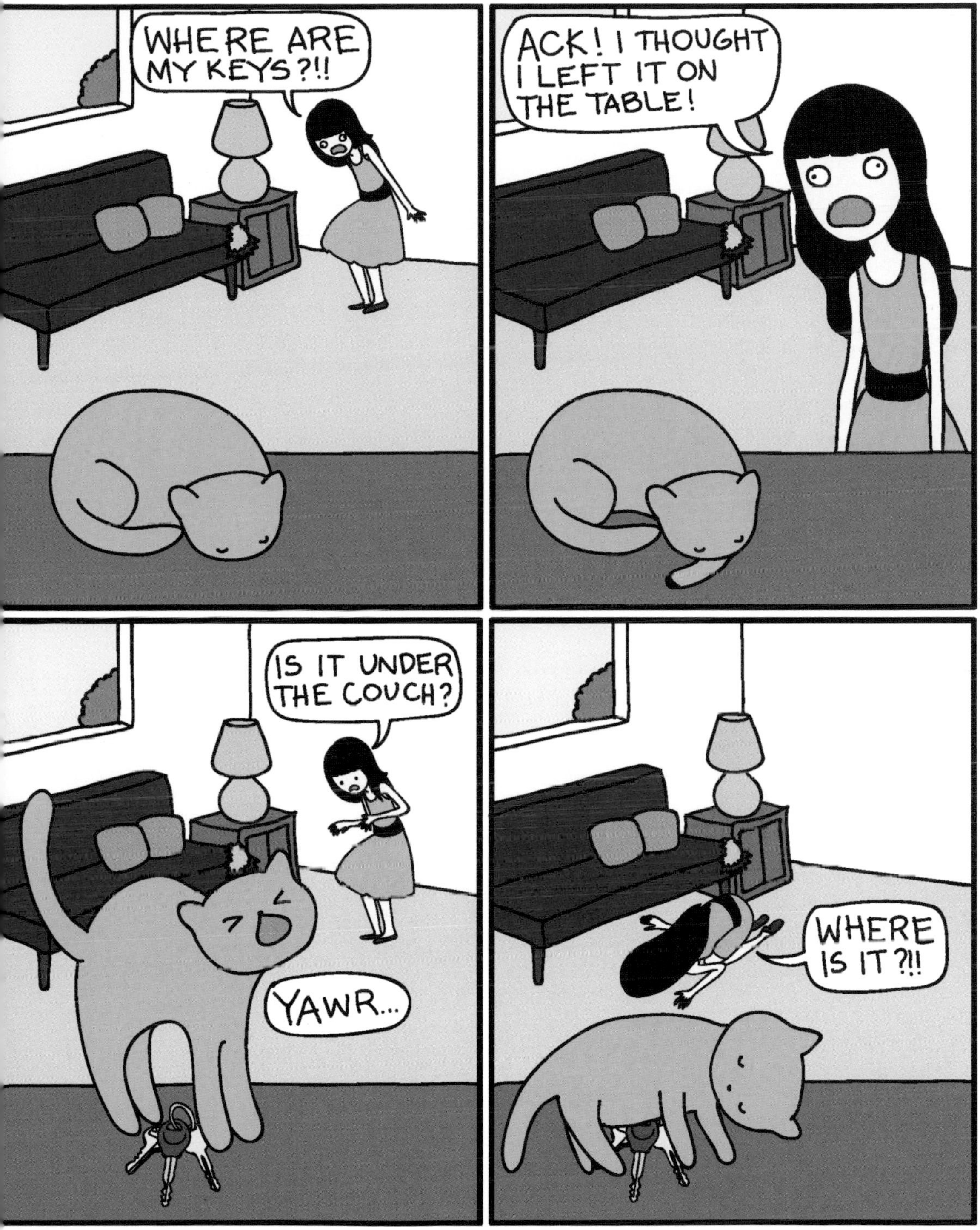
WHERE ARE MY KEYS?!!
ACK! I THOUGHT I LEFT IT ON THE TABLE!
IS IT UNDER THE COUCH?
YAWR...
WHERE IS IT?!!

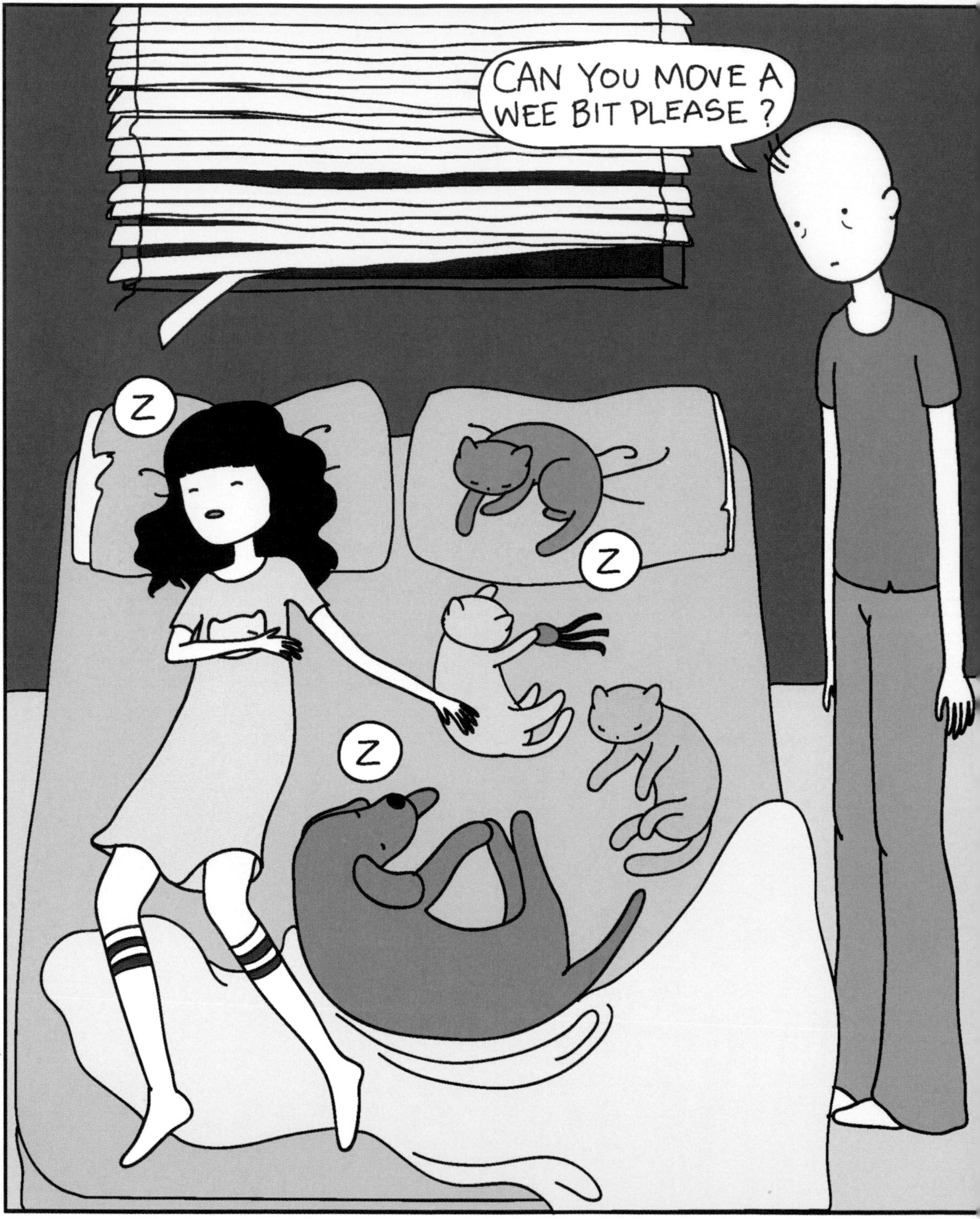
CAN YOU MOVE A WEE BIT PLEASE?
Z
Z
Z

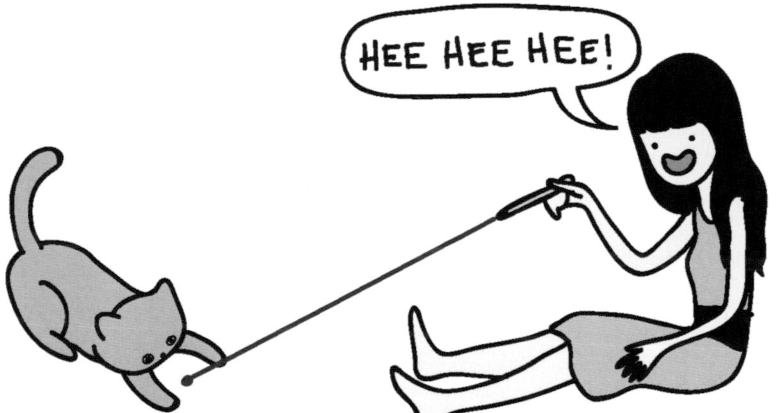
HEE HEE HEE!

Photography by Victor Surovec

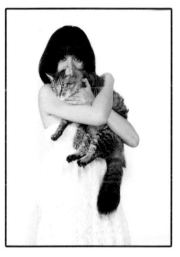

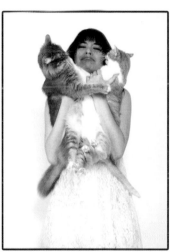

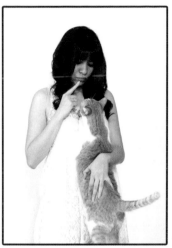

YASMINE SUROVEC IS A
DESIGNER AND ILLUSTRATOR
BASED IN THE SF BAY AREA,
WHERE SHE LIVES WITH
HER HUSBAND, PUPPY,
AND THREE CATS.

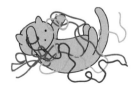

CATVERSUSHUMAN.COM

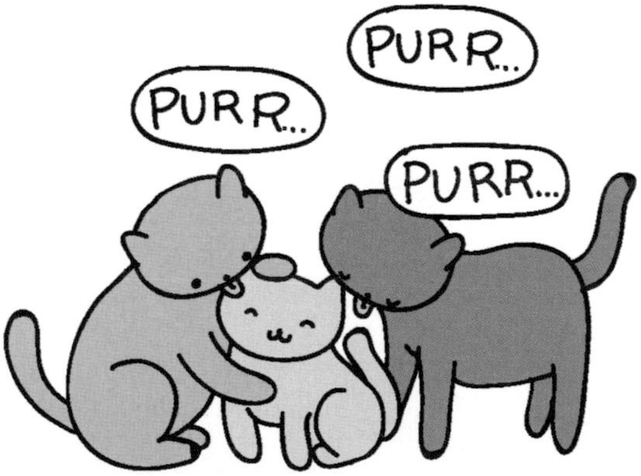
PURR...
PURR...
PURR...